Leadership
in the
Reagan
Presidency

Leadership
in the
Reagan
Presidency
Part II

Eleven Intimate Perspectives

Howard Baker   Frank Fahrenkopf
Lou Cannon   John Sears
Mari Maseng Will   William Brock
Ed Harper   Peter Hannaford
Edward Wright   T. Burton Smith
Edwin Meese

Edited by
Kenneth W. Thompson

Volume II
The Miller Center Reagan Oral History Series

UNIVERSITY
PRESS OF
AMERICA

Lanham • New York • London

The Miller Center

University of Virginia

Copyright © 1993 by
University Press of America® Inc.
4720 Boston Way
Lanham, Maryland 20706

3 Henrietta Street
London WC2E 8LU England

Co-published by arrangement with
The Miller Center of Public Affairs,
University of Virginia

The views expressed by the author(s) of this publication do not necessarily
represent the opinions of the Miller Center. We hold to Jefferson's dictum that:
"Truth is the proper and sufficient antagonist to error, and has nothing to
fear from the conflict, unless by human interposition, disarmed of her
natural weapons, free argument and debate."

ISBN 0–8191–9051–9 (cloth : alk. paper)
ISBN 0–8191–9052–7 (pbk. : alk. paper)

The paper used in this publication meets the minimum requirements of
American National Standard for Information Sciences—Permanence
of Paper for Printed Library Materials, ANSI Z39.48–1984.

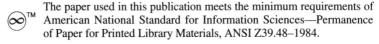

To

Carolyn

talented and courageous

loyal yet independent

An example for everyone's

daughter

CONTENTS

PREFACE

One sign of the contemporaneity of the Reagan administration is the projected publication of four or five volumes on the Reagan presidency by the Miller Center. In approaching the Reagan oral history, we have reaped the benefits of participation by a larger number of witnesses and subjects than with any previous postwar presidency. With the Miller Center's Roosevelt oral history, no more than a half dozen high-ranking officials from that administration were available. With the greater availability of the Reagan official family, we have already exceeded 50 participants.

On the other side of this advantage, we lack the authoritative historical sources, the monographs, and scholarly articles and the reconsiderations or revisions that enrich the study of earlier presidencies. No point is served in discounting the benefits of historical perspective. Such perspective is clearly lacking in the search for truth in the 1980s. With the Reagan presidency, if not all postwar presidencies, we approach a historical era the end of which is not yet in sight. We are dealing with a story viewed only from its beginning, its midpoint, and a few high points. At best we have only the most fragmentary knowledge of the consequences. Our task is the more complex because of the ideological divisions surrounding the Reagan presidency. Within and outside the administration, historians and scholars as well as policymakers cluster together around different value systems.

However, the limitation of sources and possible observer bias are nothing new in the annals of political history. James Madison wrote of such limits, saying:

It has been a misfortune of history that a *personal knowledge* and an *impartial judgment* of things can *rarely meet* in the historian. The best history of our country therefore must be the fruit of contributions bequeathed by contemporary actors and witnesses, to successors who will make an unbiased use of them.

But Madison took heart from the fact that future historians and scholars might find in such early histories the sources on which more detached and objective studies could be written. His optimism about historical interpretation is one we share. It lies at the center of our commitment to oral histories. We make bold to suggest that future historians of the Reagan administration will draw on these early findings. The participants in our inquiry have helped lay foundations for future research.

Madison concluded:

And if the abundance and authenticity of the materials . . . should descend to hands capable of doing justice to them, then American history can be expected to contain more truth, and *lessons . . . not less valuable*, than that of *any country or age* whatever [italics added].

INTRODUCTION

This is a book about Ronald Reagan as leader. Most people seem to agree that Reagan had many of the qualities of a successful leader, but at that point the agreement ceases. Some attribute his leadership skills to his power as a communicator. Columnists coined the phrase "the Great Communicator" to characterize his talent. Others point to his decisiveness saying that especially in his first 18 months he made hard decisions that changed the character of American government for years to come. Reagan had certain core convictions such as building a strong national defense and reducing taxes. Because of his core beliefs he knew what he believed and who he was. He was not tormented by anguish and self-doubt. Others insist Reagan's strength was his luck. He was seemingly invulnerable to attacks; hence, he was called the teflon president. Events broke his way. Sooner or later he recovered from any embarrassment, including the Iran-contra scandal.

We propose in volume II of the Reagan oral history to turn to leaders who worked closely with Mr. Reagan and knew him well. Basically, the first section attempts to explore his philosophy of leadership. Senator Howard Baker served as Reagan's chief of staff from 1987-88. When Reagan called for him he was in Florida with his family trying to decide whether to run for president in 1988. He had served for 18 years in the Senate where he was one of its most successful minority and majority leaders. Despite his own hopes and unfolding plans, he accepted the office of chief of staff without question when President Reagan asked him to serve.

In his testimony, Senator Baker describes President Reagan as one of the nation's most underestimated presidents. He predicts that future historians will write that he was strong, determined, well-focused, and effective. Reagan made a difference in the fundamental public policy of the country in a way that no one since Franklin D. Roosevelt has done. Baker recites some of the common criticisms that were made of Reagan and refutes each one in turn: his laziness, his falling asleep, his disregard of detail. He was unquestionably an outstanding leader.

At the same time, Baker makes clear that he didn't agree with all of Reagan's policies. From the first, he called his economic program "a riverboat gamble." With characteristic fairness, Baker underscores the successes and failures of Reagan's program. He acknowledges that President Reagan was "dispirited and demoralized" by the Iran-contra affair; one of Senator's Baker's first tasks was to collect the facts and determine the truth about that event. Another task was to pull the President out of the doldrums and help him return to his former decisiveness in leadership. In the end, Baker concluded that "Reagan was not involved in the affair and was telling the truth." In his contribution to the volume, Baker responds to questions concerning his work as chief of staff.

Frank J. Fahrenkopf, Jr. was chairman of the Republican National Committee. He, like Baker, enjoyed a unique vantage point in assessing Reagan as a leader. Some of his comments overlap with Baker's, but he goes on to describe the way Reagan conducted Cabinet meetings. He writes about the "troika" who were together Reagan's chief of staff in the first term (Jim Baker, Meese, and Deaver). Fahrenkopf provides a textbook outline of Republican party strategy and organization. He reviews and analyzes Republican political activities. He reveals the blow that Reagan suffered from the Iran-contra affair. However, people still supported Reagan even when they disagreed because of his convictions and ability to lead. Fahrenkopf speculates about some of the similarities and differences between Reagan and Bush, particularly in the first phase of Bush's actions in Panama. He also compares Reagan's intentions with those of critics such as Richard Viguerie. Fahrenkopf dissects and evaluates the media's view of Reagan. Finally, he reports on the transition from Reagan to Bush and the process by which Dan Quayle was chosen as Bush's vice-presidential nominee.

Lou Cannon is the third authority on Reagan to analyze his qualities as leader. He notes that liberals and conservatives alike find confirmation of some of their views of Reagan as leader when they read his book, *President Reagan: The Role of a Lifetime.* He both accepts and criticizes the idea of Reagan as the teflon president. He agrees that Reagan was underestimated but shows how that sometimes worked to his advantage. He finds it paradoxical that Reagan's domestic policies were a disaster, yet when he ran for president he was acclaimed for his experience in the domestic field. He supposedly knew nothing about foreign policy, yet this was the arena of his greatest success. On the deficit, Reagan blames the Congress, but Cannon quotes George Will, who said that if the Congress had accepted Reagan's budgets as he proposed them, the country would still have about 90 percent of the deficit it has today. Cannon asserts there was an ethical void in the Reagan administration. He discusses in depth Reagan's attitude toward the military buildup and toward taxes. With respect to his policy toward SDI, Cannon discloses some of its practical if unintended effects. What surprises Cannon most was the extent to which Reagan let the budget deficit get out of control. He had not expected that.

The second section of the volume deals with President Reagan and the practice of leadership. John Sears, who played an important role in managing both the 1976 and part of the 1980 Reagan campaign, presents an unusually insightful interpretation of Reagan's leadership. He finds that in the end his strengths as a leader were bound up with his unique political instincts. Sears comes to this conclusion after first discussing the highly individualistic character of American life and politics. Reagan, he observes, was unique in offering the country hope after others had talked of the people's malaise. Reagan also demonstrated that the country was governable and that not only was the office of president workable but he could make it work without having to devote incredibly long hours to the details of the job. He also proved that he could take control of the bureaucracy and reduce a certain amount of waste despite the view that problems such as this were said to be intractable. Reagan disproved the idea that governmental problems are "so difficult even the president could not deal with them." In the main body of his text, Sears presents his view of contemporary politics and the President's success in coping.

With the emergence of television and the expansion of the media into every sector of American politics, presidential speech writing has come to play a decisive role. Mari Maseng Will was a top Reagan speech writer who later became assistant secretary for public affairs in the Department of Transportation and director of the Office of Public Liaison. She offers unique insights on the various ways Reagan worked with his speech writers, his skill as an editor and writer, and his respect for each individual with whom he worked. She acknowledges that Reagan had good and bad times in office and by far the worst came with the Iran-contra affair. As director of Public Liaison she undertook the rehabilitation of the President. She and her colleagues sought to return the President to the communication strategies that had been successful in his first term in office. Few portraits of Mr. Reagan include more discerning personal *aperçus*. The President comes alive in successive actions and problems in his presidency. For those who would see President Reagan as a moral absolutist, Maseng discloses that Reagan taught her that "there are a lot more grays in the world, that things are not black and white, and that compromise is necessary." She quotes him as saying: "We'll go and get what we can now, and then we'll come back for more later." In this attitude and in other ways, she helps us understand that Reagan was quite different than he has been portrayed.

William Brock came from a different background than some other members of the Reagan administration. He had supported President Gerald Ford against Ronald Reagan's challenge in 1976. He had also been chairman of the Republican party. For these and other reasons, his revisiting of the Reagan presidency is particularly important. Moreover, he served both as U.S. trade representative and secretary of labor. His oral history is especially valuable because he calls up specific actions and events that illustrate President Reagan's approach to decision making. Secretary Brock also discusses what he considered the fundamental determining factors in Reagan's approach. In brief compass, the secretary transports readers to the scene of action on choices that show Reagan's leadership style.

The third section of the book is devoted to problems of leadership. Ed Harper discusses certain dimensions of President

INTRODUCTION

Reagan's approach when problems confronted him. The most far-reaching of these was the national debt. Dr. Harper believed that economics was an area in which Reagan had distinct limitations. The President was skeptical that economists had answers to problems of the economy. He said they were often wrong. His staff sought to discourage him from using numbers in response to press conference questions, but sometimes he persisted, to their dismay. He was excessively tolerant of others in at least two rather costly ways: He showed tolerance for people who had not earned his confidence, and he was sometimes more tolerant of infighting than Harper thought he should have been. Harper engages in a fruitful discussion with his interrogators on the national debt. Because of his role as deputy director of the Office of Management and Budget in the Stockman era, Harper's analysis of the economy is especially illuminating.

The second essay is one by Peter D. Hannaford on "The Reagan Presidency: Campaigning, Managing, and Governing." Mr. Hannaford, who is chairman of the board of Hannaford Company, Inc., was associated with Governor Reagan in the California governor's office and continued to work in an advisory capacity to President Reagan. He was a partner of Michael Deaver in Deaver and Hannaford, Inc. He writes of Mr. Reagan's career from a broad background of experience. In the spirit of the third section of the book, he comments on at least three areas of the Reagan presidency, including problems confronted in each area. Hannaford explains Reagan's pattern of delegating authority, both its strengths and its weaknesses ("Sometimes you pick the wrong people, and they bring discredit not only to themselves, but also to the person who picked them"). He tells of a problem Reagan faced in Winterpark, Florida, the training site of the White Sox, when his cue cards blew away. His campaign in 1976 was hampered by financial crises as the money threatened to run out. The question of the deficit apparently concerned Mr. Reagan as he left office and Mr. Hannaford devotes part of his concluding comments to this problem.

The concluding section is entitled "Perspectives on Leadership." The first essay is by Edward N. Wright, formerly assistant to the attorney general for national security affairs. He is currently a professor at the University of Southern California. Wright discusses his initial impressions of Reagan against the image of the President conveyed by some in the media. He reveals the close relationship Mr. Meese enjoyed with President Reagan. What follows in his discussion is a series of vignettes that throw light on the manner in which President Reagan made decisions on issues that mattered most to him. Wright's picture of the President making decisions in such high-priority areas provides a rather different perspective of Reagan as leader.

The second piece in the section is addressed to President Reagan's health. It is difficult to imagine an effective president who suffers from chronic ill health. Alexander Hamilton placed "energy" first in his list of the requirements for leadership. Dr. T. Burton Smith had been Reagan's physician in California, and when Dr. Dan Ruge retired as presidential physician at the end of Reagan's first term, Dr. Smith replaced him. Dr. Smith had examined Reagan before his run for the governorship in California. He advised him that his recurrent urinary tract infections would continue if he persisted in his quest for the office of governor. Smith muses that if Reagan had accepted that advice he would not have been governor and thereafter president.

Dr. Smith's account is a very personal and open review of his responsibilities to the President, but also to the entourage who traveled with him. Dr. Smith was responsible for selecting a hospital for the President, examining him on a regular basis, and a host of other duties. From Dr. Smith's observations, we learn a lot about the President, his physicians, and medical care for the staff in the White House.

Edwin Meese's relationship with President Reagan extended over the period when Reagan was governor of California and the years of the Reagan presidency. In the first term, Mr. Meese served as a member of the White House "troika." He was attorney general in the second term. One of his contributions to the Reagan administration was through his role as rapporteur at Cabinet and committee meetings. Not only did he assure a full and accurate report of proceedings, but some have said this task increased his influence within the government. In the forum, Meese discusses a wide range of issues touching on both personal and institutional questions.

I

PHILOSOPHY
OF LEADERSHIP

CHAPTER 1

THE REAGAN WHITE HOUSE

HOWARD H. BAKER, JR.

NARRATOR: Senator Howard H. Baker, Jr. was United States senator from Tennessee from 1967 to 1985, minority leader from 1977 to 1981, and majority leader from 1981 to 1985. He was White House chief of staff during an extraordinarily complicated period in American government and carried out that role with the same wisdom and dispatch he has brought to every other task he has had. Historians are beginning to say that he may well have been the most effective minority and majority leader in the last 25 years. It is a great pleasure to have him with us today.

SENATOR BAKER: Thank you very much. I'm anxious to hear what questions you have, and I'm also anxious to hear what answers I can contrive, so this promises to be a pleasant time.

I will tell you a little about my experience in the Senate. First of all, I will be forever grateful to the people of Tennessee for giving me the opportunity to represent them in the United States Senate for 18 years. That, in my view, is the high point of my career, and I count it a first responsibility to represent one's fellow citizens, neighbors, and friends in the United States Senate. It is a high and unique honor, and one for which I will always be grateful.

I am also grateful to my Republican colleagues in the Senate for having given me the opportunity for eight years to represent them as either minority leader or majority leader. Maybe I will give you a little insight into how that works, because the leadership, not the generic term, but the leadership in the more formal sense used by the Congress, is a little-understood institution. The majority and

3

minority leaders of the United States Senate have extraordinary responsibilities and a good bit of power, but the office is not a constitutional one, as you know. You may also be surprised to know that they are not statutory offices; they are purely a product of necessity.   With a group as large as the United States Senate—100 highly individualistic members—someone has to try to lead.

Furthermore, it is only in the last century that the offices of minority and majority leader have grown up. The antecedents of those offices go back to the earliest Congress. Then, the closest parallel we can find to the leadership as it exists now in the Senate was a pair of senators who called on the President of the United States to notify him that the Congress was in session and to formally request his recommendations on legislation and the legislative agenda. Thus, it is as a direct lineal descendent of those notifying senators that the offices of minority and majority leader of the United States Senate were created.

When I was elected to the Senate in November 1966, the Senate Republicans were a distinct minority, and not many people expected that we would ever have a majority. Indeed, when I arrived there was not a single member of the Republican caucus who had ever served in a majority except Strom Thurmond, and he was a Democrat at the time.

After the 1976 and 1978 elections in which we did fairly well, it began to dawn on some that there was a possibility that we Republicans might have the opportunity to serve as the governing majority. By that time I had been elected minority leader, and in anticipation of such an occurrence, I did something that many people thought an absolute folly and others thought a waste of time: I convened what I called the committee of ranking members.

When you are a committee chairman, the name is self-explanatory. Who the ranking members were was less clear, but I gathered the senior Republicans from each of the committees in my office once a week and told them that we were going to play a little game. We were going to pretend we had a majority, and they were going to act as if they were chairmen. Once a week they would bring in an agenda with recommendations on what they would do with their committees. We would bid for a floor time and build a schedule of legislative proposals. We were going to try to practice what we would do if we, in fact, did become the majority of the

United States Senate. Soon this practice became not only a good game, but a useful legislative exercise, because it tended to focus the role of the minority in the legislative process in a unified way. Before long we had a program, an alternative; then, in the wake of the Reagan election in 1980, we did in fact have a majority.

I remember vividly the election night in November 1980. I had set up a big campaign headquarters at the Washington Hilton in the grand ballroom, and as the numbers came in, John Heinz, then chairman of the Republican Central Campaign Committee, came up to me and announced that if numbers held, we were going to have 51 members in the Senate. At that, I turned to Bob Dole, who was standing nearby, and said, "Bob, just think, if these numbers hold, you're going to be chairman of the Finance Committee." Bob, with his typical great wit, turned around and asked who was going to tell Russell Long. I recall that there were days when I thought nobody had told Russell Long.

As a result of the practice obtained through our committee of ranking members pantomime, we took on our new responsibilities in January 1981 having had at least some experience as a majority party, even though none of us had ever been either in the majority or a chairman. We also had a degree of unity and purpose that I believe served both us and President Reagan well. I was privileged then to preside once a week not over a meeting of ranking members, but a meeting of chairmen, and it worked very well.

I had the best of all worlds, however, because this was a unique and different experience for the Republican senators, and since they had not yet figured out how much power a chairman really has, they were at that time more willing to be led than they were later on. Thus, Bob Dole had a much tougher job as majority leader during the two years after I had retired from the Senate.

I did retire from the Senate, however, and I could give you a long lecture on my philosophical reasons for that decision, but I will not do so. I believe I could have been reelected in Tennessee, but I also have an abiding belief that as long as the Congress is a full-time Congress—and it is essentially that—it should not be a lifetime undertaking. I used to deliver lectures about how we ought to return to the day of the citizen legislature—how we should be in session only part of the year and then return to our homes and communities to resume our business as farmers, doctors, lawyers, shop stewards, or whatever. This was the case for many years when the Congress was essentially a board of directors charged with the responsibility of setting broad, general policy instead of passing the thousand-page bills it does now.

After a while I began to think that if I really believed in such a system, I had better retire; so after 18 years in the Senate, I decided not to run for reelection. I have always been happy with that decision. I returned to private life with gusto and enthusiasm. I am happy, my family is happy, and not inconsequentially, my banker is happy.

You should also know that in 1980 I ran for the Republican presidential nomination. You might not know that unless you play Trivial Pursuit, but I did run. Any of you who might be thinking about running for president should know that when you make that undertaking, you contract a terrible illness; that is, you think that you will not be able to live another day unless you run for president again. It was in February of 1987 that I had an especially virulent attack of this sickness; it was so bad that I gathered up my family and took them to Florida for a family conference on whether I should run for president again. That idea was dismissed pretty quickly, so, for lack of something better to do, I took my five-year-old grandson to the zoo. While I was at the zoo, President Reagan called, and according to my wife Joy who took the call, their conversation went like this: "Joy, where is Howard?" "Mr. President, Howard is at the zoo." My wife said there was then a presidential chortle on the other end of the line, and Ronald Reagan was heard to say, "Wait until he sees the zoo I have in mind for him!"

When I returned from the zoo and learned of this, I called the President, who then asked me to come to Washington the next day. He did not tell me why he wanted me to come, but, if you recall, in February of 1987 we were in the midst of the Iran-contra affair and thus not exactly the high point of the Reagan presidency. I assumed that the President was going to ask me to join his administration on some basis, and I was marshaling arguments as to why I could not, the principal one being that I was at that moment thinking of my own political career and a possible run for the presidency. Besides, I had already done my public duty by serving for 18 years and had returned to private life.

I had my arguments pretty well lined out when I flew to Washington. I was met by a White House car and taken to the southwest gate—the gate you enter if you want to try to avoid the press—and into the diplomatic reception room entrance, which is, again, the discreet way to enter the White House. I was then taken to the third floor, which is the floor where we keep presidents. When the elevator door opened, there stood Ronald Reagan by himself in the hallway, and without any formality, he said, "Howard, I have to have a new chief of staff, and I want you to be it." I then heard myself say, "All right." That, my friends, is how I became chief of staff to the President of the United States.

I should also tell you that I have known Ronald Reagan since he was elected governor of California in 1966, the same year I was elected senator. We knew each other as politicians know each other, but we did not know each other well until I became majority leader during his first term and then worked with him closely. I thought I knew Reagan well then, but I really didn't know him as well as I thought I did until I worked with him daily at the White House. Forgive me if you think this unduly partisan, but I must tell you that I have a deep admiration for Ronald Reagan. I think he is the most underestimated President we have had in a long time, and I predict that historians will record him as a strong, determined, well-focused, and effective President. He did what no president really has done since Franklin Roosevelt: He made a difference in the fundamental public policy of our country. That is not inconsequential.

Some say that President Reagan was not very intellectually active, and that he dozed off in conversations and took afternoon naps. That is not true. He was a very bright man, and I can tell you firsthand that none of that happened while I was there, except that on trips overseas he would occasionally nod, and I would wake up long enough to notice it. In fact, President Reagan was very alert. He generally stayed in the office from 9 o'clock in the morning until 5 or 5:30 in the afternoon without a break, and almost always had lunch in the Oval Office or in the adjacent study.

It is true that Ronald Reagan did not like to be bothered with the usual burden of detail that comes the president's way if the president permits it. However, it is also true—and this is the most important characteristic of the man in my view—that he had what I call a central core of convictions. He knew who he was, what he believed, and where he wanted to go. His decisions flowed from those three traits.

Reagan was a very predictable president. He believed in a strong America, militarily; he wanted to be resolute, determined, and outspoken diplomatically; he believed strongly in the free-market and private-enterprise system. For Reagan, government was a major burden, and he wanted to reduce its intrusiveness and the burdens of taxation. He believed that we spent too much rather than taxed too little. He stood by all of these convictions for eight years.

I did not always agree with him, however. One of the things I said, which tops the list of things I should never have said, concerned the President's proposed economic program. This program consisted principally of massive tax cuts and efforts to reduce the level of the budget. I was asked by Sam Donaldson during an interview outside the West Wing what I thought of the proposal. I responded that I thought it was a riverboat gamble.

In the end, President Reagan won part of that gamble and lost part of it. We had the longest continuous peacetime economic expansion in the history of the country. We spent over $1 trillion making America strong and fostered a change in relations between the United States, the Soviet Union, and the rest of the world. In fact, we have now seen the second revolution in this century in the Soviet Union in Russia, and this one is as profound as the Bolshevik Revolution. We have also witnessed the reinvigoration of the United Nations, which, as it works its will in the Middle East, is perhaps now doing what it was meant to do in 1945.

We have also seen massive deficits, however, which President Reagan did not anticipate, and which were part of the gamble that he took and did not win. Altogether, however, I believe Ronald Reagan was a historic president who was virtually unrivaled in the last 50 years and whom I think history will record in that way. For me, it was a great privilege and pleasure to work with him in both difficult times and times of triumph.

QUESTION: How would you evaluate the political action committees (PACs) and their effect on your leadership, either minority or majority, in the Senate? Will they continue to erode our democratic form of government and election process?

SENATOR BAKER: First, let me take issue with you on the question of whether they erode our democratic form of government.

I believe that in some ways they do, but in others they do not. Perhaps it would be useful to go back and examine the origins of PACs.

The campaign reform bill that was introduced, debated, and finally adopted after the Watergate affair was far-reaching, extensive, and much of it was very good. However, during its examination on the floor of the Senate—rather than in committee—the bill was thoroughly debated on the grounds that there is a tight limitation on what individuals can contribute to presidential or congressional campaigns. They would not be able to contribute anything if we adopted public financing for the presidential campaigns. Moreover, corporations were not able to contribute at the federal level, but there were no limitations on such contributions by organized labor. Thus, the political action committee was created in an effort to counterbalance the virtually unrestrained ability of the unions to make unlimited contributions on behalf of their members and from their treasuries. That was not necessarily a bad purpose. PACs, however, have since grown to the point where they probably now have a distorting effect on the political system. They certainly are commented on far more than is the power of organized labor.

I personally believe that no one should be able to contribute to a candidate for whom he cannot vote, and therefore that PACs should not exist at all. However, I also believe that labor unions should not be able to make contributions. There should be no limitation on the amount that can be contributed to a candidate by an individual, but there should be a full and timely disclosure of contributions. Whether a lavish contribution to a particular candidate is a good or bad thing is a political judgment, but it should not be a legal judgment. In a little book that I completed years ago, I wrote that in federal elections no contributions should be allowed two weeks before the election, and that contributions should be disclosed publicly so that people could make their own political judgments.

I also believe, however, that the time to change the system is at hand, and I predict that before long, PACs will be eliminated. My hope is that eventually there will be another way of either restraining or balancing the force of organized labor and organized business associations. The best way to accomplish this would be to prohibit contributions from anybody who cannot vote.

There was a fellow who worked at my father's house in Tennessee, and in 1952 my dad asked him if he was going to vote for General Eisenhower. When he said no, my dad asked him why not, since he had been a Republican all of his life. His response was that he never voted for anybody who didn't know him.

QUESTION: On a previous occasion in this room, the statement was made that the significant changes that have occurred in Russia, including the reaction to that form of government and its philosophy, were the result of a self-generating upheaval and were not significantly influenced by the U.S. military buildup or foreign policy. I take it from a previous statement of yours that you disagree with that conclusion.

SENATOR BAKER: I do disagree with it. Although there obviously is some element of truth to that view since there has been an evolutionary change in attitudes in the Soviet Union, I do not believe that those changes were dominant. I do not know this firsthand, but I believe that at some point Mikhail Gorbachev and perhaps a small core of his advisers, which probably included Sergei Akhromeyev, took a look at their economic situation and the challenges they would face in matching or exceeding America's military commitment, especially to the "Star Wars" program and the advanced systems associated with the submarine forces, and decided that they simply could not compete on those terms and still maintain their East European empire. This would not have happened without the challenge of America's rearmament.

QUESTION: As a long-time, strong admirer of President Reagan, I have always been troubled by two things. First, why didn't President Reagan take charge of the Iran-contra affair instead of leaving it to the lawyers and courts and Special Prosecutor Lawrence Walsh? Second, before Reagan left office, why didn't he pardon North and others who did what they did not for personal gain, but rather because they believed that what they were doing was in the interest of the President?

SENATOR BAKER: I do not know why President Reagan did not act in a decisive way from the beginning. I do know that he was greatly dispirited and demoralized by the affair when I arrived in

February 1987, and that my first duty, as I perceived it, was to find every possible scrap of information on the matter and make my own judgment about the facts. Once I had concluded in my own mind— forgive the implications of this remark—that the President of the United States was telling the truth, I believed that my responsibility was to try to pull him out of the doldrums, to create an organized program for him, and to then ask him to act in a decisive way. You may remember President Reagan's speech on television, which gave him an opportunity to make a definitive statement about his relationship to these facts.

Returning to my desire to determine the facts, I had accepted the chief of staff's job on one condition, and that was that I could bring my own lawyer. I chose A. B. Culvahouse, one of my law partners and an extraordinary young lawyer who was a Root-Tilden Scholar at NYU and was very bright and well-prepared. The President gave him a free hand, and before long Culvahouse had assembled a staff of 70 lawyers and archivists. Finding archivists who can go through highly classified material is sort of tough, but he assembled his team and we went through every scrap of paper, every computer disc, every bit of data we could find to ascertain what was the President's knowledge of these affairs. We concluded that the President was not involved directly and was not aware of the details of the undertaking.

Discussing this subject with the President early on during my time at the White House, I also challenged him somewhat on certain points about Oliver North. Perhaps you know that President Reagan can be very assertive and even petulant sometimes in his remarks. At that time he told me that while people kept telling him about what North did and what he'd instructed him to do, the truth of the matter was that he did not believe he would know Oliver North if he walked into the room, except for having seen his picture. North was only a junior lieutenant colonel on the third-ranked staff of the National Security Council. Prompted by that remark, I went to the presidential logs and, if my memory serves me correctly, found that Oliver North had been with Ronald Reagan exactly four times and never alone. As for why Reagan didn't pardon North, my guess is that he didn't pardon him because he was mad at him for having created such a problem for his administration. I don't know that, but I do suspect it.

In any event, I am convinced that Reagan was not involved in the affair. The final bit of evidence was a unique set of documents, perhaps unrivaled in the American presidency, created by the President's daily diary entries. Every night except for those nights when he was in the hospital, Ronald Reagan retired to his private study in the White House, and from there or wherever he was, wrote a few lines or sometimes a few pages in longhand in his diary. The diary consisted of leatherbound, not loose-leaf books, and his entries were in pen so erasures would have been virtually impossible. Those books provided a contemporaneous record of the Reagan presidency. Based on their entries and our search of the data, along with my own contact with Reagan and the opportunity to judge his responses, his conduct, and his demeanor with whatever talent was left to me as a trial lawyer from years past, I concluded that the President was telling the truth.

Regarding your question of why President Reagan did not try to resolve this issue and defend his way from the beginning, I do not know the answer to that. He should have done so.

That same question, however, might apply to Richard Nixon. I am also convinced beyond a shadow of a doubt that Nixon knew nothing about the break-in at the Democratic National Committee headquarters ahead of time. His mistake was that when he did find out about it shortly thereafter, he didn't try to liquidate the issue. He could have lined up a bunch of people on the south lawn of the White House and fired them before live television and been a moral giant and a great hero, but he didn't. The reason he didn't probably has more to do with the nature of the man and his loyalty to his staff than anything else.

Perhaps there is also an analogy there in terms of why Ronald Reagan did not promptly resolve the Iran-contra issue. He had people he worked with daily and a competent staff. It was only later that he discovered that they were doing things without his knowledge and authority.

The one thing you must never do on a presidential staff is to assume that there is anything the President does not want to know. The president is the president, and no one has a right to act on major issues without his consent and knowledge. I think that did happen in the Iran-contra affair.

As for the role of Special Prosecutor Walsh, one of these days we are going to have to get a handle on special prosecutors. They are a wonderful thing, but they violate the rule against perpetuity as they go on and on forever without any supervision of their work. They are free agents or loose cannons, if you will. Thus, I believe we need to re-address the question of special prosecution in connection with the alleged misconduct of public officers. I couldn't say that while I was in government, but I can say it now.

NARRATOR: Could you tell us about the actual experience of advising the President, especially on issues where you may have been more knowledgeable about the congressional setting? I am thinking in particular of the veto of the highway bill in 1988.

SENATOR BAKER: I am speaking out of school now, and I almost never do this, but I told the President in that case that we would not be able to sustain a veto. That judgment was not based on my superior knowledge, but rather it was based on my superior instinct acquired during my time in the Congress. There were just too many people with projects too dear to their hearts to sustain that veto. It was not as though we were dealing with the United Nations or the Soviet Union, France, England, or even with the New York Stock Exchange. Rather, we were dealing with a piece of road in Wyoming, and while one might act as a moral giant on some matters, that almost never happens when one's own piece of the pie is at stake.

I told the President essentially what I just told you, and he said that it was still a matter of principle; the bill ought to be vetoed. My response was that the principle of being overridden and its effect on his presidency should also be considered. President Reagan could become very stiff and formal and even very angry with me from time to time. He said that he was going to veto the bill anyway. I told him that I would do my best to sustain his veto, and when he asked what he should do, I told him that he should go up to the Capitol and ask for permission to attend the Tuesday policy luncheon with the Senate Republicans and then ask for their support. That was the absolute maximum that he could do. In the end, however, the President was rejected and the veto was overridden. In that particular case my judgment was not necessarily superior to his, but my experience in terms of what the Congress would do on a highway bill was. Had the issue been a civil rights bill or something else, it would have been different. On a highway bill, however, I subscribe to the theory that all politics is local; highway bills, in particular, are very local pieces of legislation.

QUESTION: I am interested in the relationship between the chief of staff and members of the Cabinet. As I understand it, historically, the Cabinet was intended to be sort of the official family of the President. Does the chief of staff act as an intermediary between the Cabinet and the president, or does the president still maintain direct access to the Cabinet?

SENATOR BAKER: I have to guard my words here and trust that certain people who are my friends will remain friends when we finish this encounter. The truth of the matter is that the Cabinet officials' first responsibility today is to administer large departments or organizations. They see the President infrequently and long ago ceased to be his official family in terms of advice, interaction, and conversation.

The Reagan Cabinet met every two or three weeks or every two or three months, and to tell you the truth, President Reagan generally did not look forward to it. These meetings always had an agenda, which was pretty well adhered to, and there was very little spontaneity involved. In the Reagan administration the chief of staff controlled the gate, and only the secretary of defense and the secretary of state had standing rights to visit with the President. Every other member of the Cabinet had to have my consent first. That is probably not the way it ought to be, but that is how the system worked and I suspect has worked for a long time. Cabinet officials are very important. They are in the line of succession to the presidency, they require confirmation by the Senate, and they administer large organizations. Ordinarily, however, with the exception of the secretaries of defense and state, they do not have the ear of the president. I understand that in previous circumstances the director of Central Intelligence has also had free access to the president, but recently that has not been the case.

It is the White House staff, on the other hand, that has assumed the role of the president's family. They are the ones with whom he speaks daily and who have the first cut at identifying the issues, at writing papers, and at giving the president his options. In that scheme of things, the Cabinet functions through the secretary of the Cabinet, who is a member of the White House staff, and through domestic and economic policy council meetings, as well as National Security Council meetings, where such matters are discussed and then sent to the chief of staff's office for the president's decision. Once again, that may not be the way it ought to be, but that is the way it is.

QUESTION: Any comment on the 1992 election?

SENATOR BAKER: I think that President Bush will run again and that Vice President Quayle will be his running mate. Who knows what is going to happen in the Middle East or with the economy, but assuming those matters are handled reasonably well, I believe they will be reelected by comfortable margins in 1992.

QUESTION: Will you verify for us Donald Regan's account regarding President Reagan's fifth day postoperative? The press reported that NSC adviser Robert McFarlane and Donald Regan met with the President and that Iran and the hostages were discussed. The President later said that he doesn't remember the conversation. As a physician, however, I can tell you that five days postoperative or post-anesthesia was not the time to discuss such a matter. In your research, did you discover anything about what happened during that time period, or is your predecessor telling us a story?

SENATOR BAKER: I don't think that he is telling a story, but I do not know how much they discussed. As I noted earlier, President Reagan's diary contains no entry on that subject on that day, or any entry at all for that matter, and when A. B. Culvahouse asked the President about that particular event, the President again responded that he did not recall that incident. Perhaps that is a convenient dodge, but I came to believe Ronald Reagan and I still believe him. I am not challenging Don Regan's account, but if it did occur, it did not register with President Reagan and he issued no instructions at that time. You are absolutely right, however, that five days postoperative does not sound like the optimal time for a 75-year-old man to address an issue of that consequence. We did focus on that particular point, however.

QUESTION: Assuming it will take a combined reduction in government expenses and an increase in taxes to balance the budget, why do the Republicans want to avoid any change in the income tax and prefer instead to alter other taxes?

SENATOR BAKER: First of all, I am out of the business of giving the Republican position. I don't do that any more. I now give the Howard Baker position, and I can do that freely and even arrogantly. I agree with President Reagan and President Bush and many others who say that we don't tax too little; rather, we spend too much. I also agree that certain levels of taxation have a demonstrably stultifying effect on creativity and economic energy. The budget, however, cannot be allowed to produce deficits that accumulate to the point where they have a depressing effect on the economy, and that is the point that we are at now.

I believe that sooner or later we will have to adjust the tax codes in some ways, whether we alter excise taxes, the merchant rate on the income tax, or capital gains and investment tax credits, or all of those exotic things. Those decisions I will leave up to others, but we are going to require more money, even as we attempt to reduce the level of federal expenditure.

The truth of the matter is that the principal problem for 10, 15, or 20 years now has been institutional in nature. The budget process simply is not working. There is virtually no link between what we collect and what we spend at the federal level, and we live from continuing resolution to continuing resolution. By the way, this process is likely to be unconstitutional because it probably violates the "presentment clause" of the Constitution, which says that every bill, before it becomes law, will be presented to the president for his approval or disapproval. Waiting until the last minute and then sending the president one big congressional resolution that appropriates the entire federal budget is not in keeping with the requirements of the Constitution. I am not going to litigate that, however, so we still have to approach the problem through the political process.

My own view is that there are several steps we should take. First, we ought to stop dealing the president out of the budget-making process. Keep in mind that I am a man who spent 18 years in Congress, so I can say this with some sense of perspective. The President is all-powerful in some matters and very powerful in others, but he is virtually cut out of the budget-making process, which is ironic, considering that he is the only official in the government who has the constitutional duty of presenting a budget. Too often these days, however, the Congress legally declares the president's budget dead on arrival and goes on either to create one of its own or not to do one at all, which has happened once or twice in the last few years.

Thus, the first thing that should be done is to approach the institutional problem and to provide, perhaps by constitutional amendment, that the president's budget must be considered in a timely way by the Congress. To make such a provision truly effective, however, it would probably also be necessary to make it less convenient to overturn the president's budget. The fact that a simple majority of a quorum can now do that is ridiculous and negates the value of a presidential budget as required by the Constitution. I believe that we ought to allow the president's budget, in its several parts, to be overturned by the Congress by something more than a simple majority of a quorum; maybe by an absolute majority of the membership or maybe by a two-thirds majority, but the presidential budget should be given greater strength and validity.

I waffle on the question of a line-item veto. I believe such a provision would make a fundamental shift in the respective powers of the president and the Congress on appropriations, and I think the separation-of-powers concept is better than a line-item veto. I used to make this argument to Ronald Reagan, and he would listen for a while and then look me in the eye and say, "Howard, just remember I am President; you are not." I told him that I remembered that fact, but I still think the current concept is better.

There are other options as well. We could provide for enhanced recision or deferral authority, although that would be tricky too since the fundamental authority of the Congress is the power of the purse, and if the president were allowed to spend money that the Congress appropriates, we would come awfully close to changing that balance too. Frankly, I think the best answer would be to provide that the president's budget must be considered in a timely manner and that it could not be overturned by accident. It would have to be handled in a deliberate way before it was returned to the president for his approval. I do not know a single soul who agrees with me on this issue, but that is what I believe.

As I touched on earlier, I also believe that until we return to the idea that the Congress is a board of directors rather than a bunch of elected bureaucrats, we will continue to have problems such as those we've had with highway bills and other matters that are near and dear to politicians' hearts.

QUESTION: How did your relationship change with your former colleagues when you became part of the executive branch?

SENATOR BAKER: That is a very perceptive question, because my relationship with those people did change. I'm sure that the President asked me to take this job in part because he thought that I could bring the Congress along, and because I had good personal friendships and longtime relationships there. However, those individuals, while they were unfailingly courteous and friendly, were not unfailingly obedient. I instantly became something different. Although it was extremely valuable to have had that experience in Congress, the Congress was not about to take every suggestion that I or the President made lying down.

It is interesting, however, that now that I have left the White House, my relationship with Congress returned somewhat to the way it was. Forgive the immodesty here, but from time to time former Senate colleagues will call me and privately ask for my ideas or insights about a particular matter. They would never have done that while I was at the White House.

QUESTION: Senator Baker, would you comment on the significance of minority caucuses in Congress?

SENATOR BAKER: I don't have any problem with minority caucuses. There have always been groups with similar views or prejudices who have gathered together to amplify their effectiveness. It is somewhat due to the nature of the Congress that such groups would form, and we have to deal with that fact. Not all proposals from these groups are rational, and opposition leaders are not always principled. However, I simply do not have much of a problem with that. I am a devotee of the Congress and all of its pluralism, including all of its warps and advantages. The Congress is the essential element in the American system, and without it our government would be very different. I accept the Congress for what it is: a group of men and women who are not perfect. That reminds me of the story told about Will Rogers, who was not only a great humorist, but also a great philosopher and a great newspaperman. He wrote a column from Washington for a small paper in Oklahoma, where he had been during the 1930s, and when he returned someone asked him whether it was true that Congress was made up of thieves and rascals. Rogers responded that of course that was true, but it was also a good cross section of its constituency. Congress is the best cross section of the country that we have anyplace in representative government. Notwithstanding that story, it is not made up of thieves and rascals.

NARRATOR: Senator, during the Reagan administration you were in the control tower, in a sense, on arms control matters. Can you tell us anything about the President, your relationship with him, and the relationship between the departments of State and Defense in terms of the evolution of arms control agreements?

SENATOR BAKER: That is such a broad subject that we could spend another hour on it, but let me pick two or three points that may be of interest. First, contrary to skeptical newspaper accounts, Ronald Reagan from his first day as President did indeed wish to "rid the world of nuclear weapons." Although some of his efforts—Reykjavik, for example—were perhaps not as well-prepared as they might have been, my point is that Reagan did not change his position on arms control. His view was a stated principle from the beginning of his administration.

Secondly, when I first arrived, the President was, as I said earlier, somewhat despondent and dispirited. He once said to me, "Howard, I think I'm the only person in this city who still wants an arms control agreement." My response was: "No, Mr. President, at least there are two of us, and you ought to persevere." I am not claiming credit for what happened, but following that, the President made it clear to the National Security Council staff and to the secretary of state that he wanted to continue the arms control process.

As matters progressed, however, it became clear that the President was being inundated with conflicting advice and a sea of complexities. Frank Carlucci was national security adviser during the first part of my tenure as chief of staff, and he and I talked one day after one of our regular 9 o'clock meetings with the President. I told him that I thought the President would sink in this sea of complexities unless we outlined the process so he could make some presidential choices. Frank agreed and compiled a list of approximately 80 issues that required a presidential decision if we were going to achieve an arms control agreement.

You may remember the pope's 1987 visit to Miami. President Reagan was there to greet him, and while the pope was participating in one of his own events, the President, Frank Carlucci, and I met in a Holiday Inn suite, and for four hours we went over that list of 80-some odd points. The President listened to them; I am convinced that he understood them, and during those four hours he made a prompt and effective presidential decision on every one of them. Had it not been for those decisions, I do not believe we would have had the INF Treaty.

The final point I want to make is that the President had a clear view of what type of system he wanted in place after he left office. He had reconciled himself to the idea that he wasn't going to achieve a START treaty during his term, but he was also convinced that had it not been for his insistence on the "Star Wars" program such a treaty would never be achieved. He thus left office convinced that there had to be remaining commitment to "Star Wars." I generally don't comment on what sitting presidents say or do, but I am also convinced that George Bush was well aware of President Reagan's intentions and was determined to employ the same strategy that President Reagan had—i.e., to go forward with advanced, new, and even exotic systems to convince the Soviet Union of our terms on strategic weaponry.

NARRATOR: People often assign the phrase "feet of clay" to those who work in Washington. On the way back from Washington and a meeting with Senator Baker about two months ago, however, Wilson Newman and I remarked that Senator Baker might well be an exception. We are thrilled and delighted to have had this opportunity to hear him speak. We hold him in the highest regard and hope that he will find a way to come back and speak with us again.

CHAPTER 2

REAGAN AS POLITICAL LEADER

FRANK J. FAHRENKOPF, JR.

NARRATOR: Mr. Fahrenkopf was chairman of the Republican National Committee from 1983 until 1989. He is currently co-chairman of the Committee on Presidential Debates and a member of the oldest law firm in Washington, Hogan and Hartson.

Mr. Fahrenkopf was born in Brooklyn but quickly "escaped" and spent most of his childhood in the Lake Tahoe region of Nevada. He received his bachelor's degree from the University of Nevada and his doctor of laws degree at the University of California, Berkeley. He practiced law in Nevada and taught criminal law at the University of Nevada and the National Judicial College in Reno. Soon thereafter, he became chairman of the Nevada Republican Committee and served from 1975 to 1983. He was a delegate to the Republican National Convention in 1972, 1976, and 1980; was national chairman of the Republican State Chairman's Association; is vice chairman of the National Endowment for Democracy; and is a member of the board of the American Political Foundation. He has been the recipient of numerous awards, including the Distinguished Service Award of the U.S. Jaycees and the Humanitarian Award of the National Conference of Christians and Jews. He received recognition as someone who brought new concepts of leadership and organization to the Republican party. We are delighted that he has made time in his busy schedule to join us for this inquiry into the Reagan administration.

21

MR. FAHRENKOPF: I would like to begin by explaining how I got to know Ronald Reagan and how I ran the Republican party once I became chairman. I also wanted to spend a moment discussing what was really a product of the Reagan presidency, namely, the method the Republican party uses in approaching presidential campaigns. We approach them from a strategy standpoint that is totally different from the Democratic party, and I think perhaps that's why as a minority party—which we still are—we have won five out of the last six presidential elections.

I went to law school at the University of California, Berkeley, as a somewhat moderate Republican. I was there during the free-speech movement, and after seeing what happened at Berkeley for three years, my wife and I came out as hard conservatives. I then went back to Nevada and started practicing law.

One of my dearest and closest personal friends and colleagues in politics for the last 25 years has been Senator Paul Laxalt of Nevada. I first met Paul when he was running for lieutenant governor of the state of Nevada at the same time that the gubernatorial nominee of the Republican party was an old cowboy actor named Rex Bell, who was married to Clara Bow. (I hadn't thought about this, but Paul has been around a lot of cowboy actors.) About six weeks before the election, Rex Bell died of a heart attack. There was no way, however, that Paul could then suddenly move up and become the gubernatorial candidate. A runoff had to be held, and someone else ran for governor on the Republican ticket. A Democrat actually won the governorship, but Paul won the lieutenant governorship and then four years later became the governor of the state.

It was during that period of time that I met Ronald Reagan for the first time. At that time the states of Nevada and California were very concerned about saving Lake Tahoe from pollution and overdevelopment. The two neighboring governors, Ronald Reagan and Paul Laxalt, decided that they would work together on a compact between the two states to save the lake, and as a result they became close personal friends. They had known each other earlier, during the race for the White House in 1964. Paul had actually run for the United States Senate back then against Senator Howard Cannon and lost by 86 votes. Anyway, these two men working together became very close friends. Governor Laxalt would very often have Governor Reagan over at political events in Nevada, and that's when I first got to know Ronald Reagan.

I really became active politically in the late 1960s. I became the chairman of the Reno Young Republicans and then became the national committeeman of the Young Republican organization in the state of Nevada. In 1971 I ran unsuccessfully for the national chairmanship of the National Young Republicans; I was defeated by a fellow who is a good friend of mine, now a congressman from Tennessee, Donald Sundquist. Don and I campaigned all over the country against each other. You might be interested to know that one of the reasons I lost was that somebody unit-ruled California against me, so that while I had a good portion of the votes in that state, she unit-ruled it against me. Her name was Maureen Reagan. It's a true story. We were on the other side of the fence in those days.

I then became involved in what we would call the senior party in Nevada. Governor Laxalt had decided to retire from the governorship after four years and was out of politics. We then decided that something had to be done about politics in our state, and we convinced Paul to run for the United States Senate. He ran and won. We called him "Landslide Laxalt" because he won the Senate seat by 625 votes. His close relationship with Ronald Reagan continued even though Jerry Ford was in the White House and was seeking the Republican nomination. Paul had the courage—and it took a lot of courage—not to support an incumbent; he announced that he was going to chair the Reagan for Presidency Committee in 1975. In a close election at the convention in Kansas City, Ronald Reagan lost his nomination bid to President Ford. Jerry Ford was nominated, and then unfortunately we lost that race to Jimmy Carter. The American people saw the illogic in that very quickly.

In 1980 Paul again assumed the chairmanship of the Reagan campaign, and we were successful in winning in a landslide over Carter. It was at that point, when the new administration was being put together, that I was approached. I had become the chairman of the Nevada Republican party in 1975, the chairman of all the Western Republican chairmen in 1977, and the chairman of all the Republican state chairmen in the country in 1980. I was asked whether or not I would like to move to Washington and become the national chairman of the party; I said thanks, but no thanks. My kids were still at an age where I just couldn't do it, and my law practice was going well. I enjoyed my lifestyle at Lake Tahoe, and so I said no. At that point an attorney from Utah who had worked very hard for Ronald Reagan for a long time, Richard Richards, became the chairman of the Republican party.

You may recall that the November 1982 elections did not go well. We got our clock cleaned, as they say. I was the chairman of all the chairmen at that time, and I got a call on the Wednesday after the election from the White House asking me to come back to Washington on Saturday to brief President Reagan as to what had occurred in the country. I said, "I don't want to do that. I'm leading a delegation of Republican state chairmen the following Monday to go to Taiwan on a ten-day trip. You can get somebody else to do that." The White House was very insistent and said, "No, you have to come back." Well, I got sandbagged. As soon as I got inside the White House the man popped the question, and you do not say no to a President of the United States. If you do say no, you only get to say it once.

In this way, I became the chairman of the Republican National Committee. It was a very unique situation that required a great deal of planning and strategy. What we structured in 1983 was a two-tiered party arrangement; Paul Laxalt was known as the general chairman of the Republican party while I was the chairman of the Republican National Committee. There never had been a general chairman of either party before that. Our logic was that we were hopeful that Ronald Reagan was going to seek reelection in 1984, but we had no guarantees. He would not tell any of us whether or not he was going to seek reelection. We felt it was important to make sure that we had tied together the leadership of the Republican National Committee, the Republican Senatorial Committee (a free-standing committee with its own budget and fund-raising), and the Republican Congressional Committee of the House. Paul acted as Ronald Reagan's eyes and ears on the Hill—he was "the President's best friend." This gave Paul the opportunity to start preparing for the 1984 campaign, pulling all the loose ends together at the same time that we were using party funds, not illegally, no impropriety involved, but it gave us an opportunity to make sure that we had total control of the party going into 1984, and it worked very well.

As party chairman I worked closely with the political operatives in the White House. I received a phone call a few minutes before this forum began from a reporter who asked, "Don't you find it unusual that they don't have a strong political director in the Bush White House, like Reagan had in Lyn Nofziger and Ed Rollins?" I did not know that the White House political director today doesn't even sit in on the senior staff meetings. I had a very close working relationship with Lyn Nofziger and with Ed Rollins, who followed him in that job. Both men were involved on a day-to-day basis with planning. As chairman of the party, every seven to ten days I sat in on a meeting in the Cabinet Room of what was called the Republican Policy Committee. We would meet from about 9:00 a.m. to 10:15 a.m. The President would sit in the center; to his right would be Bob Dole, the Republican leader in the Senate; to his left would be Bob Michel, the Republican leader in the House; and then their deputies and key committee chairmen would also be present. There would usually be about seven Republican senators, along with Trent Lott, Jack Kemp, and Dick Cheney from the House. On the other side of the table, Vice President Bush used to sit directly across from the President. Behind the President would sit his staff—the chief of staff and principal people. I would sit behind the vice president, usually alongside the secretary of state, secretary of defense, and other Cabinet members, depending upon what the hot subject matter was on the Hill at the moment. If it was a matter of dealing with the crisis in the Middle East, the secretary of defense might give a briefing, or if it was an economic matter, Secretary of the Treasury Don Regan might be there. These meetings were a regular occurrence during the six years that I was the chairman of the party. They were an attempt to work with the leadership of the Republican party on the Hill.

It was an interesting experience to watch Ronald Reagan during those meetings. You've all heard the criticism that I've always felt to be unfounded: Ronald Reagan had to have his cards, and if he didn't have his cards there he didn't know what to say, and it was the cards that told him what to do and how to do it. Well, he would always come in with that sparkle in his eye and always a joke to start us off. He would have an opening statement, and he did read from cards, but that statement would set forth what his message was to the leadership. It was an open, to-and-fro discussion. Ronald Reagan did not need the cards to make clear his position on such issues as increased taxes or whether he was going to veto something. I saw him more than once take off his reading glasses and throw them on the table so hard that they would go up and hit the top of the ceiling in the Cabinet room. He was very forceful. He knew what he believed in, and he knew what he wanted to see accomplished. He was a very strong leader in that regard.

I don't think there is any question that the team around the President in the first four years was more effective than the team that surrounded him in the second. There was a great deal of criticism of the so-called tri approach of James Baker, Edwin Meese, and Michael Deaver when they first went in, in 1981. During the first four years a great deal was accomplished in turning around policies that had gone the other way for a long time. It was very productive.

Being chief of staff to the President of the United States is a most thankless job. Most people don't realize it. You never get a day off; you never even get an hour off. You are always on call—there is no such thing as going away for the weekend. It's a tough job. I thought that Jim Baker did an absolutely marvelous job.

Don Regan is a friend of mine, and I thought Don Regan brought some excellent skills to the job. But because it is a tough job, you also have to have the temperament to deal with it. It is hard to have been a colonel in the Marines and also have run Merrill Lynch and then suddenly be involved in the give and take of politics. His leadership will always be under the shadow. I haven't read Nancy Reagan's book yet, and I'm a little worried about what she is going to say, but I'm sure she is not going to say nice things about Don Regan. There was no question that there was a great deal of friction. In fact there was a week during which I was the loop between Nancy Reagan and Don Regan. They weren't talking to each other. She would call me and say, "Frank, would you tell him that?" and I would tell him, and he would say, "You tell her . . ." and I would say to myself, "I've got to get out of this loop. I'm in harm's way in that loop." I did get out; I got out as quickly as I could.

One of the things we developed early, starting in 1983, was the planning for the 1984 election. The reason I want to discuss this now is that I want to tell you the philosophy and approach the Republican party has developed. The initial planning was done by five of us: Senator Laxalt and I, Mike Deaver, Jim Baker, and my good friend Richard Wirthlin, who conducted polls for Ronald Reagan during my years there. He started with him in California and then continued that polling when we were in the White House. The five of us started meeting on a regular basis in 1983, a full year before the President actually told us he was going to run again. We began our strategy and our polling, and then we widened the organization and got ready.

Let me tell you how we approach the campaign. Our approach is very different, and with it I knew that we would win the 1988 election. If you remember, Michael Dukakis left Atlanta with a 17-point lead, but I knew we'd won the election when he said, "I'm going to conduct the campaign in every state in this union, a 50-state campaign." As soon as I heard that I chuckled to myself and said, "This campaign is over if he really intends to do that." You may remember that Richard Nixon said that when he ran against John Kennedy. He lost because that is not the way you put together a presidential campaign.

I don't know whether it was through the ingeniousness or mischievousness of our Founding Fathers, many of whom came from this wonderful commonwealth, but the electoral college they created makes presidential politics as different from every other type of elective politics in this country as apples are from oranges. The general rule is that whether you are running for a county commission seat or a United States Senate seat, the one who gets the most votes wins. That is not the rule in presidential politics. We've had some occasions in our nation's history when the candidate who won the most popular votes ended up losing. That is because of the electoral college system.

We in the Republican party approach presidential campaign planning with the electoral college in mind, and winning the popular vote is just a subordinate mechanism to the electoral college strategy. Never in our planning—certainly in 1980, 1984, and 1988—did we face the question of campaigning in every state on an equal basis. On the basis of research begun a year before the respective campaigns, we isolated respectively 27 states in 1984 and 25 states in 1988 where we determined that between 75 and 85 percent of our time, energy, and financial resources would be spent.

That doesn't mean that the other 25 states are totally disregarded; they aren't, but they get the back of the campaign's hand. Take the state of Nevada, for example. If a Republican candidate can't win Nevada, they are not going to win the election. You don't have to put a lot of time and energy and resources in Nevada, Utah, or Wyoming. They are conservative, Western states that are going to go for a conservative candidate.

We take what is a universe of 50 states and the District of Columbia and narrow the universe for targeting purposes. We are now down to 25 states. It was 27 in 1984; in 1988 it was 25 states that had 362 electoral votes. Remember, we are looking for 270 electoral votes. So we decided to concentrate 75 to 85 percent of our time, energy, and resources in those 25 states. We know from history that the Democratic party could nominate Genghis Khan, and Genghis Khan will get 40 percent of the vote in those 25 states, and whoever the Republicans nominate will get roughly 40 percent of the vote. You start with that as a given. Each party has a base of approximately 40 percent of the vote.

In 1964 Lyndon Johnson crushed Barry Goldwater. Barry Goldwater got about 38.4 percent of the vote. When Richard Nixon crushed George McGovern, McGovern got about 37.5 percent of the vote, the lowest count in many years. When Ronald Reagan defeated Walter Mondale in 1984 with the biggest electoral vote victory of 525 electoral votes (he won every state but Minnesota and the District of Columbia), Fritz Mondale got about 43 percent of the vote.

What are we focusing on in those 25 states? We are focusing on 20 percent of the vote and *only* 20 percent of the vote. Usually that 20 percent are people who don't care about party label. The people who care about party label are in the 40 percent on either side. Our job is to focus on the 20 percent.

Our research data has also told us over the past 30 years that of the 20 percent, roughly 5 percent will define themselves as conservatives philosophically on three issues: national defense, domestic spending and the economy, and foreign policy. This will vary from state to state by a few percentage points. They say, I'm not a Democrat, not a Republican, but I am conservative on those three issues. Two percent would describe themselves as being liberal on those three issues. From the Republican side our initial attack always has been, "This is a choice for the American people between a conservative Republican and a liberal Democrat." We keep pounding out that message, and what happens? That 5 percent falls our way without a great deal of dedication of resources. We lose the 2 percent, but we are now at 45 to 42 percent. There is only 13 percent of the vote now left to focus on, and we don't even have to win a majority of the 13 percent to win the campaign. We only have to win 6 percent of it to reach the majority threshold. So all our advertising, direct mail, and other campaign strategies are targeted at the 13 percent with the goal of winning at least 6 percent. It is a totally different approach from trying to deliver a broad message to everyone. You must target, particularly if you are a minority party, and you must do that kind of planning. It worked extremely well in 1980, 1984, and 1988.

Unless the Democrats change their party rules, I don't see how they are going to win the presidency in the near future. Their rules are made up in such a way that a Northeast liberal has all the advantages. A Chuck Robb or a Sam Nunn or what we define as a conservative Democrat in their system doesn't stand a chance of winning the nomination under the present Democratic rules.

As you know, there has been a split. I was at an analysis of the presidential race in the Kennedy School of Government at Harvard in December, and most of the leadership in the Democratic party was there along with us. They got in a roaring fight among themselves—we Republicans just sat and watched—over whether the party rules should be changed in the Democratic party. They are not going to be, although Bob Beckel, who was Walter Mondale's campaign manager in 1984, jokingly said he was going to nominate me to be the chairman of the Democratic Rules Committee. I told him he didn't want to do that because I wasn't necessarily going to change them the way he thought I would.

So the system, the approach, is very important. That is also what we were doing in 1983, preparing for that 1984 race. We laid out that sort of strategy and approach.

I'll return to my subject: Reagan as leader. President Reagan is a remarkable man, a man comfortable with himself. You saw that when he got off the airplane after his operation and took the baseball hat off. He had hair on one side and was bald on the other. Here is a man who doesn't care how funny that looked; he knew that himself. He can take his ego and push it down. He was that sort of person to work with.

I think there is something about the man's metabolism that has enabled him so late in life assume the toughest job in the world and be able to do it the way he did, always in good humor. One incident I remember during the 1984 campaign was Cinco de Mayo, which is a Mexican holiday on 5 May, and we were in San Antonio, Texas, with the President. We had flown in from Washington. He was going to address a Cinco de Mayo event. It must have been 120 degrees in the shade. He had a dark suit on with a bulletproof vest under it. He was up on the stage, and people were passing out left and right (the event was held outside). They were giving him Mexican hats and serapes. It was so warm that Mike Deaver, Jim Baker, and I had not even gone out front. We were sitting in the shade under a big tree behind the stage drinking lemonade. Ronald Reagan doesn't sweat. He stood there, without sweating, and went through this hour-long ceremony with people dropping and everyone soaking wet.

The Iran-contra controversy hurt the President personally very badly. He felt let down. It provided a means whereby those who didn't like him were given the opportunity to attack him and take cheap shots, in my view, that he didn't know what he was doing, he probably slept through it, and so forth. I was in a lot of meetings with him, and I never saw him fall asleep in the Cabinet room or elsewhere, although some of those meetings were boring. I think I fell asleep in some of them. Those charges hurt him inside. He felt that he had been let down. Of course he was a president who enjoyed tremendous popularity with the American people, regardless of where he might have been on issues.

That is what is so interesting right now in the current controversy. For example, the abortion issue has become a hot issue. It is an issue in this state and in this campaign, as it is in the New Jersey gubernatorial campaign, and likewise all over the country. Ronald Reagan was always clear where he was on the issue. He said, "I'm not free-choice. I'm against abortion." Yet people could still vote for him. My own view of it is that the American people viewed Ronald Reagan as being a man of tremendous principle, a man who stood for something. You didn't necessarily have to agree with his views.

When Americans go into the privacy of that voting booth and vote for president, their party probably plays less of a role than it does elsewhere. Most American men and women go in there and say, "I want to vote for someone who is going to lead this country and who stands for something." You knew that Ronald Reagan, perhaps more than any other president in recent times, had strong principles and stood for something even if you were on the other side. That's why he was able to win a majority of women voters even though he was viewed in some of those polls as being against many of the things that the majority of women stood for. That was an unusual attribute of his presidency that helped him weather some of the storms among the American people.

I will stop here. Please feel free to ask anything about which you might be curious. I feel that this approach to presidential politics is very important because it came from the Reagan presidency. It was the strategy that led to his initial election, it led to his reelection, and it was used again most effectively in the 1988 campaign.

NARRATOR: If I understood you correctly, you said regarding the Panama Canal activity that you thought President Reagan's action might have been a little different. I tend to believe a couple of fellows who were down there when they say that the situation was confusing and ambiguous. Dick Cheney, who has been here about three times, and Brent Scowcroft, who co-chaired a national commission we had on the presidency and science advising, are such honorable people and so clearheaded in their thinking that I believe them. I know how absolutely confusing those situations are. Yet you may be right when you say that people think President Reagan either would have done something or he would have taken Noriega out.

MR. FAHRENKOPF: I think he would have. He was tremendously frustrated by the Panama situation, and certainly George Bush is frustrated by it. I tend to agree with you. I happen to think that Brent Scowcroft and particularly Dick Cheney are real shining stars of my party. Ronald Reagan's approach to things of that nature was very much like his approach to Grenada, for example—limited downside and an opportunity to do something. Windows of opportunity open and then they close. A leader knows when to go through the window. Again, I don't know any more than I've read in the newspaper about what happened. Just knowing the President and having been around him, I think that as soon as he received news that a coup was under way and they had Noriega in their possession for two or three hours or however long it was, Ronald Reagan would have said, "Go," and they would have gone over and dragged him out. Who would have been there to defend this drug runner and this murderer, to say that was something we shouldn't have done? Sure, we would have had the normal hue and cry, but that's just my perspective from being on the outside. I think he would have done that.

I visited Panama in 1984 and met with Noriega and the then president. I was there to meet with the leaders of Panama's Republican party, which was the party of the president, but not of Noriega. I also met with Ricardo Arias Calderon, who was the leader of the Christian Democrats in Panama, and he told me at that time of the difficulty and how bad Noriega was. Two days after the failed coup, I saw him on CNN. He was one of the two vice presidential candidates who won the election that Noriega overturned, and he said something that I thought was very prophetic. We are very sensitive to the Latins' view of us, the "Yankee-go-home" view. He said, "If a dog barks a lot, it had better have teeth, or it should stop barking." What he was saying was that this administration—and I agree with him—led officers in the Panamanian defense force to believe that they were saying, "If you act, if you throw this rascal out, we'll be there to help you." What he was saying is that some did act, and whether or not the United States didn't have sufficient intelligence because of its own weakness—our deficiency as to what we should have known and been able to pass to Dick Cheney or to Brent Scowcroft—we led those people to believe that if they moved, we would help. I have to believe we knew something. We barricaded two roads that were coming in and didn't barricade the third. The information we are getting out now is confusing, and I don't have any more than you do. All I know is what I read in the paper. Just knowing Ronald Reagan, he probably would have moved. I'm a great supporter of George Bush, and I'm not in any way criticizing him. I'm just saying when questioned, I believe Reagan would have done something.

George Bush in the long run may be right. It was too confusing or the cost in human life, American lives, would have been too high. That's a judgment only presidents can make. Having been around both men, I know they are different, and their approaches to problems are different.

NARRATOR: In 1984 you were dealing with people like Richard Viguerie, who were beginning to say, "This President isn't strong enough; he isn't decisive." Most of it was aimed at social issues and what Reagan hadn't done. As we saw with the Korean airline (KAL) incident, isn't there also the side of Reagan that you can sum up in the word *restraint*? How does restraint relate to decisiveness and saying "let's go"?

MR. FAHRENKOPF: In making a decision on when to move, you've got to weigh the upside and the downside. One of the things that Ronald Reagan always did was to weigh things very carefully. There is a difference between being dumb and pugnacious and being smart and pugnacious. If you are pugnacious and smart, you know when to move; you weigh it very carefully. Hopefully, you have good intelligence and know how to move, and that's what he did in Grenada. Obviously, with KAL that was not the case.

When you bring up Richard Viguerie and Howard Phillips, who are people I have known for a long time—and I've said this publicly—I never thought that they spoke for a very large constituency. I thought that they were only interested in their own affairs and that it was in their own personal best interests to be in opposition and to criticize. I'm not speaking out of school because I've told them that to their faces many times. No one would ever satisfy them. They would always criticize because they are interested in developing their own little constituency to whom they could write letters, and hopefully money would be sent back to them. So I don't think, and I've got to be very honest with you, that the Vigueries and the Howard Phillips of the world ever played a part one way or another in moving Ronald Reagan with their criticism. Those two said some of the worst things about Ronald Reagan that I've heard anyone say about a sitting president. Democrats didn't say some of the things about President Reagan that they did. As I said before, it is a question of having judgment as to when to move and when not to move.

QUESTION: I am tremendously impressed with the priorities that you assigned to strategic planning and how you have used the mechanism in order to achieve the desired political result. While you were discussing this, I wondered why, when it has been so effective on the national basis, it doesn't achieve the desired result in legislative campaigns. Would you comment on that?

MR. FAHRENKOPF: First of all, take the presidential race, because of the electoral college, and put it off in another world. It is very unique, and you can use that sort of strategy for it. The failure of the Republican party in state legislatures is why the Democrats have controlled Congress, because Congress is the product of state legislatures. The Republican party—and I was part of it at the time—was totally deficient between 1975 and 1980 in preparing for the 1980s.

If you were to go back and look at the political literature during that time frame, you would read story after story about how the American people were becoming mobile. People were migrating from the heavily industrialized upper Midwest and Northeast to "the Sunbelt." As a result of this movement, there was a dramatic change in American politics following the 1980 census and the 1981 reapportionment process. That would take place because the more liberal states in the Northeast and upper Midwest lost representation in the House after the 1980 census, and the states that picked up new House seats were those in the Sunbelt. Those states tended to be philosophically more conservative, and many therefore reasoned that this would inure to the benefit of the Republican party, being "the conservative party."

I think the leaders of our party took that anticipated benefit for granted, and thus began preparing much too late for the 1981 reapportionment process. In most states—and it varies from jurisdiction to jurisdiction—the members of the state legislature draw the congressional lines and districts that govern for the next ten years the nature, scope, and demographics of congressional districts in the state. They do that based on the population results of the census. What the Republican party didn't realize and get to work on was that in the late 1970s most of the state legislatures in this country were controlled by the Democratic party, and it drew districts that protected Democratic candidates for Congress. The Sunbelt states did pick up some House seats, but there was no way the Republican party was going to win enough House seats. I said when I was elected in 1983 that there was no way the Republican party was going to control the House of Representatives in the decade of the 1980s. It was impossible. It just could not be done.

The only way that the Republican party is going to become competitive in the House is if the Republican party does a better job making sure that they control state legislatures, because they are the ones who draw the congressional district lines. I spent a lot of time in my six years focusing on governors. My goal when I left was for us to be in a position, particularly in those Sunbelt states that are going to pick up seats in the 1991 reapportionment process, such that we would have a Republican governor and at least a third of one of the houses to sustain a veto of an egregious gerrymander put together by Democrats. That was particularly true in the South, because even though Republican candidates have been successful in presidential races—tremendously successful in Senate and House races in the South in the last few years—at the local level there has only been one party for a hundred years. It is the Democratic party. If you wanted to be involved in choosing the sheriff—and that's real political power historically in this country—or in choosing your mayor, or in other issues concerning local politics, you had to be a Democrat. If you were a registered Republican in states that had registration by party, you were out of it. Not only didn't you have a party organization, you didn't have any candidates running because usually in most of the Southern local races it was all "D"s on the ballot. So many, many people would go out and register as Democrats, where there was registration by party, to participate in the process. Sure, they might vote for a Republican for president, but that was easy to do. That is still something we fight in the South in getting control of Southern state legislatures. You look at the strong support of Republican states for Republican presidential candidates and then look at the makeup of their state legislatures.

We did very well during my chairmanship. I put a lot of time, energy, and resources there in picking up the governorships of North Carolina, South Carolina, Florida, Alabama, Texas, and Oklahoma. We picked up New Mexico, and we picked up Arizona for a short period of time before losing it, and we picked up California. I concentrated there because those are the Sunbelt states that are going to gain congressional seats. In most of those states, we've slowly been picking up state legislative seats so that we would be in a position to sustain a veto by a Republican governor of an egregious gerrymander.

The real problem that the party has is the result of Watergate. I haven't spoken much about this. I'm writing an article, and I'll speak about it now. It took the Republican party until 1986 to get back to where we were in the state legislatures of this country immediately prior to Watergate. Everyone talks about the impact of Watergate being on the presidential level and the congressional level, and while that was devastating, let me tell you where it really hurt. It hurt at the local level. I think we lost over 3,000 legislative seats in the aftermath.

What are the minor leagues for future Senate candidates, congressional candidates, governors, and attorney generals? The minor leagues in most states are the state legislatures and the courthouses. Men and women get elected to the state legislature, serve a term or two, get some experience, and then they either run for attorney general, for Congress, or for governor. We in the Republican party had a whole generation of potential congressional and senatorial candidates wiped out by Watergate.

If you were to go back and look at who ran for the United States Senate in 1986 and 1988, you would find something very remarkable. Most of the Senate candidates of the Democratic party were former governors or attorney generals in their states, or congressmen who were stepping up. They had been in the public spotlight serving in lower offices, and then stepped up to become United States senators. You look down at the Republican candidates, and it is amazing how many are first-timers, men and women who had never served in a state legislature, or had never been a governor. You know if you have a sitting governor running for the Senate against someone who has never served, right away you get the experience issue shoved down your throat.

That's not an excuse, though, that I've given you. I'm just trying to explain what has happened. That's why we spent so much time on it in my six years, and I hope that it is continuing. I can't tell you if it is or not, because I'm not there day in and day out with the new administration, building county party organizations. I've always felt that this was the building block. If you have a strong county organization, which is usually the lowest common denominator in political building, then strong counties produce strong legislative candidates; a strong party organization in the state creates a stronger national party. That's the weakness, and that's the difference between presidential and legislative politics.

QUESTION: I'd like to put the focus on the presidency. You said several times that all you knew about the situation was what you read in the paper. Considering the intelligence and information that the general public receives through the media about the President and your having known him and worked with him so closely, would you indicate two or three of the most important discrepancies as you see it? You have mentioned President Reagan going to sleep, his use of note cards, and so on. My more fundamental question is this: Is the media, whether for partisan reasons or because of their limited economic resources, projecting the President's personal character in a negative manner? Or are they projecting him as you saw him?

MR. FAHRENKOPF: No, I don't think they projected him as I saw him, but I also don't think that the vast majority of them do it intentionally. We are all products of our environment, the way we were brought up, and what we believe in. The vast majority of men and women in the media are liberals. They are liberal in their approach to life, and that creeps into their work. I truly believe that the overwhelming majority try to be fair, but we are all human beings, and what we believe creeps into what we report.

I'm often asked, who is your favorite media person? Many people are surprised by my answer. I say, "My favorite is Sam Donaldson," and they say, "He was so terrible to President Reagan. How can he be your favorite?" I say, "Because Sam Donaldson is consistent. He is miserable to everybody." What I mean is that if Sam is interviewing Ronald Reagan or George Bush, he is going to be miserable and rude to them, and he is going to be tough on them, but he is the same way to Democrats. He is going to be just as miserable to Ted Kennedy, and that is fairness to me.

What bothers me is that there are many reporters—again, I don't think they do it intentionally; it is built into their system as human beings—who will be miserable to a Ronald Reagan or George Bush and then turn around and not be as miserable to the other side. What we want is not someone who favors us; we want someone who treats both sides the same way.

I must tell you that I am not one who rails against the press and says, "Oh, the press is so unfair." I have always felt that many Republicans make a big mistake. All they do is whine and cry about the press. My philosophy has always been—when I was a state party leader and during the time I was a national party leader—that journalists' biases are a given in life. Assume that such people are well intentioned, but assume that they have built-in weaknesses and frailties that you are going to have to deal with, just as you have to deal with other things in life when you are planning your campaigns or when you are running your governorship or your Senate term or your presidency. Assume it. That's a given. Deal with it, prepare for it, plan for it, and quit whining and crying about it, because you are never going to be able to do anything about it. That has always been my philosophy and approach to it. I must tell you that this approach always worked well for me. You must treat reporters as people out there trying to do a job. They've got families to support; they are doing their best. You do have some who want to put into their work their own personal views and do things for partisan reasons, but that's the exception, not the rule.

COMMENT: I want to comment on your discussion of legislatures. Virginia contradicts what you've said. I have been very active with the Republican party here, and we had nine out of ten congressmen, between 90-95 percent, who are Democrats. The reason is that the Virginia Democrats are very conservative. In the county when I was chairman, a very prominent Democrat gave me a check for $25 for Mr. Nixon. They won't vote Republican, but they give money.

MR. FAHRENKOPF: But you have a tradition. Each state is different, and that's the marvelous thing. That's why when people talk about doing away with the electoral college, I say, "No way." That college respects the individuality and tradition of states. Virginia is not alone. There are many states where Democrats are Democrats for their own purposes but will support Republicans—I'm speaking in broad generalities when I talk about that. By the same token—and I'm not making gibes—the Republican party in this state has not done a good job. They gave former Governor Chuck Robb a free ride. That's why Gerald Baliles is now [1989] the governor. He is a friend of mine; I like him very much personally, but my view is that the free ride that the party gave Chuck Robb let Jerry Baliles walk into that governorship. Congressional races tend particularly to be decided by local politics, and there is very little that a president can do.

If you were to look at the three special elections that we've had in the last year, Dan Quayle's seat, which was held by Republicans for years, was won by a Democrat. Trent Lott held a seat in Mississippi for 17 years, and a Democrat recently won it. Claude Pepper held the seat down in Florida for years, and Ileana Ros-Lehtinen, a Republican, won it. I know that the President and my successor as chairman of the party are going to take some hits. There is very little impact that the national party can make, particularly in special congressional elections, because when you start getting down to that level, people know people. They know who they are, they know their family, and they know whether they've been interested in the community. Then the question comes up as to whether that post office is going to be closed or whether there is going to be an expansion of the veterans hospital. Local issues play a part.

QUESTION: I want to go back to Richard Viguerie and the PACs who have their own agenda, who are raising their own money and doing their own thing. How does that dilute or hinder the work of the national committee, or does it help?

MR. FAHRENKOPF: It hurts. I can't tell you how many times I would get calls and letters from someone saying, "I sent you a thousand dollars to help you and President Reagan." I said, "Oh?" It turns out they sent it to some United Republicans for Victory in the World, or whatever. I say, "Wait a minute, the United Republicans is not us," and I spent a tremendous amount of time, as did the President, telling people that unless it says Republican National Committee, Virginia Republican party, Republican Senatorial Committee, Republican Congressional Committee, Republican Women of Virginia, or any official organ, don't send it. If you have any questions, call us. It does hurt; it probably hurts the national party less than it does state parties and county parties because they are the ones that have a rough time raising the money.

QUESTION: What about their advertising?

MR. FAHRENKOPF: It's sometimes very bad, and of course it is disruptive. A candidate can have in his mind in a particular state how to run a campaign, and then suddenly there is injected another factor. The best example I can give you of that—and people can say whether it helped or defeated Mike Dukakis—but those ads that showed Willie Horton's picture were not the Bush ads, and they were not the Republican National Committee's ad. We were very careful that we never showed Willie Horton's picture. We never mentioned Willie Horton's name. You cannot find a Bush-Quayle ad or a Republican National Committee ad that even mentions his name or his color or shows a picture. We were talking about the furlough program and not being able to understand it. These other groups injected their views, and then of course Dukakis picked it up because he thought he could turn it around and use it to his advantage. What he did, however, was exacerbate his own problems.

NARRATOR: You said that you and the President were concerned about strengthening the role of the party. Could you say just a little bit more about the extent to which the President troubled himself about party matters, and was he a party leader?

MR. FAHRENKOPF: He really was. I think George Bush may be better, however, just from the fact that George Bush sat where I sat. I know George Bush is the only president of either party to have been the national chairman of his party. He was the Harris County, Texas, party chairman. He may also be the only president who has ever been a county Republican chairman, and that's getting down where the rubber meets the road. He understands. He has probably been out hammering those signs in the ground. That's what you call a grass-roots politician. That's the person who starts out holding the campaign poster stake while somebody else is hitting the top.

Ronald Reagan's great ability in the party was fund raising. I'm a little embarrassed about it now, but during my six years of chairmanships, we raised about $360 million. It broke every single record. Ronald Reagan's name was gold on a letter. Everyone says I wrote every day, but I did not. He could sign a letter, and it was like opening a bank door. The money would come in. He had that remarkable ability. He would go out and make a speech somewhere, and it would be sold out within an hour. The man had that kind of charisma. Any time I asked him to do a special event, to raise money for the Governors Association or a state legislative association, he would be there.

We had a dramatic impact. The Reagan years changed the makeup of American politics demographically in many ways. It truly was in 1980 and even more in 1984 the breakup of what was the old New Deal coalition of the Democratic party. We received in 1984 a majority of the Italian-American vote that always had been strongly Democratic. We received a majority of the Irish-American vote and more of the Catholic vote and the Hispanic vote than we had in the past. Ronald Reagan in 1984 got 45 percent of the Hispanic vote. He got a third of the Jewish vote, and it probably would have been higher. We were running about 45 percent of the Jewish vote until the Mondale campaign ran the Jerry Falwell ads: "Do you want Jerry Falwell picking your next . . .?" and scared the Jewish community. They ran that ad very heavily in New York and those areas where Jewish voters played a very important part.

The only part of the old New Deal coalition with which we were unsuccessful was black voters. We spent a tremendous amount of time, energy, and resources and ended up with 9 percent of the vote. Bill Brock, one of my predecessors, spent four years as chairman of the party, spending a tremendous amount of time, energy, and resources trying to make an impact in the black community, and we failed. That is something with which we were troubled. We work on it very hard, but sometimes it is just like banging your head against the door.

George Bush, when he was vice president, spoke to the NAACP (National Association for the Advancement of Colored People)—I think it was in 1983. He walked into the room, was introduced, and a funeral dirge was played by the organist. I spoke to the NAACP Convention in 1986 in Dallas. I was on the very same platform where I had been two years earlier when we renominated the President and Vice President. When I was introduced the remark was made, "Now we are going to introduce the chairman of the Republican party. Maybe now we ought to do the benediction." Then as soon as I mentioned Ronald Reagan's name, I had to stand on that podium while he was booed and jeered. We've worked very hard at it, in any case.

George Bush, hopefully, is going to be able to do a better job at outreach because he has a very strong civil rights record and will work very hard at it. One of the areas in the press on which Ronald Reagan was constantly criticized—wrongfully, I think—was that he was insensitive to minority needs. There is not a prejudiced bone in Ronald Reagan's body in my view, and I've been around him a long time. He got beat up on that count for a long, long time. That was the one area where we were unsuccessful.

The biggest area of success was young voters. Traditionally, the vast majority of young voters when I was growing up were Democrats. When young people went out and voted for the first time and registered, they were Democrats. Ronald Reagan turned that whole thing on its head. The strongest demographic support group for Ronald Reagan in the Republican party beginning in 1982 were young voters. I remember when those numbers started showing up in 1983. I went to the President and said, "Mr. President, I've got some good news and bad news. The good news is that you have changed American politics dramatically, that young voters who automatically were Democrats, the vast majority of them are now Republicans." He said, "That's great. What's the bad news?" I said, "The bad news is they are the worst voters," and they do in fact have the worst voting record. We spent a lot of time and energy and improved the participation of young voters over the years.

The demographic change at which we were unsuccessful as a party was among black voters. George Bush, I think, got 13 percent of the black vote in 1988, which is still very low. It's unacceptable.

QUESTION: Regarding the mechanics of elections, I wonder what your judgment would be about the voting machine being a factor given that more people tend to split their vote. Years ago, when we voted by hand, all you had to do was put an X at the top and you voted for every Republican or every Democrat. Does that affect the coattail factor of a president's influence?

MR. FAHRENKOPF: I don't think so. Doing away with it has helped the Republican party because in some places, like Chicago, where they pulled that one lever, we got our brains pounded out.

Let me try to explain it this way. I said a little while ago that in voting for president, party probably has less to do with how people vote. When they go into the voting booth, I think most Americans say, "I'm not just voting for me; I'm voting for my family

history. I'm going to vote for the best man or woman." When you
get lower down the ticket—when you start voting for state
legislature, county commissioners, and city council (where in some
parts of the country they run as partisans)—the party becomes more
important. The reason it becomes more important is that those are
the political races that usually get lost in the public perspective,
because they are overshadowed by the presidential, senatorial, and
gubernatorial races that get all the ink, all the television coverage,
and all the press. While this isn't true in rural areas where people
know the candidates, in the big cities and large metropolitan areas,
most of the time people go in and say, "I saw Senator so-and-so
debating so-and-so, and I liked what he or she said." They get down
to the bottom of that ticket and look and say, "It's a choice between
Judy Jones, a Republican, and Shirley Smith, a Democrat. I don't
know either of them." Those candidates usually have low budgets;
maybe they got a door hanger from one. "Oh, yes, I remember. I
got that cute door hanger that had that little plastic thing that
helped me open the mustard jar." You've all got them. They make
decisions based on less than that. They say, "Well, I don't know
either of them, but I'm a Republican, so I'm going to vote for the
Republican," or "I'm a Democrat, so I'm going to vote for the
Democrat." It is at the bottom of the ticket where party affiliation
is more important and where the realignment wrought by Ronald
Reagan is taking place.

One new poll has 32 percent of the American people
considering themselves Republicans, 32 percent considering
themselves Democrats, and the rest nonaffiliated. We've been
close. In 1984 we were within the margin of polling error, according
to one of the surveys taken. It is the first time that this particular
poll has ever shown that we are at the same level. That's very
important, and that's where in the long run, if we do our homework
in preparing for reapportionment in 1991 and 1990, it will pay off
by electing more Republicans to the state legislatures, so they will
be there drawing the lines for 1991 that will determine the
congressional layout.

QUESTION: I want to follow up on the question about President
Reagan's interest in building a party. I would ask you to think back
to your preparation for the 1986 midterm elections. You came in
after a midterm election in 1982 that didn't go so well. Obviously,

in the 1984 elections the President would have been preoccupied with his own reelection, but by the time you get to 1986 you are back in the situation where the President could be utilized to deflect some of these problems that you addressed in terms of the local elections. What kinds of strategies were developed? Exactly how did you attempt to go about using these?

MR. FAHRENKOPF: I'm really glad that a graduate student asked that so that history could be set right. Most people say that 1986 was a disaster for the Republican party because they lost control of the Senate. The untold story of 1986 was that the Republican party had a net gain of eight governors, seven of whom were in the Sunbelt states.

I must also tell you that the Senate races weren't my bailiwick. The United States Senate races are handled by a separate, free-standing committee that I didn't have any control over. Lee Atwater doesn't have any control over it today* because under the federal election law we must keep an arm's distance. They have their own budget.

Ronald Reagan was instrumental in working for the Republican Governors Association, raising money and helping me put together the team. We went out and got good candidates and were tremendously successful in the governor races.

Let me tell you what happened in the Senate. No one ever thought about the Republicans capturing the Senate in 1980, but when Ronald Reagan was elected in 1980, he carried into office with him 12 wins for Republican Senate candidates with a margin of victory of 1.5 percent or less. I'm not going to name names, but he carried in a lot of turkeys. (Republicans have turkeys who are elected to the United States Senate just like the Democrats.) These turkeys who were elected had six years to do their homework and become thoroughbred racehorses. Many of them, however, didn't take care of their constituencies and thought that suddenly in the last year they were going to pay attention to the home folk. These are people who during those six years had not been riding in their local Fourth of July parade at home; they were in Washington

---

*Chairman Fahrenkopf made this statement prior to Lee Atwater's death.

watching the fireworks around the Washington Monument. What happened? These people had to go out and run on their own. Ronald Reagan wasn't on the top of the ticket, and they got beat. Who beat them? Look back at 1986 as I mentioned, and you are going to find an amazing number of Democratic former attorney generals and governors, people who were well-prepared candidates who tended to the home fires. We took the President out campaigning, though; I went out with him for two weeks. Everyone said Ronald Reagan didn't have any coattails because those guys lost, and you lost the Senate. He really did, though, because when we got the President out, there were some of those guys who were down to 42 percent of the vote, and we went out and did the work, and they finished with 48 percent of the vote. Ronald Reagan had moved the electorate six points, but not enough to get them over the hump.

The President was very involved with me at the National Committee, focusing on the governorships, which were my big challenge. He also attempted to the best of his ability to help the party in the Senate race, but there is only so much you can do for a weak candidate. Therefore, we lost some of those states, and some of them were Southern states. We lost in Georgia, Alabama, and Florida. However, the one whom everyone said in 1981 would be the first one to get knocked off, a fellow named Alfonse D'Amato in New York, was instead carried to victory. Everyone said, "This guy is a buffoon, and the Democrats will knock him off in six years." Well, Al D'Amato went out and worked for six years. You would have thought he was a state legislator instead of a United States senator. He was home every night making speeches; he rode the shuttle back and forth; he worked, and he was reelected by about the same margin that Governor Cuomo received in New York.

You've heard the joke: You are a realtor; what are the three most important things in valuing a piece of property? Location, location, location. Still, in politics—with all the things I've talked about—the three most important things are the candidate, the candidate, the candidate. Even with this description I gave you of the way we approach presidential races, let me tell you that if George Bush hadn't gone out there on that podium that night in New Orleans and delivered that great speech, or Ronald Reagan hadn't been the indefatigable campaigner that he was, all that strategy would have been for naught. You can never replace the candidate. We had weak candidates in the Senate races; in the meantime, we had strong gubernatorial candidates, and that's the answer.

QUESTION: How close was the Reagan-Bush relationship? To what extent and how well did President Reagan prepare Mr. Bush to become president?

MR. FAHRENKOPF: My experience is that he did an extremely good job. I must tell you interestingly enough, that the relationship emulated in many ways the relationship that Jimmy Carter started. Jimmy Carter changed the role of the vice president in that he brought Fritz Mondale within the tight loop and had him present at national security briefings. He gave the vice president more to do. It wasn't that warm bucket job that the former vice president from Texas [John Nance Garner] described it as being. That's what Ronald Reagan did with George Bush. At all Cabinet meetings and NSC briefings, he really had Bush in the loop, and then they themselves originated the weekly luncheon. Many times I was in the White House and I'd be walking across the trellised area from the main house to the west wing (I think it was Wednesdays at noon), and the President and vice president would be alone eating outside, having a weekly lunch, just the two of them—no staff. So I believe Reagan did a good job in working with and involving the vice president and helping to train him.

I also think that George Bush was probably the most magnificent vice president that we've had in a long time. It is a miserable, tough job. In order to be a good vice president and in order to serve the man with whom you were elected and who chose you, you must take your views and your own personality and swallow them. Your job is to be there as part of the team, to assist, and to help. I was present in my party chairmanship role at these policy meetings I told you about, and there could not have been a more loyal, dedicated, or helpful vice president than George Bush.

That's why it has always been so difficult for a vice president, and why so many of us in the party were concerned as to whether or not George could step out from under the shadow of a strong president. It's most difficult when the president you serve has been strong. Harry Truman had that problem. No one gave Truman a chance. If you look back now and read about him, everybody says, "He was strong and dynamic." But if you read the literature, it was a joke because Roosevelt was such an overpowering figure. In many ways, Eisenhower was a very popular president, a powerful figure, a great war hero, and Nixon was under him. So we were all concerned. Could George step out from under that shadow and convince the American people that he was his own man? I think he did. He did a marvelous job in New Orleans. That the campaign of Mr. Dukakis was so miserable was a great assist. Ronald Reagan's including him and involving him was one of the reasons Bush was able to do what he did. There has not been, in my view, a better prepared president than George Bush.

COMMENT: That is true, given all the positions he has held.

MR. FAHRENKOPF: He was county and national chairman of the party, so he knew the political end. He was a congressman, our ambassador to the United Nations, our first envoy to China, our CIA director, and vice president for eight years. That's not bad training.

QUESTION: To what extent is the abortion problem going to become a single issue to bring candidates down?

MR. FAHRENKOPF: That is the unknown. Candidates mishandle it and are stampeded on the issue, and they shouldn't be. Like school prayer, the abortion issue is neither a Republican issue nor a Democratic issue. It cuts across the fabric of politics in this country. Candidates, wherever they are on the issue, could learn a lesson from Ronald Reagan. Most of them waffle on the issue; they ought to stand up to the line and say, "I'm Catholic; this issue means something to me personally. Here is what I believe, and that's what I believe. I understand people can have the other view, but that's what I believe and that's my own view." People who oppose abortion tend to waffle the most and end up hurting their campaigns. Ronald Reagan attracted the votes of people who disagreed with him totally on the issue of abortion and school prayer because they'd say, "Well, I don't agree with him on that, but at least he believes in it." Sure, there are people who are single-issue voters. They are always going to exist, whether it is abortion, school prayer, or whatever it may be. You are going to lose them. You are not going to win everybody, but you should stand for something: "This is what I believe in and understand. When you vote for me, this is my belief. I'm sorry, it is part of my makeup, and there is nothing I can do about it." That is the problem with candidates. Issues like that hurt them when they don't convey to the voter that they have any inner strength one way or the other.

QUESTION: Concerning the 13 percent of the vote that is uncommitted, how do you go about winning that?

MR. FAHRENKOPF: You do it in many ways. Let me give you an example. Our polling data made very clear to us that in that 13 percent, George Bush and Republican candidates were losing by about 24 percentage points among women who did not work outside the home. I started running ads directed at this group of voters between the two conventions. I ran these ads during daytime television with some of the game shows in the morning and some of the soap operas in the afternoon—shows like "Donahue" and "Oprah," where our statistics told us we could reach these voters.

You may recall the two ads. One of the ads won the best ad of the year and the other won the second best ad of the year. It was a little girl sitting on a porch with a coloring book. She was coloring, and a voice said, "This is a very fortunate little girl. During the seven years of her life, inflation has been down, unemployment . . ." and then the camera came in at the very end, and she looked into the screen with these big blue eyes and said, "Why would we ever take a chance of losing what we've done in the economy?" I've always thought that the gender gap was based on economic issues, not on social issues. The other one was a comical ad. I had done some research and found that the American people have become so used to seeing color television that if something is on in black and white, it automatically draws their attention. I had produced an ad in black and white that was captioned, "I remember you. You're the one who made me feel so blue." It was in black and white and showed Jimmy Carter's pictures, gasoline lines, and so forth. Then the voice said, "Republicans have been working very hard in the last seven years to make sure that you don't have long lines and unemployment. Tell them you remember." There was a little, catchy tune. We ran those ads to the saturation point; I spent

$4 million on them. We saw that 24-point margin that Dukakis had on us among that tier of voters, the 13 percent, go right down to nothing. We eventually won the majority of those voters.

So you take your advertising and focus. You deliver your message to those voters.

NARRATOR: Do you have any thoughts about the way we select and nominate vice presidents?

MR. FAHRENKOPF: I will tell you the process and how it worked in New Orleans. George Bush called me into his office about a month before New Orleans when it was clear that he was going to be the nominee. He asked me if I would become involved and get a feeling from around the country from Republican leaders as to who the vice presidential nominee should be. I know that he also asked Senator Alan Simpson of Wyoming to get the views of members of the United States Senate. I can't remember whom he asked in the House, but he asked one of the House members to do a little informal survey among House members. He asked the chairman of the Republican Governors Association, Governor Mike Castle of Delaware, to do the same among governors. He said, "It is going to be confidential. You are not all going to be called in together. I'll call you in by yourself and what you tell me will be confidential, and I hope it will remain that way." I spent a lot of time on it. I went in and spent an hour and a half with George Bush about ten days before New Orleans and told him what I had found out. I'm not going to tell you the results of what I told him, though, because that's confidential, but I gave him my thoughts and what the feeling was of the party chairman and the Republican national committeemen and committeewomen around the country and of county chairmen. I spent some time on it.

I then went off to resume my responsibility of putting on a good convention, which is a tremendous burden. I did two, and I'm so happy that I'm not going to have another one. You have no idea what is involved in one of those.

I went off to New Orleans. The next thing I heard, which upset me greatly, was that George Bush was going to announce the selection of his running mate at a breakfast of the Texas delegation on Thursday morning, the final morning of the convention. When I heard that, I went nuclear. I called Jim Baker; I talked to everyone I could talk to. I talked to those people around the vice president. I never did tell the vice president this directly because he was busy campaigning, but I talked to his people. I said, "That's idiotic. If he does it Thursday morning, the last day of the convention, then the Friday morning talk shows and the Friday morning newspapers are not going to be focusing on his acceptance speech Thursday night when he has to step out from under the cloak of Ronald Reagan and show that he is his own man. They are going to be focusing on the vice presidential campaign, and the speech will get lost." My suggestion was that we do what we did in Detroit in 1980. When Ronald Reagan went over the top on Wednesday night, we brought Reagan to the convention center in Detroit, and he went out on the podium to the cheering crowds on Wednesday night and said, "Thank you for the confidence you've shown in me, and tomorrow I want you to nominate George Bush as my vice presidential running mate." The focus of the Thursday morning papers was "Reagan Wins Nomination, Selects Bush as His Running Mate." Then Friday morning the focus was on the acceptance speech. So I said, "Please, please. You've got to do that."

In the meantime we were arranging what we called the farewell to Ronald Reagan—the kissing of Air Force One and Air Force Two. If you remember the convention, George Bush was not in New Orleans at the opening of the convention, which was on Monday. That became Ronald Reagan day. The President came in on Sunday, and we had a big welcoming ceremony for him. He addressed the convention on Monday night. On Tuesday morning the President went out to a naval air station outside of New Orleans. Air Force One was parked on the ramp, and George Bush flew in with Barbara Bush. The two airplanes parked alongside each other. George Bush came down and Ronald Reagan welcomed him. That point in time was the first time to my knowledge that George Bush told anybody who his running mate was going to be. He said, "I'm going to choose Dan Quayle." He has admitted that he told Reagan. Reagan then went up the ramp, got on the airplane, and flew away to the ranch in California.

Vice President Bush then called his traveling party and entourage into a holding room at the naval air station and said, "I want you to get Jack Kemp, Bob Dole, Elizabeth Dole, Pete du Pont, Paul Laxalt on the phone for me. I'm going to call them and tell them it is not them." To my knowledge that was the first time he told Jim Baker, Bob Teeter, and people around him that he was going to select Dan Quayle.

While all this was going on I was down on the wharf outside the Hilton Hotel with 15,000 screaming people waiting for the riverboat. We took Bush from the naval air station to the river, put him on a Mississippi paddleboat, and brought him down the river to the site outside the Hilton where I as the party chairman was waiting with the crowd to welcome him to New Orleans. Here I am, dumb and happy, and I'm saying to myself, "I'm going to tell him not to make the announcement Thursday morning; he's got to do it Wednesday night." I had in my mind that the Marriott where he was staying had a glass elevator. I had the camera angled; he was going to get in while the votes were being tallied, and he was going to come down in the glass elevator and get in the limousine. We'd have a camera on top of the Superdome, and then he'd go closer–I had it all planned. Dumb me, standing there in 8,000 degree heat and humidity with sweat rolling down and the Dixieland bands playing. Suddenly down the river comes the boat, and it docks. I'm waiting there, and there was no George Bush. Suddenly Jim Baker got off the boat and came up to me. I'll never forget it as long as I live. He said, "Frankie, it's Quayle, and the old man wants to announce it right now. Quayle is out in that crowd somewhere, and we can't find him." If anyone were to go back and look at the tapes of that welcoming ceremony, I was on the stage with Jim Baker on one side and Bob Teeter and Roger Ailes on the other, and we were looking for Quayle in the crowd.

What had happened, of course, was that these 15,000 people had been in there like sardines for an hour and a half, so when Quayle arrived (he didn't have Secret Service at that point), no one knew who he was. Finally after a few minutes we found him, the Secret Service got him through, and George Bush made the announcement.

The decision to my knowledge was made by George Bush and George Bush only. It was totally his decision, and that's the prerogative of the nominee of the party. Whether that should change or it should be done differently, whether it is right or wrong, I'll be happy to comment if you want to involve me in that study.

NARRATOR: We'd like to.

MR. FAHRENKOPF: I'm not sure it will ever change.

NARRATOR: It is interesting that all executive branch people say it ought to change. All of you who are the politicians say it may never change.

MR. FAHRENKOPF: I doubt it. I have tremendous respect for individuals like George Bush and Michael Dukakis who become candidates for the presidency of the United States. I have respect for the winners and losers. It is a terrible, tough thing they go through. Nowadays, you are running for four years. You really are. You don't just run the last two years; you are at it all the time. It is a tremendous burden, and I think they are always going to feel justified to say, "Under the system, I've got the right to choose my veep and nominate my veep, and I'm going to keep that." So even if all the great thinkers in the world were unanimous in saying, "That's not a wise way to do things," it will be for naught. Thank you so very much. It's been a pleasure being with you.

A JOURNALIST'S PERSPECTIVE

LOU CANNON

NARRATOR: Some observers and historians have called Lou Cannon the first of the revisionist historians. He may want to rebut this, but suffice it to say that Lou Cannon tells it like it is. Lou Cannon's style was always evident in his *Washington Post* columns throughout the Reagan administration. A lot of us miss those columns because, like Walter Lippmann's column in an earlier time, one never quite knows where Lou's column will lead, and that is refreshing in journalism.

His recent biography of Reagan, *President Reagan: The Role of a Lifetime*, has some of these same characteristics, and true believers and critics alike can find points that appeal to them. Throughout its 900 pages, the biography is well researched, carefully documented, and profoundly observant.

It is a rare privilege to welcome Mr. Cannon.

MR. CANNON: Thank you for that kind introduction.

I have almost reached the point where I have nothing left to say about Ronald Reagan. If I were a revisionist historian, I would wonder whose work I was revising, since I have been writing books about Reagan since 1969. Perhaps we Reagan historians are all revisionists since Ronald Reagan has always been more complex as a person and as a political leader than either his cheerleaders or his critics believed.

I have thought a lot about this since the book was published. I have had very favorable reviews, which I suppose I shouldn't complain about, but it bothers me sometimes that liberals, for example, will see in what I write about Reagan only confirmation of their beliefs. These are the reviewers who invariably quote the passages of the book that show Reagan's detachment from his job. For example, in Williamsburg, on the eve of the only economic summit held in the United States during the Reagan presidency, Jim Baker prepared a stack of briefing books for the President. When he came back the next day, he noticed that the briefing material was undisturbed. Baker asked Mr. Reagan if he had reviewed the briefing books, and Reagan replied, "Well, Jim, *The Sound of Music* was on last night."

Reagan was largely untarnished with the public by such reports because most people knew he didn't read his briefing books and liked him anyway. Yet any reader of my book will know that I don't totally subscribe to the Teflon theory. Reagan's popularity sank to near 40 percent in the midst of the recession. Even Eisenhower's popularity fell during a recession, and if the Reagan recession had continued, his presidency might have been far less notable. There is no Teflon if the economy gets bad enough.

To a degree, though, Reagan was the Teflon president. In his first campaign, the Democrats had portrayed Reagan as an actor who was basically reading his lines and who had been upstaged by a chimpanzee in *Bedtime for Bonzo*. Then when he got into office and seemed to be doing OK, they wanted to hold him to account. Of course, it is hard to hold someone accountable whom you have portrayed as a puppet in the first place.

The origin of the Teflon presidency was an underestimation of Reagan. He was underestimated so much that in some circumstances he simply had to give an average performance in order to be seen as exceptional. But I believe Reagan's opponents had more to do with this than Reagan himself.

The conservative reviews of my book haven't been much better. I actually respect one or two of them that criticize me because I don't believe in supply-side economics. The supply-side notion that lowering taxes results in more government revenue simply hasn't held true.

Favorable conservative reviewers find evidence in the book that Reagan was true to his principles. Reagan had some things he wanted to accomplish and in many cases was successful, but still these people ignore the fact that Reagan's managerial style was more than an inconvenience: It was a prelude to catastrophe in Lebanon and in the Iran-contra affair.

Once you are a former president, everything changes. Harry Truman said, soon after he left office, "Yesterday everybody was hanging on my every word; today I could speak for an hour, and nobody would care what I said." Reagan is now in the penumbra of his presidency. Immediately after leaving office a president—any president, even FDR—suffers badly. For some reason, this is when a president looks the worst. The flaws loom large: For example, the Truman and Eisenhower administrations looked much worse right after their presidencies than they look today. It will be some time before we can fairly judge the Reagan presidency.

Several things about the Reagan presidency stand out, and taken together, they form an enduring paradox. First of all, Reagan had no background in foreign policy. When asked in 1980 what his experience was in foreign policy, he would rattle off the names of all the foreign policy leaders he had met. What became exasperating after you heard that question asked and answered a few times was not Reagan's response but the fact that he thought it answered the question very well.

Reagan seemed well trained in domestic politics. He had been governor of a state that if measured in terms of its economy would have been larger than all but six nations in the world. He faced a divided legislature in California as well and would face a number of the same issues as President that he had seen in state government. Yet, I think you could probably say that Lebanon and Iran-contra notwithstanding, Reagan was successful as a foreign policy president, particularly in dealing with the Soviet Union, but that his presidency was a domestic disaster.

A central question about the Reagan presidency concerns the budget deficit. It is absolutely true that Congress made the deficit worse during the Reagan years. It is also true that Ronald Reagan never once submitted a balanced budget. I believe it is George Will's calculation that if Congress had been some Third World country parliament and simply approved the Reagan budgets as they were submitted, the country would have about 90 percent of the deficit it has today.

Don Oberdorfer, a friend and colleague at the *Washington Post*, has written a fine book on United States-Soviet relations in which he quotes the British historian J. V. Sedgewick as saying that history is written backward but lived forward, and those who know the end of a story could never know what it was like at the time. The only thing that I tried to do in writing about Reagan was to capture what it was like at the time. I wince when I read some of my past columns, but that's the way it was at the time—or at least the way it seemed.

QUESTION: The savings and loan fiasco strikes many of us as a magnificent example of a lack of responsibility certainly shared by the executive branch and Congress. As early as 1983 there were pretty clear signals of an impending disaster. Was the Reagan administration conscious of the magnitude of the savings and loan crisis, and what defined the administration's attitude toward the problem?

MR. CANNON: The savings and loan mess was a shared scandal. There are some fiascos of the Reagan administration—the HUD scandal, for instance—for which Reagan should be held more accountable than the Congress. But the root of the savings and loan scandal was really Congress raising loan limits and allowing insured loans for purposes other than home-buying.

   William Seidman has made the point that in the savings and loan scandal there was a complete collapse of government checks and balances. That is to say, if it were a congressional scandal one would expect the administration to point that out; if it were an executive branch scandal, we would hear about it from the Congress. With the savings and loan crisis, we saw what amounted to a conspiracy of silence, or at least a conspiracy underestimating the magnitude of the scandal. The Democrats—not just the Democrats, but they ran the Congress—really depended upon these people as contributors. Also, Democrats were somewhat historically associated with the savings and loan industry through their housing programs aimed at expanding the middle class.

   The Republicans, by and large, were prisoners of ideology rather than political contributions. They believed that deregulation would take care of everything. As Ed Gray pointed out, they did not make the distinction between deregulation of a market in which the government has no investment and deregulation of an enterprise in which the full faith and credit of the United States government is vested. The S&Ls were not a market economy; we were putting up the money for these guys. The Republicans never made this elemental distinction. The people who complained about it were Bill Seidman and Ed Gray, who were dismissed as "re-regulators" by the Donald Regans and the David Stockmans of the world and the people who worked for them. To be accused of being a re-regulator in the Reagan administration is now like being accused of being a Bolshevik in Russia—it's a pretty bad thing.

Near the end of the Reagan administration it slowly dawned on Congress and the administration that this was a terrible crisis. Both branches hoped the crisis would not surface until after the next election. There is this wonderful story told by Burt Ely, a prominent savings and loan expert. At one of the hearings in 1986, Burt went up to a principal official in the Treasury Department and asked him when Treasury was going to tell people what was really happening. The answer was, "Not on my watch."

I think the savings and loan scandal is hard for us to understand because there are too many villains. In the early days of the crisis, the administration did not realize how bad it was going to be. The real tragedy is that if the crisis had been addressed in 1985 or 1986, it would have cost a minuscule amount compared to today's bailout figures. The "not on my watch" attitude has cost us dearly.

QUESTION: In many ways Reagan exemplified notions of old-fashioned virtue, even if his administration was awash with ethical failings. Still, he seemed to have an almost complete blind spot toward misdeeds and corruption in his administration. How do you account for this ethical contradiction?

MR. CANNON: One of the problems in making ethical failings stick as a political issue was that there were so few saints in Washington. Jim Wright and Tony Coelho often pointed out "sleaze" in the Reagan administration but themselves resigned just ahead of the sheriff, so to speak.

I once wrote a column for the *Washington Post* in which I quoted a president as saying that attacks on his administration colleagues were really veiled personal attacks on himself. The president was Harry Truman. This is uncannily similar to what Ronald Reagan said the day they almost caught up with Ed Meese. It is more than just a coincidence that the quotes are similar.

Truman, with a completely different background, had a simple, uncomplicated way of looking at things that were thrust upon him. He was doing a good job and was popular. Hence, his critics went after Harry Vaughan and the rest of the crowd.

The difference between Truman and Reagan in this regard is that a number of the Truman people, like T. Lamar Caudle, were tried and convicted. Reagan broke new ground by having the only sitting Cabinet member, Raymond Donovan, ever to be indicted, though Donovan was later acquitted. Both Truman and Reagan saw things in highly personalized terms. Reagan was not analytical; he often acted based on personal experience, which sometimes failed him. Once you worked for Ronald Reagan, as far as he was concerned, you were solid gold. So if people were critical of Reagan's Cabinet, he saw it as an attack on him.

It is like most things: It is not totally untrue. It was pretty obvious to everybody that Meese was a more vulnerable person than Reagan. Reagan's critics were usually more willing to attack Meese than the President. The petitions for the removal of Jim Watt that all the conservationist groups circulated deliberately did not mention Reagan's name. He was popular, and Watt was not.

I argue in my book that there was an ethical void in the Reagan administration. Apparently, Reagan never gave much thought to ethics in government; he simply assumed that people who worked for him would be honest. He did not view government as a noble profession entailing Grover Cleveland's idea of public office as a public trust. You will not find the word *ethics* in all of Reagan's quote books—he never spoke to the subject.

This meant that everyone in the Reagan administration followed their own ethical standards. Sometimes those standards are quite high. When he was White House chief of staff, James Baker recused himself from discussions of energy issues because he owned some Texas energy stocks. A number of people at lower levels were scrupulous in the way they behaved, but it was not because the President set clear ethical standards to be followed. I fault Reagan for this ethical void in his presidency.

QUESTION: How do you rate the competence of the people surrounding Reagan?

MR. CANNON: I don't think the blanket charge of incompetence against the Reagan administration stands. The level of competence in many of the departments was high, but across the administration, competence was very uneven. George Shultz was competent. Caspar Weinberger, with whom I often disagreed, was highly competent. Ed Meese was a valuable counselor in the White House but was not, in my view, a competent attorney general. I think William French Smith was. It varied a lot from office to office and position to position.

QUESTION: The wisdom of the Reagan military buildup will probably be debated for years to come. Was the buildup based on military advice or on philosophical notions of Reagan and the Republicans?

MR. CANNON: It was both. There was never any shortage of experts telling us about Soviet military superiority. It's also good politics. John F. Kennedy campaigned on the missile gap, which after taking office he found didn't exist.

Concern about U.S. military vulnerability was not limited to Reagan's people; Carter's people had similar concerns. Indeed, the military buildup began under Carter, a fact that curiously both sides like to forget. Those who want to give Reagan credit for the entire buildup tend to forget it, but people who think the Reagan military build up was excessive also forget the role of the Carter administration.

Ronald Reagan was absolutely clear on the buildup. People wanted it; he believed it was necessary. When Reagan visited the *Washington Post* in June 1980, we asked him if he feared an arms race with the Soviet Union. He replied that he welcomed an arms race because he was convinced the Soviets couldn't compete with us.

Reagan believed that showing we were serious about a buildup would lead to negotiations with the Soviet Union because their economy could not support an arms race. Reagan was right. Of course, one never knows what the road not traveled might have held. Still, it seems that the fact that the United States was intent on technological competition with the Soviets was certainly a factor influencing a wise leader like Gorbachev in deciding to negotiate a lower level of armaments.

QUESTION: Did Reagan make federal tax cuts so popular a notion that people in state and local government didn't dare risk their political careers by raising taxes to make up that shortfall?

MR. CANNON: With popular leaders like Reagan, you always wonder if he's riding the tide or summoning up the waves. There was a feeling in this country that taxes were too high, that taxes were becoming counterproductive. I believe Reagan was reflecting this feeling.

Reagan had a deep antipathy toward taxes, but he proposed a relatively mild restriction on tax limits when he was governor. It failed. Proposition 13 in California, which was the forerunner of all these tax cuts and which crippled state government in California, was passed by the voters in 1978, two years before Reagan was elected President. Similar propositions followed on many state ballots. Had Ronald Reagan never come along, it is clear we would still have seen the tax revolt. Reagan might have popularized the tax revolt, but anti-tax sentiment was there already.

Personal explanations often account for Reagan's policies. Reagan made a lot of money for the first time in his life right after World War II when marginal tax rates reached 90 percent and individuals couldn't income-tax average. At a time when Ronald Reagan called himself a liberal Democrat, he went around lobbying for a human depreciation allowance. The idea didn't catch on, but the fact is that Reagan opposed taxes out of his personal experience. This is quite different from a belief that taxes have gotten so high that people simply try to shelter their money rather than use it productively. There was a core of accurate perception in the tax revolt, but cutting taxes is not the answer to everything. Like a lot of revolutions, cutting taxes got out of hand.

QUESTION: How does one reconcile the economic growth and prosperity of the Reagan years with the disaster on the domestic economic scene today?

MR. CANNON: Much of what you are seeing today is rooted in the 1980s. I'm of the school that believes deficits do matter. Even Ronald Reagan used to say that deficits matter: He thought the Carter deficit of $33 billion was too much.

In all fairness, it has been harder for Bush because he didn't start anywhere near ground zero. When Bush became President, he had a deficit of hundreds of millions and a national debt that had tripled during the Reagan years. But having said that, I think that neither Congress nor Bush have confronted the deficit. They have pushed it away, and even the Senate compact is something of a joke from an economic standpoint. Bush and the present Congress deserve responsibility for continuing the deficit, but those who originated it deserve the greater blame.

QUESTION: How much personal credit would you give Reagan for the "Star Wars" program?

MR. CANNON: I would give him a lot of credit. Ronald Reagan did have a notable sense of where he wanted to come out on some particular issues; the Strategic Defense Initiative (SDI), or "Star Wars," was one of them. SDI was his vision or, some would say, his fantasy. When he referred to SDI as "my dream," as he did when he unveiled the program, he was referring to it correctly.

Ronald Reagan did not know until he visited the North American Air Defense Command (NORAD) in 1979 that the United States could not defend itself from a missile attack. He was genuinely shocked. That might seem hard to believe, but many Americans didn't know it either. Reagan has some odd beliefs that he has fashioned into a whole scheme that makes sense to him. For instance, he seriously believes Armageddon to be a biblical prophecy of nuclear war. No one else I know who believes in Armageddon as a prophecy also thinks that human beings can avert it, but Reagan set out to avert it. There is a lot of scientific support for the idea that by defending your missiles, another country is less likely to attack. That is controversial, though plausible. Reagan wanted to build a shield that missiles couldn't penetrate, even though scientifically there is very little support for such a notion.

In a curious way, SDI worked for Reagan—very well, in fact, because it was SDI's multiple technologies that the Soviets most feared. The evidence is clear on that. The fact is, nobody knew what shape SDI would take. Hence, there would be a lot of research into different space-based weapons, ground lasers, and the like. It was this technology and its spin-off that most worried the Soviets. So SDI turned out to be very useful in getting the Soviets to the bargaining table. Reagan was right, but for the wrong reason. SDI advocates will now attempt to make a scientific case that such a defense system can protect us from a Saddam Hussein who has one or two weapons, so now we will have to refight the whole political battle over SDI.

What is interesting about SDI is that almost all the people involved in it, with the exception of a handful, knew it wouldn't work, at least as Reagan envisioned it. They knew it wouldn't work but saw its utility in leveraging the Soviets.

QUESTION: What do you know about the so-called "October surprise"–the accusation that the first Reagan election committee interfered in the Iran hostage situation?

MR. CANNON: I looked at that less for this book than I did for the book *Reagan*, which I wrote ten years ago when Bill Casey was alive and when some of those events were a little closer in history. I am clear that whatever happened, Reagan himself would certainly never have been involved.

You have to look at the genesis of the Iran-contra affair. Without the Iran arms sales, there would not have been any profits to divert to the contras. The testimony is overwhelming that Reagan was so caught up with the plight of the Americans held hostage that he disregarded his own policy about trading arms for hostages to try to free them. So Ronald Reagan would not have been involved in any plan to delay the release of American hostages.

As for Bill Casey, I don't know. The first charge, which has been disproved, was that Bush met people in Paris. I have never been convinced that Casey met people in Madrid either. Nobody has ever shown me that the Iranians would make such a calculation. Lloyd Cutler, who was Carter's chief counsel–and who doesn't believe this story, by the way–said that they (the Carter administration) very effectively used the argument that the Iranians wouldn't get a better deal from Reagan to get the hostages back. There was no reason for the Iranians to think that they were going to get a better deal from Reagan.

The so-called "October surprise" needs to be fully investigated. One of the things that bothers me about the investigation is that the charges have come from people who are not outside the process.

Gary Sick, who I'm sure is sincere in what he alleges, worked for Jimmy Carter. He isn't an outside historian researching this. The Carter people never thought that they would lose, that Reagan could beat them fair and square. They *wanted* Reagan to be nominated, so they find it hard to accept the fact that Reagan beat Carter.

The Reagan people provide a very partisan response whenever this issue is raised. I just hope that the congressional investigators are able to get beyond the pronouncements of the Carter and Reagan people and look at it objectively. As with any conspiracy theory, the burden of proof is on those who make it, and they haven't met that burden yet.

QUESTION: Did Reagan often consult Bush when he was vice president?

MR. CANNON: The thing that was least satisfying to me in my book was that it was impossible to determine the extent of Bush's influence. There were some circumstances in which clearly Bush was consulted, such as the withdrawal of U.S. troops from Lebanon and the firing of Don Regan.

I don't know the extent to which Reagan and Bush consulted on a regular basis. They did hold weekly lunches, and they kept the content of those luncheon discussions very secret. Among the high command in the Reagan administration, Bush alone did not divulge what Reagan said to him. Bush saw that his best chance to become president was to be the super loyalist, and he was. I expect Reagan did consult with him because Reagan would ask anybody with whom he met regularly what they thought about issues. But I see no sign that George Bush ever took chances by trying to argue Ronald Reagan out of anything. Vice presidents who want to become president, as he did, don't take those kinds of chances.

QUESTION: Like other presidents, President Reagan frequently told untruths. Was he aware of what he was doing?

MR. CANNON: Generally, the answer is no. Being truthful was very important to Ronald Reagan, who was basically a truthful person. If he said something that was totally opposed to what his policies had been, he managed to convince himself that whatever he was saying was consistent with his past positions.

When he was governor of California, Reagan signed what was then the nation's most permissive bill on abortion. Abortion has been a settled question in California, if not the country, since 1967, largely because Ronald Reagan signed that bill. When he signed it, in all fairness, Reagan had been in office only three or four months, and he did once tell me that he wouldn't have signed the bill if he had been more experienced.

When Reagan signed the California abortion law—the bill permitted abortions to preserve the mental health of the mother—those opposed to it made it clear that this was a loophole so big as to permit any woman who wanted an abortion to have one. Reagan later claimed that psychiatrists were distorting the meaning of the law and were permitting abortions that should not have been performed. When Reagan signed the bill, he was told this would happen, yet he still believes that it was doctors who, after the fact, distorted the bill.

Reagan believes that the budget deficit was not caused by unbalanced budgets that he submitted but by the Congress, and because he believed in this, he was very effective. Jesse Unruh, the Democratic leader in California who ran against Reagan in 1970, once complained to me that whenever he [Jesse Unruh] said something that was right, people thought he was a lying politician. If Reagan said something that was completely wrong, people found him wholly convincing. Even Unruh found him convincing.

There were times, though, when Ronald Reagan did know he was telling a lie, and one of them was in the famous November speech that he gave denying the arms-for-hostages deal with Iran. As I watched the speech on television, I could see by his face that he knew he was lying. He felt terrible about it because he knew his effectiveness was based on his credibility with people, even people who disagreed with him. People usually thought Reagan was telling the truth. That is why people who didn't agree with him were scared by him. The whole effort by Nancy Reagan, Stu Spencer, and John Tower to rehabilitate Reagan after the Iran-contra affair was an effort to restore Reagan's confidence in himself and get him to tell the truth. The truth was that he traded arms for hostages. Getting Reagan to admit that his heart and mind told him one thing but the facts told him something else was a big step. Once he did that, he was comfortable with that issue. History may judge him harshly, but at least Ronald Reagan could live with himself. He *had* to believe in himself, and most of the time he did.

NARRATOR: You covered Ronald Reagan as long as anybody. What surprised you most about his presidency?

MR. CANNON: I suppose what surprised me most about the Reagan presidency was the extent to which he let the budget deficit get out of control. Many people were surprised by the foreign policy developments and the fact that you finally wound up with Reagan and Gorbachev strolling through Red Square proclaiming a new era. I wasn't surprised with that because I knew Reagan envisioned this sort of rapprochement. In his first term, Reagan used to say that he was willing to get along with Soviet leaders, but they kept dying on him.

It should have been clear by 1983 or 1984, certainly after Reagan's reelection victory, that economic problems had to be tackled. He needed to get beyond cuts in discretionary programs and tackle entitlements, notably Social Security. He was unwilling to take on Social Security because his popularity was at stake. Ronald Reagan maintained his popularity during his second term by not confronting entitlements and leaving the bill to be paid by others. That surprised me a little bit—maybe it shouldn't have—but it also disappointed me.

NARRATOR: We thank you very much for a wonderfully informative view of Ronald Reagan.

II

PRACTICE
OF LEADERSHIP

CHAPTER 4

REAGAN'S POLITICAL INSTINCTS

JOHN SEARS

NARRATOR: John Sears was born in Syracuse, New York. He received his bachelor's degree from Notre Dame and his LL.B. and J.D. degrees from Georgetown. He served as a clerk in the New York Court of Appeals and became an associate of the firm of Nixon, Mudge, Rose, Guthrie, Alexander, and Mitchell. He then became a member of the staff of Richard Nixon and was deputy counsel to President Nixon from 1969 to 1970. He has been a partner of several law firms and ultimately established his own law practice. He managed Ronald Reagan's presidential campaign from 1975-76 and from 1979-80 and was a fellow of the Kennedy Institute of Politics. He presently lives in McLean, Virginia. Mr. Sears has been a frequent participant in discussion on television and radio of contemporary American politics. We're especially pleased that he has returned to the Miller Center.

MR. SEARS: Thank you very much, Ken. I'll make just a few remarks about the Reagan presidency because I'd rather hear your questions. The investigation of political scientists and historians of anybody's presidency comes down to a simple matter of what did they do and why did they do it. I think, however, that kind of investigation sometimes gives short shrift to other items which may be more important for anyone's presidency.

We live in the only country in the world that is made up of individuals. I've traveled to 57 foreign countries—most of them many times. I can tell you from my own experience, that everyone in the developed or underdeveloped world—with exceptions in

Canada and Australia—adheres to some tacit or recorded set of beliefs. We call them cultures, and people have a certain confidence in them even if things are very bad economically or politically.

We have no such shared set of beliefs. The closest you can come to it is our strong belief in freedom, but each of us defines that a little differently. Everyone who came here and stayed in this country was an individual. For every poor person who came from Ireland, Italy, or any of the other places from which people migrated to the United States, there are five or six just like them who stayed where they were and are still there. So what we had was a group of adventurers, or as one European wrote, "a group of spoiled brats." I would take out "spoiled," but we are certainly brats. We survive here not because of our common beliefs, but because of our individual beliefs. We are a society that is capable of accomplishment that other people feel is impossible, because when you are part of an organized culture, you think that your own experience is the guide of how you should live. Therefore, things that have been tried before and have failed are not tried again.

When you come from a society that is individualistic in nature, it only takes one person to decide to try something. In this country, if someone takes a chance and he succeeds, he's a great hero. In most places, such a person is considered a fool even if he does succeed. Our president is the most individualistic identity that we have had in the culture at any time. So much of what he does or doesn't do for the country has a lot to do with what examples, strengths, and feelings people derive from the man in the office. During Ronald Reagan's presidency, most of those were very valuable for the country. He gave the country hope when, because of the failures of the Vietnam War, Watergate, and perhaps the Carter presidency, people were not sure whether they should be hopeful anymore. The immediate problems of the country when Reagan took office seemed to preclude any examination of the future. He gave the people hope for the future. He said things weren't so bad. He sometimes sounded foolish because of his optimistic views of the future. However, on the whole, that was good for all the individuals in the country, and the country moved ahead individually under Reagan's example.

Before Reagan became president, people believed, generally, that maybe it was not possible for a president in our system to govern the complicated problems we faced. Indeed, many people were writing in the 1970s that because of the problems we'd had under Nixon and Carter, perhaps the powers and obligations of the presidency should be altered and perhaps something should be done to change the system. Reagan proved that he could be president, address the country's problems, and still go riding once a week. In a strange way this was a relief to the country. Reagan proved a man could endure eight years of office and actually look just as good when he left as he did when he started. When newspapers printed that he really didn't spend much time on the job, people were relieved to find that you could run this very complicated job without having to spend all your time on it.

A third thing I would say that happened under Reagan was that Reagan changed the notion that the establishment of the federal bureaucracy could not be altered in any meaningful way. Indeed we had gotten used to the idea that various parts of it were just untouchable. Today, there is a tacit agreement in Congress that the way we spend our money, what it goes for, and indeed some responsibility for its efficiency is a bipartisan concern. Prior to this new agreement, people could agree it might damage the economy, but there was certain agreement that you had to tolerate a certain degree of waste. We still have waste in the government. However, a combination of the politicians, people from within the bureaucracy speaking out, and the press give instant attention to at least those instances of waste and mismanagement that can be pinpointed. Hopefully this will lead to more efficient and responsive government in the future.

Reagan rarely if ever appeared before the public looking strained whereas Carter often conveyed the idea that circumstances were so difficult that even the president could not deal with them. This was sometimes true of Nixon and was true of Johnson in his last two years. Reagan's approach was a great relief, and perhaps in a country of individualists this was his greatest contribution. Thank you very much. I'd be very glad to hear any questions that you have and shall do my best to answer them.

QUESTION: You've been closely associated with both Nixon and Reagan, and both being representative of the relatively conservative wing of the Republican party, how would you compare the policies and the admitted incompetence of Mr. Nixon with Mr. Reagan?

MR. SEARS: Nixon and Reagan were entirely different men with entirely different attitudes about policy. Mr. Nixon chose to have his hand in everything he possibly could. No president actually can accomplish much with his hand in every decision that's made. Mr. Carter tried to do the same thing. Mr. Reagan, of course, was the other extreme. He delegated perhaps more responsibility than any president we've had in modern times, possibly because there was more to delegate than ever before.

Mr. Nixon had strong ideas on almost any question that had to do with government. He believed he was a student of government, having served in the House, Senate, and as vice president. Mr. Reagan did not have that kind of experience, although he had been a governor, and didn't have an informed opinion on most issues. Therefore, he was very willing to take advice.

When I went to work for Mr. Reagan, people thought that he was an intractable person, that he had strong and very conservative beliefs. As I got to know him, however, I found out he was actually a very malleable man who was capable of doing the right thing in the right circumstances if, indeed, the right thing were presented to him.

You couldn't pick two people who were more different in approach, style, or personality than Mr. Nixon and Mr. Reagan. Mr. Reagan could do all the things relative to the symbolic side of politics very well. The other part of the presidency, which is to be the toughest player in the Washington power politics game, he couldn't do at all. Others had to do it for him. Mr. Nixon was very good at the second part and awful at the first.

QUESTION: Mr. Bush is spoken of as a consolidator of the changes wrought by Mr. Reagan. Is Mr. Bush capable of going off in a new direction?

MR. SEARS: I hope so, because, being individualistic, we are experts in change in this country. The word *change* here is a positive word. In most countries, change is a very frightening word, because it implies that what everyone has believed in and lived by is perhaps wrong. Therefore, change causes people to feel that they themselves are corrupt. Here, we love the word. We are experts in change and we advise it for everybody.

That being the case, for a president to have no recommendations for a world that is changing more rapidly than it ever
has before is, in my view, a very serious problem. I hope that if Mr.
Bush wins a second term, he will concentrate more on this problem.
Certainly, one cannot argue with the need to deal with the change
that's naturally occurring. We as a country need to have important
things to do or our institutions all suffer. There are many reasons
why, but I hope that as he comes to a second term, Mr. Bush will
present us with what he feels we should take as a new direction.

QUESTION: Will the violent campaign style seen in California be
picked up nationwide, or will it pass?

MR. SEARS: Like everything in this country, whether it's
something you like or dislike, it will pass. The question is really
when will it pass, what will replace it, and what parts of it will we
keep. We experience all kinds of things in this country. Sometimes
we incorporate a great deal of that experience into our system and
sometimes we incorporate very little.

Television is here to stay; we're not going to get rid of it. So,
as a means of communicating with voters in elections, it is going to
remain. The nature of the medium itself, however, is not
contemplative. Even in the news divisions, it is an entertainment
medium. This presents a problem for any candidate who wishes to
take a position on an issue and to try to persuade the people to
accept his position. Serious debate is vital to the political process,
if it's going to be honored, accepted, and practiced by the people.

When Harry Truman first proposed the Marshall Plan, we
didn't have polls, and it was a very unpopular thing. I wonder if a
poll were taken on a proposal similar to the Marshall Plan today
and it was found to be unpopular, would anybody support it?

The horrible condition of our politics today will change, and
the real thing that will propel the change is the tremendous lack of
interest on the part of the people, and ultimately the politicians.
Fewer and fewer people vote, so the politicians feel illegitimate. I
think this will cause more and more of them to disregard whatever
they read in the polls, hopefully soon.

Indeed, the polls really aren't useful for what they are being
used for. People take polls about the issues. These days, you can't
tell whether the answers are a real expression on the part of the

people or whether the people are taking intelligence tests because there are so many polls in the paper. We ask people what is the most important question facing the country, and they all reply, the federal budget deficit. You don't know whether they are saying, "I know the answer to that," or whether they really mean it. There's a lot of evidence that they don't really mean it, because they never seem to vote in regard to differences of opinion among the candidates on how to solve the federal budget deficit. My party has argued about the federal budget deficit since 1932 and gave it up in the last eight or ten years, so this is not a recent issue. We never won any elections on it. The Democrats argue about it, but they don't seem to win any elections on it either. Frankly, the people are fairly intelligent about this. They say, "If I ran my own household with that kind of a deficit, I couldn't survive. Evidently you people can, somehow, because you do this all the time. You talk about solving it, but you never do it, and nothing bad happens. I've been frightened about it for a long time, but some way or another nothing bad has happened. If you ask me to treat it now before we see what damage will occur, I'm not going to do that. Show me the damage and maybe I'll know what to do then. I'm not going to vote a person in office because of something in the air." Yet the budget registers all the time as a number one issue. You don't have to be very bright to know there must be other things more interesting to the people. They've heard about the budget since 1932. The validity of taking polls these days is suspect in the sense that there is so much information available on what previous polls have said and so little being contributed to public debate. We will get back to more public debate, because someone will come along and start presenting their ideas. Much of what we think about how to run campaigns will then change, I hope.

QUESTION: The Iran-contra affair continues to be exploited by certain interests. Is there something that President Reagan might have done before he left office that would have put the affair to rest?

MR. SEARS: I don't know that there is anything he could have done to put it to rest. I think the fortunate thing for him was that the people did not view this as Watergate reincarnated. As people looked further and further into the Watergate scandal, they found more and more things that didn't pertain to the original investigation. I don't think that would have happened in the Iran-contra affair. In this scandal Reagan was fortunate, because people kept to the scandal itself. They believed that, for whatever reason, Reagan didn't have much to do with it (he didn't, I don't think). Frankly, that's getting off pretty easily.

The scandal still crops up now and then, especially in connection with Mr. Bush, but I don't think the people are anxious to get back into it. So, while stories appear every now and then, you know it is not because the people want to protect those who were involved, but because people are tired of scandal. They must address scandal when it appears, but they are tired of it. I don't think anything remains about "Contragate" that will be particularly damaging to Mr. Bush or anybody else.

COMMENT: The special counsel seems to be pursuing this whether or not there is a basis.

MR. SEARS: Yes, that's true. The press has given up trying to make it into another Watergate. They tried for quite a while. I don't mean they were trying to be partisan, but television is in the entertainment business. If this were another Watergate, it would be the best entertainment that news can give, according to them. They gave up because the facts aren't there to really sustain anything meaningful.

QUESTION: What are your thoughts on the primary system in presidential races? Do you think that having four regional primaries close together in time would be better than the current 18-month campaign which eliminates well-qualified candidates early in the race?

MR. SEARS: We got into this system of having so many primaries because the Democrats felt, after their experience in 1968, that they needed to open up the process. They wanted to give some voice to the many groups in their party that they weren't able to handle in the old manner. So they opened up the process, and in so doing destroyed their own party. The Republican party is perhaps marginally stronger today than it was in 1968, but not much.

Rather, it is the decline of the Democratic party which has made the Republicans seem so much stronger.

The Democratic party was the majority party when I first entered politics, and it was a grand thing to behold. It clearly could compel high numbers of votes from people who were not getting anything for themselves. It had order and it had structure. As a Republican, when I would see a poll in some race where our Democratic opponent was under 50 percent, that was an occasion for great joy because it was technically possible that we could win the election. Although we still might be down 20 points, we would be happy, because usually our opponent would begin with well over 50 percent. That is how strong the Democratic party was.

So what did the Democrats do? They destroyed their order. They left a system in which it was possible for individuals to decide arguments and lay them to rest, and they put into motion a system of primaries which decide only who will run, not what the Democratic position is. Now the people, and even most Democrats, don't know what is true of the Democratic party. The people used to have a very clear vision of what the Democratic party was. It was a kind party that looked out for all individuals, even those no one else would look out for. It was a strong representative of the country in the international sphere. It isn't that people necessarily have negative views of the Democratic party now, but they don't know what it stands for anymore. I blame the primary system for this.

On your particular question, I think that would be the wrong way to go. I think our problem in politics today is that we have too many primaries. There are men getting nominated for president who, if they were subjected to any kind of review by people who knew them, would flunk. After primaries were opened, the Democratic party nominated George McGovern in 1972. I happen to know George McGovern, and I think he's a wonderful human being. He was, however, no more representative of the breadth, depth, and kind of feeling that the Democratic party exuded to the populace than the man in the moon. He represented a narrow part of the Democratic party. No group of politicians in the Democratic party, no Mayor Daleys, no others would have ever selected George McGovern. In 1976, the Democrats nominated somebody none of them even knew. He survived the primary schedule, but one of his problems as president was that nobody knew him, and he didn't know the people in Washington. This system didn't change my party much, because we nominated the same candidate we would have under the old system.

What I would do is go back to having fewer primaries. Most Democratic politicians would agree with this but everybody is afraid to do so, because the press would say it was all being taken into the back rooms again. I think someone like Lane Kirkland should have something to say about who the Democratic nominee is without having to fool around with a primary. He's an important element in terms of anybody's chances to be elected as a Democrat. He doesn't have a say today.

Maybe we had too few primaries prior to this, but we certainly have too many now. The trouble with having regional primaries, and Super Tuesday of 1988 demonstrated this, is that you know the position of several states on the same day. Most of the candidates under the present system know that if they do well in Iowa and New Hampshire, they can then raise the money to go on. You give them a quarter of the country to have to fund on a particular day, and you'll find that very few people can do that. The front-runners will be the ones who have already raised enough money.

In the old days, we used to have a primary in New Hampshire, and a month later there would be one in Wisconsin. There was a good feature of this. In those days, the politicians used the primaries to see how they did under game conditions. The primaries didn't have enough votes in them to nominate anyone. In 1968, fewer than a quarter of the votes at the national convention were decided in primaries. In 1988, over 80 percent were. Let's consider, for example, New Hampshire. New Hampshire is a unique place. It is not, however, representative of the country. It is an older state with older voters, and does not have all the mix of minorities that you do in the larger states. One nice thing about it is that it's a small state, so people get a personal impression of these men who want to be president. In earlier years, you could have won or lost there and it didn't matter, because you wouldn't have to run another primary for over a month. By the time you were actually close to the election in the next primary, everybody had forgotten about New Hampshire. The problem today is, especially if you schedule either regional primaries or primaries too close together, the results of the last primary create momentum for the next one. The election has nothing to do with the issues, the candidates, or anything else. If you happen to be popular in a state whose primary is down the line, it will do you no good unless you are number one or two in Iowa or New Hampshire, because you won't have any votes by the time you get to that primary.

So, I think it's a terrible system and a terrible way to do business. There is no peer review. The people who know candidates should have more to say about which ones are ready and know enough to be president. It's hard for a voter to decide who should be nominated. He can, however, decide who should win an election. What kind of people are the candidates? Are they qualified? It's awfully difficult for the voters to make that decision. It is especially bad when their opinions are rolled into a continuing consensus that leads to a Jimmy Carter, a George McGovern, or, indeed, a Michael Dukakis.

The answer isn't to rearrange the primaries. We've been altering the primary schedule because we've never liked this system, and usually when we alter things that are already bad we make them worse. That's what we've been doing in regional primaries.

QUESTION: Both parties are having a tough time attracting people of real quality and stature to run for elective office. We see the problem locally, on the state level, and nationally. Is it the media's fault?

MR. SEARS: It isn't entirely their fault, because what they are commenting on to a certain degree is there. However, it is partially their fault. When a party moves to a primary system for nominating the president, it is actually an abdication of choice on the part of the politicians. After 1968, many politicians in the Democratic party didn't want to be blamed by groups for whatever happened, so they thought, "We'll let the people decide, then they can't blame us." What they didn't consider was that they would lose their power when they did that.

The new system put the press in a strange position. In the new system, the voters have to make the choice. Well, where are they going to get any advice? Formerly when parties were stronger, they would listen to what their party said. If the local organization and nomination process had endorsed somebody, they would listen to that. That structure is no longer there, however, and this doesn't happen anymore. So the voters have only one source of advice, which is the press.

We have talked about the press, especially television. They are in the entertainment business. People don't live their lives so that they will ultimately run for president. If the press can find something that's interesting about a candidate's personality or something that has happened to him, then that becomes big news. It is not fair to the people. If Gary Hart had been running even as late as 1968, he wouldn't have gotten as close to the presidency as he did. In 1968, Hart would have found himself in a small room with a bunch of people who controlled votes to the National Convention. They would have demanded an explanation of his personal life, and Hart would have to promise to behave or else be rejected. Now, unfortunately, all that scrutiny has to be done in public and I think it is unfortunate.

When the press comments on an early poll about who is ahead and who is behind, they negatively affect the campaign process. In 1984, the press decided John Glenn was ahead. Well, if you're a voter who is more interested in this than most people actually are, you read a poll that says who is ahead and who is second, in your own mind you might say, "Well, I've got no reason to look at these other guys." In this case, the real news was that, just as expected, Mondale won. However, the amusement and entertainment side of the story was that Gary Hart beat John Glenn for second place. In the old system, if you won, you won. In this system, often you may win and lose. In effect, Mondale lost that day because Gary Hart got this great push out of beating John Glenn. So, we see that the press corrupts the process. It's not that they try to do this, but by virtue of following their own instincts about what is entertaining, they corrupt the process.

COMMENT: I think your analysis of the relative strength of the parties nationally, the role that the bosses no longer play, and the consequences of that are precisely on target. In Virginia, the roles are reversed. The Democratic party sat down and said, "We interviewed a bunch of people. We don't have anybody of any stature to run against Warner, so we're not going to make fools of ourselves, and dissipate our resources over nobody." At this time, they are stronger.

QUESTION: I can't help but notice that all your examples of the foolishness of the campaign system have been Democratic examples. How was the Republican party able to avoid such problems?

MR. SEARS: Well, I would say that the success of the Republican party, mostly since the 1960s, has been the result of Democratic foolishness, frankly. We had a smaller party in the beginning, and we were not a coalition party. Still, we had divisions between liberals and conservatives or moderates and conservatives, and these divisions came to the fore in 1964. However, we were a smaller party, so the big change in the system of nomination didn't result in much substantive change. We don't have party bosses in our party anymore either, but we used to have them. However, we have been getting the same results from the new system as we did from the old. So, there has been little rancor inside the party. People have accepted the results.

If we wound up nominating Lowell Weicker one year, we would have a problem. That could conceivably happen under the new system. In 1976, Ford beat Reagan narrowly and the primary system contributed to the ability of Reagan to make it close. Reagan wouldn't have been able to come that close to being nominated in an ordinary system.

For parties to mean anything in the new system, voters must be able to see the order and the decision-making process they go through. Voters can then have confidence in what the party says it stands for. When there is no confidence in the party's decision, the voters are left to guess whether or not a candidate is telling the truth. Usually, a voter comes away from that experience saying, "Probably not." Once he does that, he asks himself, "Do I need to vote, really? What difference does it make? This guy says he'll do this, but I don't trust him. I don't even like what he says."

As another example of the difference, in 1967 and 1968 there was a man in Philadelphia named Billy Mean, the Republican city boss. He didn't win many elections, although he had a Republican organization which was not dormant and indeed controlled the mayor of the city for a long time. When it was time for nominations, Billy Mean was an important person, because he had direct control of five congressional districts; under our system of two delegates (to the nominating convention) for each district, that was ten delegates of his own. Through coalitions or agreements with people in Montgomery and Delaware County, he really spoke for somewhere between 20 and 25 delegates and had something to do with the at-large delegates. So, he was a powerful person unknown to the country.

Billy Mean had never liked Richard Nixon, but he liked me all right because we had something in common: We had both attended the University of Notre Dame. I would go to see him, and finally I persuaded him to see Nixon. If you were running for president then, you spent time, in addition to running in the primaries, going around and visiting the bosses and talking with them. People on your behalf did that also. Nixon met with Billy Mean, and Billy asked him what he was going to do about the war. He got about two sentences out, and Billy said, "No, no, no, Dick, not that baloney; what are you going to do?" Nixon said, and this is the only time I've ever heard him say this in private, "If I get in, I'm going to start taking the ground troops out to reduce the number of casualties and step up the air power and the sea power for a while to make them know that we're not just giving them up. Then, I'm going to try to settle it and get out of there." The reason he had to do that was because you couldn't lie to Billy Mean. He knew enough about you and about politics and what was possible to know when you were lying to him. If you lied to him you would never get his support.

Nixon told Billy Mean precisely what he later did, but he never said it anywhere in private other than there when I was present. Maybe he did to some other people, but he certainly never said it in public. There's nowhere in this present system where anybody can get that kind of straight answer.

Billy Mean also asked Nixon another question that day. He said, "Dick, I like to win some offices here every now and then. For me to do that in Philadelphia, I've got to get somewhere between 30 to 38 percent of the black vote. How are you going to do that for me?" Nixon in the best way he could tried to describe what he could do. He could not guarantee the votes, but he had to convince Billy that he was going to do some things to try and make the situation better, and we did some things. They weren't enough to get him that much, but you couldn't lie to Billy.

A contrast with Nixon would be Ronald Reagan eight years later. Walter Cronkite asked him—it is the press who asks you now, not the political leaders—what he was going to do to get the black vote. Reagan said, "I'm going to get that vote just like I get the white vote," and that was the end of that. If Reagan had said that to Billy Mean, that would have been the end of the interview right there. Without leaders such as Billy Mean, nobody really asks the Republicans how they're going to get black votes anymore, because blacks don't vote in the Republican primaries. Republicans don't get elected with black votes. They don't do anything for blacks. Nobody asks about it. It's a bad situation.

QUESTION: You've spent a substantial portion of your career putting together national campaigns, and I wonder what you think of the notion that there is a Republican lock on the presidency? Where do you feel the Republicans' greatest vulnerability lies in presidential politics?

MR. SEARS: Well, I don't think there's any lock on anything. The Republicans have done very well at the presidential level, and had it not been for Watergate, we probably would be able to say that a Republican has been in office since 1968.

Carter was an interesting political phenomenon. He should have been beaten, even under the circumstances, but the trouble was that the Republicans were too locked into their own thinking to do the right thing. Carter won every state in the South except Virginia. The way the Republicans had been winning, they were vulnerable then to a southern candidate. They aren't now because the Democrats are unlikely to nominate one for a while. The memory of the experience with Carter, even though he has in some ways been an exemplary ex-president, is too fresh for a Southern candidate to convince voters in Iowa and New Hampshire, as one must do, that they ought to be nominated by the Democratic party. That is the practical problem. Carter, by virtue of the strength he had in the South, was able to hold the normal black vote and able to cut into the white vote that the Republicans had normally been getting. He was vulnerable in the Northeast, yet the Republicans felt so inadequate in the Northeast that they didn't really run against him there. The Republicans carried New Jersey anyway. They never spent any money in Massachusetts, and Ford lost it 54 to 46 percent. The race was closer in other places. If they had devoted the funds and the effort, I think the Republicans could have run stronger and forced Carter to try to explain that he wasn't really a Southerner, which would have hurt him.

The Republicans are vulnerable today to the right man in the right circumstances. What coalition of states or interests is that? Well, I think that the Democrats must have a candidate who can come into the race with most of the Northeast in hand but also claim some of California. If they can knock California out of the Republican building blocks, everything else gets a lot more speculative. As you will note in all of these successful years and even in the Ford election, the Republicans carried California. Without it, the race becomes scary for the Republicans if the Northeast is locked up. The Republicans are not as strong in the large states in the Middle West as they were 20 years ago. If you carry the South it's worth a lot, but it won't win it for you. California is the key to the rest of the Republican coalition. If you are a Democrat, you need to have a candidate from the Northeast who can either make himself well enough known or is likely to be popular.

QUESTION: Any suggestions?

MR. SEARS: Well, Cuomo to a large degree fits a lot of that. I don't know how he would do on California. They don't know him very well out there.

NARRATOR: Could you tell us about Reagan as a campaigner and your relationship to him? Your predecessors in the Nixon oral history indicated that Nixon himself made the big calls, and not John Mitchell, as many of us had thought. What about Reagan?

MR. SEARS: Reagan wanted to be managed. When I first went to work for Reagan, a lot of people, many of whom were my friends, either enthusiastically or unenthusiastically expected to support Ford. Reagan was thought to be a loon. They all told me not to do it when it looked like I might. Then there were friends of mine who had worked for Reagan in the past who told me not to do it either. They told me the reason was that no matter how inviting it might look or how nice he might be about it, in the end he would not bring himself to decide to run for president. So, I would look like a fool, because there would be no race. I listened to them, observed a few things, and ultimately was able to lick that problem, because I never asked him if he was running. There came a day in August or September 1975 when I had to say to Mr. Reagan, "Well, in November, you are going to announce your candidacy, and here's a proposed speech. We're going to take a trip here, and we will fill you in more on that and see what you think of the speech," and I walked out of there that day. Nobody said no, so we went ahead. Actually, the same thing happened in 1979. On neither occasion did I ask him if he wanted to run, whether he was going to run, or if he had made a decision.

You may think that's pretty strange, but here was a fellow from Tampico, Illinois, who had never been outside of town until he went to college, and college wasn't that far away. Afterward he made the move all the way to Davenport, Iowa. There, he did radio re-creations of Cubs games in the "big city" of Des Moines. After that he went to Hollywood and became a movie star.

Reagan was very serious about being a movie star. There are two kinds of stars in Hollywood: those who take it very seriously, watch their weight, take care of their health, and work hard, and those who are very talented and don't control themselves, but are tolerated because of their great talent. Reagan was in the first category. When he was working, his car would arrive, pick him up before the sun rose, and take him to the set. The door would be opened for him, he would go in, and people would make him up. Somebody would go over his lines with him. While some stars might say to the director, "Well, I think I could play it a little better this way than that," usually Reagan listened to what the director told him. When he walked on the set, he didn't question whether the people who wrote the script, handled the lights, or directed could do their jobs; he just did his. He did a scene over and over again until the director said, "We've done that one enough." The next day, he did the same thing.

It might be true that the director would get fired during the course of a picture or that arguments would go on all around Reagan, but it didn't bother him. When the picture came out it was perfectly natural that the acting was criticized if people said it was a bad picture, but Reagan knew it might just as well have been the writing or the directing. When it was a good picture, he knew he would get most of the credit.

Some of these are very interesting and, to some degree, healthy habits for politics. It was not that Reagan didn't have ideas or classify himself, but this was his discipline. Once he had assembled his advisers, he didn't usually question them, just like he wouldn't question the director or the writer. What was most important to him was to do well at the part he played. Things turned out pretty well for him.

It's an interesting comment on our society that we can take so much from how someone behaves rather than what he does in the presidency. I don't think that's unique. We always look to the president to give us, in a broad sense, something of value to look at, and Reagan did a good job at that. It was too much for people to expect to see his handprint on every single thing that was done. The best quality he had was to let people around him do their jobs.

The presidency has a great deal of residual power. If you try to hold it all for yourself, you waste most of it. He may have erred in delegating too much power, but given the experience of Johnson, Nixon, and Carter, there was plenty of room to delegate a lot more, and he did.

NARRATOR: The last question we always ask people is how do you think history will judge your president? Reagan's popularity seems to be declining and Carter's is rising.

MR. SEARS: Carter is coming up because he has been an excellent ex-president. Maybe I haven't read the right things, but I don't know that evaluations of the four years he spent in office are any more favorable now than they were right after he left office. Maybe they are; I just don't know.

Reagan was always destined to be viewed poorly rather quickly, but I don't know the end result. He is viewed poorly now because as people come out of the administration, they attest to the fact that he delegated a lot and didn't put his official stamp on things. He allowed things to go on often without getting a chance to look at them. This detracts from what historians and others expect out of a man who is president. We expect the man who is president to be a very active person and put his stamp on the office and what's done underneath him.

I think the real question is whether or not Reagan's eight years, as you look back from a longer-term perspective, were helpful to what happened afterward. I think on that score he will look pretty good. We're now experiencing a new era in the world and everyone who can claims a little credit for it, but the fact is Reagan was president as it began to happen. I would ask those who thought we might have a third world war while Reagan was president to note that he had good instincts. He did not have to be told, as Gorbachev became more easily approachable, that approaching him was a good thing to do. Reagan was the one man who could convince the conservatives that peace should be sought. He had the credibility to do it, and did it, so I would hope he's viewed well over the long haul.

CHAPTER 5

SPEECH WRITING
FOR PRESIDENT REAGAN

MARI MASENG WILL

NARRATOR: Mari Maseng Will was born in Chicago and is a graduate of the University of South Carolina. She was a reporter for the *Charleston Evening Post* and then served as press secretary for the Reelect Thurmond Committee in 1978. She also served as staff director of the Dole for President Committee from 1979-80. She was special assistant to the chairman of the Reagan-Bush Committee in 1980 and then continued as press officer in the office of President-elect Reagan. She then had a stint as presidential speech writer in the White House and, following that, as assistant secretary for public affairs in the Department of Transportation. She also had business experience as vice president and director of corporate affairs for Beatrice Companies, Inc. Her major responsibilities in the Reagan administration were as deputy assistant to President Reagan and director of the Office of Public Liaison. In the last year of the Reagan administration she also served as White House communications director during a very exciting period when the effort was made to assure that President Reagan left office with the same respect that he brought with him to the office. She is married to the celebrated columnist, George Will.

MS. MASENG WILL: I was thinking about what you might be interested in and thought perhaps I would be representative of how people came to Ronald Reagan and how the Reagan revolution was put together through people, because I came to him almost accidentally. I was a journalism major in the university and was a reporter. I felt then that by this time in my life I would be at the *New York Times* and have won a Pulitzer Prize in journalism.

Somehow I went astray. Senator Strom Thurmond asked me to be his press secretary. He taught me about politics. One thing led to another, and I found myself in Washington working for Bob Dole in his first presidential bid in 1979. Many people may not remember that he ran for president in 1979, but he did. By the end, there were just five people and a relative on the staff, but we were slugging it out in the primaries.

After Dole dropped out of the race, there were a series of unity dinners at which the Republican candidates came together to raise money for those who didn't make it and to bring everybody together for the general election. It was at one of those unity dinners that I first came into contact with Ronald Reagan. I was a very tired 25-year-old. I was the only political person left on Bob Dole's staff, so I did everything. I was exhausted and had left to sit in an outer room next to where the speechmaking was going on. The former candidates had been droning on, and suddenly I heard this voice—a very different voice—coming over the speaker system. I'll never forget the sensation. I had been thinking about where we were going next, and what was left to be done, but the voice was so powerful it made me turn around, stand up, and go to watch the man who was speaking.

The power must have been a combination of things. Surely it was the resonance of his voice and the compelling nature of his speaking style, but there was also power in what he was saying. It was captivating. He was speaking about freedom, about empowering individuals. He was telling Americans there was nothing wrong with us, that we could make this country great again. It was a very exciting, moving moment that I'll never forget. That was when I knew this man was going to be a great president.

The next time I remember hearing him speak I had become one of his White House speech writers. (I still think that was the greatest opportunity of my life. I was 26 years old and not very experienced.) He was giving the first remarks I had ever written for him—the welcoming of Margaret Thatcher. She made the first formal state visit of the Reagan administration.

I remember standing out on the south lawn of the White House. It had been raining earlier, so the grass was wet and the dirt was soft, and I kept falling back on my heels. I remember the air; I remember the Marine band playing Sousa marches and people waving flags—and then the silence when President Reagan got up to speak. He started talking with that same captivating, majestic voice. Then I realized that I knew what he was going to say next.

That's when I knew what the opportunities were for me and for all of us there in the Reagan White House. We were going to try to change the world. Perhaps it sounds a little grand, but I was 26 years old and tended to think like that. I think we all did. Everything was possible.

I left and returned to the White House several times, which was good for my perspective. It anchored me a little more in the outside world. But I was like most others in Reagan's administration because I was filled with a sense of purpose. Always at the center was this man with his personal force and a core of beliefs that we were all there to achieve for him.

That is how I became a part of the Reagan administration. There were many people like me who were drawn first to the man himself, and then who through the man became believers in his ideas, and who to this day work for them. He changed us and the country, and he was a great president because of that.

QUESTION: You served throughout the whole term, although you came and went, and you certainly had an experience few people had. You were what we call a "cross-cutter" because you worked as a speech writer, as his director of communications, and in the Office of Public Liaison; thus, you saw him from a lot of different vantage points. I wonder if you could give us a sense of Reagan as a person, of how you saw him in all of the different jobs that you had. How accessible was he to people on the staff? How did you see the presidency changing him?

MS. MASENG WILL: I'll start at the last question and work back. The presidency did change him, but I think I was much more changed at the end. From the time I first became associated with him to the time we were saying goodbye on his last day in the Oval Office, I remember thinking that he had changed very little, although he was perhaps a little more tired.

He changed most significantly in terms of his attitude toward the Soviets. He established what he believed was a personal rapport with Gorbachev, which affected his defense policies. That was probably the most dramatic change. Other than that, he changed very little. He is both a very warm and inclusive man as well as a very distant man, so I'm not sure anyone knows him very well.

Over the years, I had increasing contact with him. In the beginning, as a speech writer, I did not see him much. We met with him every Friday morning at 9:15 to go over upcoming speeches—to hear his ideas and get direction on the approach he would like to take. We would present our thoughts and get our marching orders. After that, as we worked on speeches, the communication was mostly by writing back and forth—with his editing, changing, inserting, and deleting.

QUESTION: Did everybody on the speech-writing staff meet together with him on Friday?

MS. MASENG WILL: Usually they did. Sometimes, depending on the press of time, it might be just someone who was working on a major speech, but usually they tried to include all of the writers.

QUESTION: How many people were writing?

MS. MASENG WILL: There were five writers. The assignments would rotate through the staff pretty much according to who was up next, so you would write on economics one day and arms reduction the next.

QUESTION: They had no specialties?

MS. MASENG WILL: They didn't at that time. Later on, some people tended to develop areas that they preferred to write about, but in the beginning it was just rapid-fire—whoever was up next.

QUESTION: What was he like to work with personally in the various interactions you had with him?

MS. MASENG WILL: He was terrific. He was the best editor I ever had; he taught me. I thought newspaper training was a great benefit in writing for him. At a newspaper you are taught to downsize paragraphs, sentences, and even the words that you choose. He was very intent on that and was, as a result, able to communicate complex thoughts and theories with very simple, straightforward communication that could be absorbed by the masses of people. He was great in that sense. However, he almost never expressed criticism directly to the staff. Usually he would dole out the praise and would write notes on speeches if he liked them or call you to say it was good. If there were a problem, you usually heard through Baker or Deaver, which was a problem for people who didn't catch on quickly. The staff argued righteously, answering Baker or Deaver with, "Well, the *President* wants it this way!" You soon learned not to do that and eventually understood that this was Reagan's method.

Only once in my time as a speech writer did he deliver the bad news in person. One particular writer tended to write more for the eye than for the ear, in big words, long sentences, and endless paragraphs. Finally the President called us all in (he didn't single anyone out) and told us about the 50-cent word and how that really wasn't what he wanted to do around here. It was a very brief meeting, but everyone got the point.

NARRATOR: Did you know who had written each speech?

MS. MASENG WILL: Yes, we did. In the upper left corner of every speech draft, until it went to press copy, was the slug that had the speech writer's name and then, after it had been edited, the initials of the communications director, and then another slash once Reagan had signed off on it, "RR." It would go that way all the way up to and including the President's backup copy. When it was put out for public release, it wouldn't have that, obviously, but with the slug you could track it all the way through the system.

NARRATOR: Did you have the same problems that Peggy Noonan said she had with the National Security Council and others in the government wanting to cut down her work?

MS. MASENG WILL: Being a speech writer was the best and worst job you can possibly imagine. I used to think, where else would they pay you to sit and read and think? It was wonderful—in a terrific environment, in the middle of a lot of history, motivated by a great cause. Then there was always that day when your speech draft would go out for circulation. It was just one day, but it was extremely painful. You would hear from a GS-8 in Housing and Urban Development about your style, or "the flow." Everyone, as Peggy says in her book, believes himself to be a writer. Sometimes that problem would arise, but usually we had a lot of defensive support from senior members of the staff. After a while a speech with too many edits loses that intangible essence of itself. A committee draft isn't a speech. It won't communicate, and communication was always very important in the Reagan White House.

We were talking earlier how different presidents, in trying to accomplish different tasks, set different styles. Reagan wanted to change the world, as I said, to change the manner of thinking in Washington and the political dialogue around the country. To do that, he mobilized the White House as a bully pulpit. It was always a wonderful place to work if you were a communicator. The entire machine was oriented to do that which I was about. Consequently, we usually had support in fighting back some of the less helpful changes. I found out later when I was communications director that the support job fell to me, and I realized how much a part of my day that took. There was always an understanding in our White House that the message had to get through, and in the end most other considerations gave way.

QUESTION: Could you comment on the technique and style of the final product? How much would Reagan edit what you had done?

MS. MASENG WILL: Mr. Reagan would redo some of the pages. He is famous for long yellow legal sheets that he would write out by hand. He changed a lot of his State of the Union addresses this way, for example, and would insert them into your speech on given issues. However, the speeches that he chose to change this way were usually on topics that touched core issues. He had broad themes and goals about which way he wanted to take the nation and a handful of key issues on which he focused. He had about five issues that he cared the most about. Taxes and defense were at the top, and he always paid a lot of attention to anything that impinged on those two issues in particular.

QUESTION: You must have had a political philosophy that fell into line with Mr. Reagan's philosophy; otherwise, you would not have been so uncritical about everything he wanted in his speeches. You started your career with Mr. Thurmond, who is seen as the epitome of conservatism. Did you start with that political stance yourself?

MS. MASENG WILL: I grew up in a conservative family. My grandparents immigrated here from Norway—one from Denmark, but all from Scandinavia—and so I was raised in an atmosphere of traditional conservative values. Ingrained in me was the belief that if you work as hard as you can and get an education, you can become anything you want in America. I grew up in South Carolina, which is a place that tends to ground you in those values.

I was most attracted to the President's political philosophy because of its controlling theme of freedom: freedom in a broad sense—the American system versus that of the Soviet Union—but also choosing freedom in each of our domestic decisions. Even within our system there are different ways and degrees of looking at that—empowering and unleashing the individual to achieve as much as he or she can. Limiting government was very appealing to me as a political philosophy, and I saw that translated into all the different forms of policy. Obviously you can't agree with anyone on everything, but that was what attracted me first to President Reagan.

QUESTION: How did the task of speech writing change during the difficulties of Iran-contra?

MS. MASENG WILL: Those were very dark days. I was then the director of the Office of Public Liaison and was a member of the President's senior staff, which I was not when I was a speech writer. Speech writers reported through several levels before they got there, so I had a little bit more of a window on the President and on the inner workings of the White House at that time.

The Iran-contra crisis broke in the fall of 1986. It first surfaced in news reports in a Beirut newspaper, and attempts to learn what was really going on were rebuffed by the National Security Council staff. As the director of the Office of Public Liaison, I reported to Pat Buchanan at the time, and I remember going in and asking Pat about it and urging him to help us get to the bottom of this. It was an amazing series of reactions, which shows you how insulated the White House can become. There was one person in a staff meeting who assured me that I was overreacting and that this would be an "inside-the-Beltway" story. I'll never forget that. I remember Admiral Poindexter assuring me that this whole thing would be settled within a couple of weeks and that when the American people knew what we've been about, they would be behind us for sure. That kind of denial went on for several weeks before it really became clear that the situation was out of control.

The speech-writing system totally broke down in that period. One of the reasons it was such a disastrous period for the President was because at that time, for poor reasons, the communication system which had worked so well for the President was abandoned. Those people who brought about the debacle, namely the National Security Council staff, took complete control of all communications on the issue. They wrote the first speech that the President gave about it, which was a terrible document—misleading at best. It was not circulated even in the tight ranks of the west wing of the White House. I saw a copy given to me by Pat Buchanan, who was one of a few people allowed to see the draft before it was given. I marked it up for him and gave it back. I had underlined and circled and marked in the margins sections that could not be true—outrageous assertions, unbelievable arguments and "facts" that could not be true. He tried to make changes and was flatly overruled. Thus, there was no speech-writing process. The rest of the White House was shut out. The NSC was in control.

The same was true with the poorly thought-through press conference that followed. It's always a mistake in communications to rush to reveal the facts more quickly than the facts are coming to you. The facts were not nailed down, but once again the same crowd was in charge of briefing the President and divining the strategy. I appealed to Buchanan to stop it. He appealed to Regan. Regan phoned Marlin Fitzwater to call it off—but it was too late. Fitzwater was already in the briefing room announcing it. The communication system was circumvented, and the press conference was a failure. It was at that press conference that the President asserted "no third countries" were involved, for example, which was clearly not true.

We didn't really rebound until the spring of next year when Landon Parvin, a member of the initial team of speech writers, was brought back in finally to create a draft in the manner in which drafts are usually created. That was when the President expressed his regret over the crisis and things began to get back on a regular footing. Of course, by that time Poindexter and North had been fired and the NSC staff almost totally replaced. It would not be, however, until Reagan's final year that he would recover from the damage done in those last two months of 1986.

QUESTION: What differences do you see between the first and second terms?

MS. MASENG WILL: It's hard to tell. There was a difference in personnel. We had changed chiefs of staff, and chiefs of staff often bring their own tone or style to the operation of the White House. Of course, the Iran-contra scandal broke in the second term. At the very end, a lot of people from the early days had returned—Kenneth Duberstein was back, this time as chief of staff; Oglesby was the deputy chief of staff; I had returned as head of communications; Tony Dolan was still the chief speech writer. We tried as best we could in that last year to recreate the tone and style of the early days.

QUESTION: In the middle period it seemed that there was an extreme distortion by the opposition in focusing on the evils of the budget cuts, and they had these very wild stories about the terrific impact that this was making; television was full of people who were being impacted in different ways. It seemed at the time that what was lacking was a vigorous counterattack. Was that a matter of policy, and was it just decided that a rebuttal wasn't needed?

MS. MASENG WILL: There was always a tension throughout the administration between the people who believed that the best defense is a good offense and the people whose goal was to lock in existing support by avoiding controversy. I personally have the view that in politics you can't stop moving; you must either keep gaining ground and momentum, or you begin losing it. There is no "status quo" option. That is particularly true for someone with Reagan's goals: He was trying to create a revolution, to fundamentally change the way business was done in Washington. To do that he needed to control the national dialogue, and by definition, accomplishing his goals meant he upset a lot of applecarts. If you ever stop upsetting them, people are going to turn them back over. There is just no in-between.

On the other hand, there are those people who think that once your support levels reach a certain percent, if you do anything controversial, you will erode those support levels. There was a constant struggle between these two points of view—during some periods one approach would have the upper hand, the other in the next. You are referring to a time when people were trying to protect the rating polls.

QUESTION: Did you have any flare-ups with Nancy Reagan?

MS. MASENG WILL: No, I never did. I had limited contact with Mrs. Reagan, and that contact was always helpful.

NARRATOR: You never hid behind a pillar like your colleague said she did?

MS. MASENG WILL: No, I didn't. Not only did I never want to, I'm not sure it could be done.

NARRATOR: Why would Peggy Noonan have been upset about that when she spoke about wearing a khaki skirt and seeing Mrs. Reagan curl her lips when she saw it?

MS. MASENG WILL: Peggy is a friend of mine, and I've worked with her and think very highly of her writing. She is a very talented person. But I would point out that in that exchange recounted in her book, not one word is spoken by Mrs. Reagan. It's all in Peggy's mind; it's her view of what happened. I doubt that Mrs. Reagan recollects it; I haven't asked her about it. Maybe Peggy felt bad about wearing the khaki skirt; I don't know.

QUESTION: To what extent would you say you were successful in changing the world and the way people think?

MS. MASENG WILL: I believe it was fundamental. As President Reagan took office our country was sliding into a recession that those of us in his administration believed was caused by past policies that stifled growth and an individual's ability to create growth. Whereas the debate before had been about how much more to spend, the President got people arguing about where to cut. The discussion had been about how much to increase taxes, but the President got people arguing about how much taxes could be cut. He talked about wisdom coming from the people to Washington, not just from Washington to the people. Jimmy Carter said it was a time of national malaise; Reagan said it was a time of national greatness. I believe President Reagan called us to our better nature and made us believe in ourselves again. What resulted was a period of tremendous growth that benefitted most sectors of our economy. Very stringent measures had to be taken, and that hurt for a while. But it worked. The President created the longest period of recovery and growth since World War II.

What he did for freedom was even more profound. He believes—and I believe—that by strengthening America and reaffirming American values, the Reagan revolution in America became the catalyst for the outbreak of freedom now literally erupting all over the world. I know that this is what he thinks was the most important contribution of his presidency.

QUESTION: Could you discuss his attitude toward women?

MS. MASENG WILL: Yes, I would love to talk about that. The topic of Reagan and women is very interesting. He is somebody I would describe as very enthusiastic about women. His attitude was not shared by all of the people around him. There were certainly those in the Reagan White House who were not enthusiastic toward women. Reagan, however, was. As I said, I was 26 years old when I came to the White House, and he made me a presidential speech writer. He promoted me again when he nominated me to be assistant secretary of transportation, and I was confirmed by the United States Senate when I was 28 years old. I came back again at age 32 to join his senior staff as the director of the Office of Public Liaison. At 35, I returned again to be his communications director, the most senior communications person at the White House. Clearly, he gave me tremendous opportunities.

When women would walk into his presence, his face would light up. That's the only way that I can describe it. It would happen when I walked into the room for a meeting; he would look up and this big smile would appear. When Lynn Martin would sit down at a leadership meeting, he would give the same look. He just liked being with women.

He was very open to their ideas and ready to accept their expertise on an issue. For example, when I was a speech writer he would listen intently to me when I would present the way I thought a speech should be put together. His respect and enthusiasm became even more apparent as my positions of responsibility escalated. When I was at the Office of Public Liaison I would be talking to him about groups and their policy goals and their political dynamics. When I was communications director, we were putting together the strategies for the final year. He took me seriously and dealt with me as a professional, but he was also someone who made me feel he was always glad to see me.

QUESTION: After hearing you speak and respond to the questions and knowing your background, I can see that you have a personal agenda of very high order and very sound values. Would you comment on the degree of difficulty in reconciling your personal agenda and the political agenda that was expedient and necessary at the time?

MS. MASENG WILL: I always began with the premise that this was Reagan's presidency and not mine. Because the overlap of his beliefs and mine was so great, I felt always that I was working to advance the larger cause. There are times when you don't agree and you have to make a personal decision as to when the balance gets to a point that you no longer want to advance the cause. It never got there with me in terms of the issues with which we were dealing. There would be battles you would win and battles you would lose over parts of a policy. There were big fights over the gas tax, for example. But usually once those were settled and the President signed off, he was the leader. This is what he wanted, and this was his view of how to succeed.

One thing he did teach me (which perhaps everyone learns as they grow up, but this was the difference between me when I first came to the White House and my outlook when I left) was that there are a lot more grays in the world, that things are not black and white, and that compromise is necessary. He was very skilled at compromise, though many of us weren't when we first came to the Reagan administration because we were so fired up. Sometimes in the early days people would think that he was letting them down or that this wasn't enough, but he would say, "We'll go and get what we can now, and then we'll come back for more later." That is how he got the big tax cuts in the beginning, but he wasn't finished and still came back in 1986 with tax reform. It was constant pressure—moving the ball, trying not to be so preoccupied with the immediate struggle that you couldn't see the big picture. That was how I would approach the broad question. Sometimes those questions are taken to mean the stratagems and specific actions in a political struggle, but that has more to do with your personal style and beliefs. There are many ways to accomplish your goals, and I always found the easiest one was fairly straightforward. That is how I would approach the internal battles.

QUESTION: Can you discuss the Reykjavík summit? At first there was a certain amount of confusion and a sense of disappointment, and then about 48 hours later they seemed to turn the situation around. Can you comment on that?

MS. MASENG WILL: I was not on that trip, so I can't speak on it at any great length. I will make one broad observation. There is a momentum that takes place when you're on one of those negotiating teams or working toward a goal; you can confuse your ultimate goal with the immediate goal of the negotiation. They were so oriented toward having an agreement that some people lost sight of what the agreement was supposed to accomplish. When they didn't get the specific agreement, the trip appeared to be a failure. When later it became clear that the President had protected one of his highest priorities, suddenly he seemed strong in standing up to Gorbachev. He didn't fail at all.

QUESTION: Can you comment on the relationship between Reagan and Vice President Bush? Did you do work for both?

MS. MASENG WILL: I did a little bit of work for the vice president after President Reagan was shot. The vice president took up all of Reagan's public engagements, so we automatically began writing speeches for him. That was the only time. Other than the occasional presence of the vice president's staff at Cabinet council meetings and sessions of that sort, there was very little interaction between the west wing and the vice president's office. When I was communications director, I did have some interaction. The vice president personally welcomed me back to the White House, which I thought was a great and generous gesture since I had been out working on his rival Bob Dole's campaign. I especially appreciated his welcome.

QUESTION: President Reagan had a minimum of press conferences, and there was much discussion about that. Do you have any comments on that?

MS. MASENG WILL: Well, his was a different style. There was one period in the middle years when he had particularly few, and that's bad. You have to have enough so that people have the impression of openness and feel in touch with their leader.

I don't think press conferences are a particularly enlightening experience for anyone, however. Sometimes the kinds of questions that the press asks are not always on the top of the American people's mind, and they often are not the message that the President wants to get out. I would rather choose those forums or methods where he can speak to the American people about what he wants.

He gave a great many speeches, so I don't think there was ever any question in anyone's mind about what Ronald Reagan stood for. In the first six months, how many times was he on television? He was on in February with his economic plan, with the joint session after he was shot, and another Oval Office address in July of that year, again on economics. He was constantly reaching out to the American people. He probably had more contact on his own than any president has ever had with the American people. In fact, his whole presidency was predicated on that. We needed to draw the American people into the battle, which is something the American people don't like to do. They would much rather let people take care of it in Washington, but these were such fundamental changes taking place that he forced people to choose. He put the questions to them and asked for their support. They would write their congressmen and call in, and it became a real bond between the President and the people.

Press conferences do have their place. They should be done. Perhaps President Bush has the best technique; now they happen so much that they don't even put them on television.

QUESTION: Could you comment a little bit about the "Teflon" characteristic that people ascribed to President Reagan? For example, is he going to be absolved from the savings and loan problem?

MS. MASENG WILL: It's hard to say because we are still in the throes of that. I don't know. I wish President Reagan would speak out more now and write more to reconnect with the American people and give us his views on things that have unfolded publicly since his presidency.

The Teflon image was something created by people who became very frustrated by not being able to undo the base of support that he created. What the American people wanted from him was to know where he wanted to go and what he believed in, and he told them that. He connected with them; they respected him even when they didn't agree with it.

It was a combination of two things. Even people who didn't agree with him gave him a certain amount of respect and gratitude in terms of his leadership. He established his base because of the core issues that he chose. That support was firm, hard, and rock solid; you would be hard pressed to go back and find another leader who had that. He established that core of people who would say, "Sure, this might happen or that might happen, but he is solid on those things that I consider most important for the nation, and I'll stick with him." That's what it was, and it's a political technique that I call "polarizing." I'm sure he wouldn't call it that, but it involved going to the American people and asking them to choose if they were with him or against him, creating a solid base and operating from there.

The second factor would be that he is such a genuinely likeable person. He likes people, and people tend to like him. He never says a harsh word to anyone about anyone. For example, he was always careful in his speeches. Sometimes speech writers would get a little rambunctious, and there might be too much of an edge or too much of a cutting remark in the speech. He would always take it out. You could go up to a line, but you couldn't go over it—never anything ad hominem. He always kept things within a very civilized range, and that protected him as well.

The "Teflon" peeled away during the Iran-contra episode when he so dismayed people by seeming to go in the exact opposite direction from what they expected. That's when the base of support came apart and his polls plummeted.

NARRATOR: In the last year, how did you try to reconstruct that earlier image?

MS. MASENG WILL: When he asked me to come back in that last year, it was to try to recreate with him the mood and the feeling and perspective for the presidency in the last year that had existed in the early days. As I said, his polls plummeted after the Iran-contra debacle; they stabilized after Howard Baker came in. The slide stopped, but the President never really regained the momentum or the good feeling that he had previously enjoyed. His polls were somewhere in the 50-percent range. There was a great worry on his part and among others in the administration that if he were to leave office with the polls at this level, it would be interpreted, as it was beginning to be interpreted, as a rejection of his philosophy, accomplishments, and value system.

Our goal in the last year was to try to put it back together again. It was really very simple. It seemed as though it would be a daunting task, but the simple premise was that you rarely have to recreate the wheel. We just looked back to what President Reagan was talking about and what constituencies he was speaking to in the early days when he had been at the height of his power and popularity. We translated those issues and those constituencies into their 1988 counterparts and put together a basic formula so that we could be sure everything the President said or did was focused under this discipline. For example, he would speak about strong defense, but the 1988 version was that strong defense had led us to peace, Gorbachev, and so on. Family values were translated into education policies and other things. We just went right down the line, put together the 1988 version and then laid out a schedule. We also determined that it was essential for Bush to be elected so that the policies would continue, and we used the platform of the presidential campaign to speak out on those same issues to those same people and recreate the base. That's what he did, and it worked the second time exactly the way it worked the first time. His polls rebounded by 20 points by the time of his farewell address. He was the most popular president ever upon leaving office. It was really just a matter of recreating the issues and the constituencies.

QUESTION: Do you go along with those who believe that the American people don't want a strong president but prefer a weak president?

MS. MASENG WILL: Again, I have a limited perspective. Many of you have worked for many other people and have seen administrations in a more close-up manner than I have. This is really my only one.

My view is that the American people are a little schizophrenic. On the one hand, they would prefer to worry about their businesses, schools, and local communities and to let someone else run Washington. On the other hand, they feel most comfortable when Washington is being run right, when there is a strong leader there. I remember seeing how the people would respond to the President. When he was strong his support was stronger, and when he was weak his support was weaker. I think they prefer to have a strong president.

NARRATOR: We always ask about limitations, and you gave us a little hint when you used the word *distant*. Your colleague Peggy Noonan made two comments on this, and I wondered whether you agree with her. First, she said that the distance and the "loner" aspect could be explained by his childhood—his father and his retreat from that family problem to his own room, and so on. The other explanation she gave was that Richard Darman explained President Reagan to her in a way that she didn't fully understand. Was there an interpreter among your colleagues who helped you understand this personal distance?

MS. MASENG WILL: No, and I always find it very dangerous to analyze people, so I don't have any great insights as to why he is the way he is. I have a feeling that his personality type was enormously successful because it protected him from some of the hurt of the personal attacks that come when one is a modern-day political leader. It also probably enabled him to deal with some of the great decisions that he had to make.

I have no idea how he came to be that way, but it worked pretty well. Sometimes people say that translates into his management style, of which, again, there is the good and the bad side. The good side was hailed by *Fortune* magazine in his first year, when he was seen as the manager of the future. The good side is how he was able to focus so intently on those things that he felt he must achieve while he was President. The bad side of it was manifested by Iran-contra. It's hard to tell.

QUESTION: With regard to the Iran-contra affair, there are those who say that President Reagan should have pardoned the individuals involved because they merely were trying to carry out what they thought were his wishes in the matter. How do you look at this?

MS. MASENG WILL: I believe that the people who were involved were responsible adults who knew what they were doing and were personally responsible for what happened to the presidency. My view of whether or not they should have been pardoned doesn't have so much to do with their own personal case, but more to do with my belief that it would have been over for the country faster if we hadn't had to go through all the trials. It doesn't seem to have hurt us, however, and we are getting through fine.

COMMENT: He could have saved the government and the taxpayers the $20 million spent on special prosecutor Lawrence Walsh by that simple act of pardon before he left office.

MS. MASENG WILL: I would have done that for that reason. It's pointless. We all knew everything we needed to know by that time, and it was just a rehashing. I don't want to get into the motives of Walsh or any of the other people, but I don't think much was accomplished by those trials, and certainly a lot of time, energy, and money was spent. That would be a reason to pardon them.

QUESTION: You were talking about the changes over time in his views of the Soviet Union. Can you tell us how those changes came about as you saw them?

MS. MASENG WILL: Again, my view was from a distance, but he used to talk a lot about it. He talked to me about Gorbachev quite often in the last year. His sense was that there was a great opening for us because Gorbachev was in power and perhaps this was a leader who might, for various reasons, be more open to making some of the difficult choices that he, Gorbachev, was being forced to make because of the deterioration of the Soviet Union's strength. Reagan found a lot of opportunity in that man. They had a personal rapport, and Reagan became very focused on the opportunity to try to bring about a new era of peace through this changed relationship with the Soviet Union. This became his priority in his last years.

NARRATOR: We all thank you for a most clear and forceful presentation.

CHAPTER 6

THE REAGAN PRESIDENCY: LEADERSHIP REVISITED

WILLIAM BROCK

NARRATOR: When did your association with Ronald Reagan begin?

MR. BROCK: We met during the 1960s, but it was very casual and very brief. We didn't actually get to know each other until probably the mid-1970s, and really not well until 1980. We worked together on more than one occasion in 1979-80 when I was chairman of the Republican party and he was a candidate at the time.

NARRATOR: What were your initial impressions of him as a leader? Did any of those perceptions change, and in what ways?

MR. BROCK: I thought he was a remarkable leader. I thought he was the most articulate public spokesman for our party that I had seen in my time in politics. He was wonderfully able to motivate people and to lift their vision to what can be achieved.

NARRATOR: Were his qualities of leadership greater than the leader with whom you worked in 1976?

MR. BROCK: I supported Gerald Ford in 1976. I did not think Reagan was wise to divide our effort by an assault on the incumbent. I knew Jerry Ford, and I liked and respected him as a human being. I also felt like he would be a fine president, given the opportunity to do so.

In 1980 I was the national chairman and could take no position, so obviously I didn't. My job was to be sure that the party was strong enough to elect whoever won the nomination, so I literally kept myself clear of the primary situation.

NARRATOR: Were you at all surprised with President Reagan's appointment of you as trade representative?

MR. BROCK: He did ask me if I wanted to serve with him. I suggested that this was an area of intense interest to me, and if given the opportunity, I would like to do that. When he named me, I was not totally surprised and certainly very pleased.

NARRATOR: What role did you play as trade representative? As I understand it, you reported directly to him and were responsible for directing all trade negotiations and formulating overall trade policy. During the first few years, there were quite a few people involved in such issues as the auto imports question.

MR. BROCK: Oh, yes. The role of the United States trade representative is very clearly stated in the law, and it is different from any other Cabinet position because the Congress felt that each of the various departments had a focus that was too narrow to represent the total U.S. interest. Thus, the United States trade representative was required by law to involve all the other departments and to coordinate trade policy. In the final analysis, it was the trade representative's responsibility to not only negotiate but also implement that policy with the support and consent of the president.

In any trade issue, as distinct from issues that directly relate to education or commerce or to the other departments, by definition, you have to involve all the other departments, and we did. I chaired the Trade Policy Committee. In that setting we debated these issues. In the end, it was fundamentally my responsibility. If things went wrong it was my fault, and if things went well, I was supposed to have done it right.

NARRATOR: What did the President stand for in terms of free trade in relationship to voluntary restraints or restrictions of any kind?

MR. BROCK: The President was wonderfully supportive of free trade. I am a free trader, and he was a free trader and remains so. There were any number of occasions when that was tested. A sort of fun vignette from around 1983 or 1984 shows what I mean. Some of the California wine interests got the support of Ed Meese and Mike Deaver to put some limits on the importation of wine from France and Italy and so forth. We had several meetings of the Cabinet council, without the President present, in which the issue was argued vigorously. I refused to yield because it was a ridiculous case in my judgment, but it obviously wasn't to them. Finally, they decided that it was sufficiently important to take it to the President in a full Cabinet meeting, which we did. I presented the factual foundation for maintaining free trade and then both of them, I think, made their cases for a different position. The President listened for a while and then finally said—and I'm paraphrasing this—"Mike, do you know why we've got more wine than we can sell? It is not because of the French and Italians. It is because of the tax laws of the United States, which have given a subsidy for every doctor and every lawyer to grow wine in California vineyards, and they ought not to be doing it! They ought to be doctors and lawyers, and I am not going to protect them from competition. It's wrong, and that is all there is to it!" That was the end of the discussion. It was a very clear, articulate stand and a correct statement of the facts.

NARRATOR: Is that essentially the way you built your conception of President Reagan's views on free trade, from specific episodes and policies that were debated?

MR. BROCK: Yes, but he was an advocate of free trade in general during the campaign and I think in virtually all of his economic statements. You test those principles in the real world by implementation.

We had a very tough time. The first issue that I had to bring to the President related to a congressional resolution that would have put a limit on importation of Japanese cars. The debate was whether or not it would be a limit of 1.2 million or 1.5 million units a year. I had to say, "Mr. President, we are in trouble on this issue. I'm not sure we can sustain our position. The options are fairly stark: We either fight it and take a chance and lose, which would be a disaster, or we tell the Japanese we have a problem and see if they want to voluntarily maintain a position close to the present level without any rollback, in order to give our industry a couple of years to recover from the shock." The second energy shock had just collapsed the sale of U.S. large cars in 1979 and 1980. The Japanese were not selling small cars until then, but at that point all those unsold Japanese cars were on the docks and started selling like hotcakes, and we had an industry that was losing money faster than any industry in history. It was in pretty desperate straits.

We really had to wrestle with that issue. He was very uncomfortable agreeing to any restraint at all, and neither he nor I felt that it was the right thing to do to demand any change.

Finally, he essentially said, "Bill, tell the Japanese what the problem is and that we are going to do whatever we can to keep Congress from enacting this. Tell them that we will not demand that they adopt any particular position, but will support whatever they decide. If they then decide to impose some voluntary limit on their car shipments to the United States, that's fine. But don't go there and tell them that they have to do it."

That is precisely what I did, and it was very frustrating for the Japanese because they said, "What do you want us to do?" The Japanese always like to have a number.

I said, "Gentlemen, I have told you what the President and I both feel, that whatever you do, we will support you. If you decide to take no action at all, we will support you and we will fight the congressional limit. If you decide to put on some limit, fine—we'll support that. But we are not going to ask you or pressure you to do it, and we are not going to suggest any particular number."

It was a terribly difficult conversation for them, but in fact, I think it did reflect President Reagan's philosophy. While it was hardly a classic action of free trade, it was a realistic step, because if we had not done that there was no question in my mind, at least, that the Congress was going to act very vigorously.

NARRATOR: As in Senator John Danforth's bill and others?

MR. BROCK: I don't think it was Danforth who was the problem at that point, although he certainly was for restraints. There were even more aggressive bills than his.

NARRATOR: Did you ever take into account the view of the International Trade Commission and Roger Smith, that the primary cause of the automakers' economic problems was not imports but something else that they themselves had to face as well, as cars continued to come in?

MR. BROCK: Sure, and that is absolutely correct. Having said that doesn't change the fact that the industry was tumbling into the chasm. We could have lost at least Ford, Chrysler, and American Motors, if not General Motors, if those trends had continued for another two or three years.

As it turned out, it wasn't Japanese restraint that saved the automobile industry; it was the turnaround in the economy that occurred. But nobody could predict that, and I'm not sure that anyone of us are wise enough, even as Monday morning quarterbacks, to go back and say, "We know precisely what would have happened under a different set of circumstances."

What we had to do at the time was to say, "The U.S. automobile industry is largely to blame for its own problems." We couldn't blame the Japanese. I don't think I ever did that in my speeches; I always said that we had to put our house in order and not depend upon the Japanese, and that it was wrong to blame the Japanese. I said that even if the Japanese did put a limit on, that it should be for a very limited duration, and that I personally would not support leaving it on for an extended number of years. In fact, that was my position. The Japanese decided to continue them, and I asked them not to.

NARRATOR: Some of the literature tends to picture the lineup in the Reagan administration in terms of two football teams: Drew Lewis, Mac Baldridge, and you lined up on one side and David Stockman, Donald Regan, and Murray Weidenbaum were on the other side, with the President having real difficulty deciding what side he was going to come down on in a particular trade issue. The lineup changed from time to time, and that made his difficulties even greater at the time of the so-called Meese-Baker-Lewis plan.

Is that the way it was? Was it a fairly evenly divided group with the President acting as arbiter between two contending views, or was it quite different from that?

MR. BROCK: That is a little simplistic, but it's not totally so. What's wrong with that is the implication that Drew Lewis, Jim Baker, Mac Baldridge, or I were protectionists in sheep's clothing. I know that wasn't true with me, and I really don't believe it was true with any of them. However, there were a couple of occasions, and the automobile case is the most dramatic, where we honestly felt that if we didn't do something, the Congress was going to do something a lot worse, and forces would be unleashed that might be uncontrollable. What we then tried to do was to temper that hazard by an application of political judgment that was consistent with our philosophy, although not totally pure.

I guess I have been involved in politics too long to believe that there are nothing but black and white choices in all cases. I don't believe people who practice that are successful in politics. I was frustrated with some purists who admitted they really didn't care what the practical effect of their action was so long as their theory was upheld—that, in effect, they would rather go down in flames. I don't think that is the way you govern, and neither did Ronald Reagan.

The thing I respected about him was that we never lost one of those fights, and it wasn't because he was a protectionist. It was because he honestly felt that in order to govern coherently, you had to make some accommodations to the real world, because that is what politics is all about. People always misunderstood Ronald Reagan. He was so clear in his articulation of conservative philosophy that people thought that meant he hewed to every dot and tittle, that he insisted everybody around him do so, and that he was unrealistic. That just is not true. He was an enormously instinctive, pragmatic politician who knew where he wanted to take us as a country more so than any other president in this century. Moreover, he did so while bending to unusually heavy breezes without letting them break him and his basic instinctive direction.

NARRATOR: How did President Reagan organize the White House? What was your relationship with it, and did any of that change? How did you feel generally about the White House? The literature says that Baldridge and Meese had a kind of private deal that was related somewhat to a turf battle that was going on between you and Baldridge. The deal supposedly involved the merger of the Commerce Department with the U.S. trade representative and the creation of a Department of International Trade and Industry, but that was voted down by the full Cabinet, 13 to 1, and Meese withdrew it.

I mention that, not necessarily to go into details on it, but simply to ask if you had trouble with the White House or the way it was organized. Was it effectively organized so far as trade and economic policy was concerned? Would you have done it differently? Did the President ever talk about it being too large, too small, or too interventionist or too noninterventionist?

MR. BROCK: Yes, I had trouble with the White House organization, and yes, I had trouble with the economic/trade governance of the White House, because it was not well done. That caused conflicts that were unnecessary.

The law required the creation of the Trade Policy Committee, which I chaired by law. Meese sided with someone who had been active in that campaign—Mac Baldridge—whom the President loved like a brother, and rightly so, because he was a wonderful man. Meese sided with him on an issue involving turf more than anything else, and created a Cabinet council on Commerce and Trade. It was entirely duplicative; we had double meetings. Mac and I fussed and fumed for a while, but the more we worked together the closer we got. I loved him; I really and truly did. I have such affection and respect for him. There were times when we just had to sit down and say, "OK, this is silly. Let's work it out." And we would do so.

All the trouble was only a matter of petulance, childishness, or poor organization that caused more anguish than was necessary. However, it turns out that in the final analysis, I don't think it affected our performance. We got the job done, and we did it with an awful lot of credit being given to the President for what we did. The fact remains, though, that there were times when my stomach was churning a great deal.

NARRATOR: I don't suppose this is the first time that has happened.

MR. BROCK: No, and in the second administration we reorganized because no one could justify the misery that we had gone through for the first four years. The second reorganization was better, but it wasn't adequate. If you really want to reorganize the White House—and a lot of thought has been given to that, and I have done a lot of work on it and spoken and written on it—there are better ways to do it.

NARRATOR: Did you have any trouble with the kitchen cabinet, the California people?

MR. BROCK: No. Occasionally they would want the President to appoint somebody to a job that the person wasn't qualified for, or something like that. You merely had to find a job that they were qualified for.

In terms of policy substance, I have never had that problem at all. Maybe they were just all free traders, I don't know.

NARRATOR: Donald Regan said that he had great difficulty in the first six to 12 months in gaining a clear sense of what the President's economic policy was. He said he never had any kind of extended, serious discussion with him and simply was reduced to reading his speeches and press clippings. Was that a problem of any kind in your orbit?

MR. BROCK: No, but that is because I sat on almost every economic group or subgroup that existed. We talked economic policy constantly. There was never any real debate in the administration on where we were going or how we were going to get there. There was a very clear sense that—and I don't want to just use the cliché of supply-side economics, because it is a cliché—the basic aim of the policy we were trying to implement was to restore growth. That meant focusing most of our efforts on reductions in the rate of taxation, the level of regulation, the rate of spending, and the generation of entrepreneurial activity by whatever incentives we could dream up within a free trade system. That's a very concise statement of economic policy.

What we discussed were component parts, but I don't think any of us really had much disagreement in terms of philosophy. We may have argued tactics, but not strategy.

NARRATOR: Did you ever have problems in communicating new ideas, for instance, your new idea about trade in services and intellectual property and investments? You said "Service trade is the frontier for expansion for export sales," and I gather it was an issue to which the insurance and banking industries responded, but then people in communications, advertising, and construction wanted to be sure that they were counted in on it too. Did the President respond to new ideas of that kind?

MR. BROCK: Sure. The fun of working for Ronald Reagan was that he really did believe in the delegation of authority. He believed that if he gave us a job to do, we were supposed to do it, keep him up to date, keep him appraised of where we were, what the problems were, what the difficulties and challenges were, and of new ideas. If we came to a conclusion, unless it was philosophically inconsistent with his own value system or his view of the world, he gave us free rein to try out different things.

That's a real joy when you have that kind of support from an executive. It motivates you to do better, I think. I like that kind of management, maybe because I've had fun doing it. I practice it in my own life too, in terms of people working with me. It works better if people are given a good deal of rein. But when they get out of line, you rein them in. He didn't hesitate to rein us in.

In the areas you are talking about, I said, "Mr. President, there are no rules that relate to the exchange in intangibles, whether it is transportation, communications, advertising, or even movies. That's crazy, because they are going to have a lot of problems in those areas. We are good and competitive, and we are going to do a lot of business. What I want to do is to start some conversation to create a world trading system in this area."

He said, "Fine. Do it. That's a great idea." There wasn't any hesitation at all.

NARRATOR: Did this sympathy for what you were doing remain essentially the same after 1985 when you became secretary of labor?

MR. BROCK: I had a great reluctance to leave Trade. The President knew that. I spent a number of days saying, "Please don't ask me, because I want to say no." Finally, Don Regan called and said, "The President would like to see you this morning, and he is going to ask you, so be prepared." I said, "Damn it, Don, I don't want to say yes." He said, "Well, he's going to ask you, so you've got to say yes." I said, "OK, if he is going to do that, obviously I will say yes."

Then I needed some support; I needed to put my own people in and maintain some relationships I had with people in organized labor with whom I differed fundamentally on philosophical issues, but whom I respected as human beings and as Americans. I said I wanted to maintain those ties, and Regan said, "That is exactly why we want you there."

When I would get into issues within the Cabinet or with others in the executive branch, I would recall that conversation. When I asked for support, I got it; it never failed. The President never turned on me. He never called me to account, to say, "Bill, you're just wrong; turn it around." I had a good debate going for a while with someone who was very close to him, like Ed Meese.

NARRATOR: Would it have been easy to talk to him about the kind of thing you and Ray Marshall have been writing about regarding the work-force issues?

MR. BROCK: We did because we had a tough time with the budget, obviously. When we were looking at the budget, I had to go before the President and defend what I was proposing to do with the work-force issues concerning our employment and training programs. Stockman was nickel and diming, and I had to be able to justify what I was doing. I would say, "This is what we are doing; this is why; this is the study we have done." We had published what some have called a seminal piece, *Work Force 2000*, and I described that to him. I said, "This is where we are as a country, Mr. President. We've got to do something about workers' skills." He heard that.

NARRATOR: How effective was President Reagan in healing the wounds or dealing with the cleavages in his administration, or if that couldn't be done, shifting people to other jobs and maybe even dismissing them? There is a widespread belief or myth about his not being able to remove anybody.

MR. BROCK: He didn't like to do that. He was very uncomfortable chewing people out.

However, there is too much said about his unwillingness to fire people and not enough said about the times when he was forced to choose between two individuals he liked very much who were proposing totally divergent positions. The Cabinet would be fairly well divided, and he had to make a decision. He didn't hesitate to make a decision; he would make it, and that was it. The nice thing about him was that he would do it in such a way that he didn't make the loser feel like he was totally out of favor. He would be so gracious, yet firm. You knew that there wasn't any appeal, but by the same token, you didn't feel as though he was saying, "You're an idiot."

NARRATOR: That's a great strength.

MR. BROCK: It is enormously important to be able to do that. We just didn't have a divided Cabinet on most issues. It was a wonderfully coherent group with many close relationships that built up over the years because of the way the President conducted himself. He simply didn't put up with backbiting.

NARRATOR: Are you saying that even the Weinberger-Shultz debates were not personal in the end?

MR. BROCK: They were pretty tough, but because they would do it in his presence, I think both of them would temper themselves. They both felt very strongly—there wasn't any question about that.

You know, a lot of us had disagreements with Cap. He had his job to do, I had mine to do, and I was ready to kill him when the Pentagon was screwing around with my area of trade and putting limits on the export of Kewpie dolls. I thought it was like a bunch of third-graders, and I went over there and told him so.

NARRATOR: If you had a yellow pad in front of you and were asked to put the strengths of President Reagan on one side and the weaknesses on the other, would there be some entries on both sides?

MR. BROCK: Sure—Ronald Reagan is a human being like the rest of us. His strengths are an enormous character, an enormous commitment to fundamentals, and the belief that if you keep yourself focused on the fundamentals, almost all else will come out right. That more than anything else brought this country back. It gave us a sense of fullness again.

You can't have just a commitment. You have to be able to communicate it, articulate it, and portray it in a way that people warm to you and to the values you are selling. He had that quality to a degree that I have never seen in another person.

One thing that has been described as a weakness was his lack of interest in some subjects because they were not subjects that involved any philosophical value system. Maybe the fact that he didn't get interested in some of those things kept him focused on the larger goals, and maybe he could have paid some more attention to certain issues.

I guess if I had a concern, it was the lack of willingness to direct the White House staff. There were too many games being played beneath him, and they did not involve real issues or basic principles, but rather petty stuff. Over a period of time, that was debilitating but not destructive; it made life just a little less pleasant than it should have been.

On balance, though, it was a very positive and remarkable presidency and almost a unique one in this century.

NARRATOR: Was this game playing worse under some chiefs of staff than others? Was it worse during times when the President had health problems, or was it a general problem?

MR. BROCK: It was probably more general than I would like to think. It was particularly bad the first year, when it was rather mean. If you didn't come out of the 1964 Reagan crowd, and I certainly did not, then you were *persona non grata* and the message was abundantly clear. That became less of a problem as you got to know people and as things calmed down.

Still, some of the residue of "us and them" remained, and I don't think it bothered me so much as it gave the appearance of a White House that was not quite as focused and coherent as it might have been.

NARRATOR: Do you think the Reagan presidency will go up or down in the judgments of history and historians?

MR. BROCK: He may get a tough time from the historians who are living now. My guess is that historians writing 25 years or more in the future are going to be very kind to him, and I think they will give a lot of credit to Ronald Reagan for the emergence of Mikhail Gorbachev, as I think they should.

NARRATOR: Nobody has said that before, but that is a very striking insight.

MR. BROCK: I ran into a major player at *Time* magazine last year when they did the cover on Gorbachev as "Man of the Decade." I said, "You know, I think that's fine and I don't have any objection of putting the leader, at least for the moment, of the U.S.S.R. on the cover of *Time*, but you are so cheap in your approach. Why don't you put his parents on there?" He asked, "What are you talking about?" I said, "His parents—Margaret Thatcher and Ronald Reagan!"

Give credit where credit is due. The consistency of the United States, the clarity of approach—not only in national defense but in the regeneration of the free world that occurred under Ronald Reagan—and the fact that almost every country in the world was trying to emulate the United States by the end of the 1980s, are all totally ignored by the press and by so-called contemporary historians, if that isn't an oxymoron.

I regret that, because I don't think it is right and I think it is misleading to ignore that fact. I really don't believe that Gorbachev would be there or would have survived were it not for Ronald Reagan. I think Reagan deserves the Nobel Prize equally as much. I think Reagan deserves credit for Gorbachev.

NARRATOR: Thank you for a most incisive and illuminating discussion.

III

PROBLEMS
OF LEADERSHIP

CHAPTER 7

THE REAGAN WHITE HOUSE: THE APPROACH, THE AGENDA, AND THE DEBT

ED HARPER

NARRATOR: Ed Harper was born in Belleville, Illinois. He taught at Rutgers University after completing his bachelor's degree with honors at Principia College and his doctorate at the University of Virginia. He was also a research scholar at the Brookings Institution.

He served from 1968 to 1969 on the staff of the Bureau of the Budget and as senior consultant at Arthur D. Little, Inc. He was assistant director of the Domestic Council in the Nixon administration. He then returned to the private sector and was an executive with several companies, in particular Air Balance, Inc. He then returned to government and was deputy director of the Office of Management and Budget in the Stockman era. He was also special assistant to the President during that time, and was chairman of the President's Council on Integrity and Efficiency in Government. Mr. Harper also served on the President's Commission on Industrial Competitiveness and on the President's Commission on Executive and Legislative Salaries. Thus, through a good part of the first term of the Reagan administration, he served in very important positions. He then returned to the private sector as senior vice president and chief financial officer of Campbell Soup Company in Camden, New Jersey.

In 1968 Mr. Harper was the recipient of the Louis Brownlow Award. He received the Person of the Year Award from the Washington Chapter of the Institute of Internal Auditors and has been recognized in numerous other ways. It is a great privilege to

123

have one of our own return to the University of Virginia, and we feel sure that his chapter in the Reagan oral history is going to be an important one.

MR. HARPER: My subject, the Reagan administration, brings back a lot of happy memories. I also served in the Nixon administration, a tough proving ground. Much of the unfulfilled good that might have happened in the Nixon administration did happen in the Reagan administration, in part because of the leadership of Ronald Reagan. His personality tells a lot about the shape of the organization and what happened during those years. As is the case with almost any organization, it reflects to some degree the personality of the chief executive officer.

The Reagan Approach

Ronald Reagan, as you know, was great at telling stories. In fact, once I told him a story from Peters and Waters' *On Excellence.* It is a story about the latest generation of super-computers. The question was asked of one of these super-computers, "When will machines be able to think like human beings?" The computer went on for days cogitating this difficult question, and finally the bells rang, the lights flashed, and the answer came out, "That reminds me of a story." As Peters and Waters went on to point out, the issue here is that human thought processes function in patterns and don't necessarily work in the linear logical flow of computers.

One of the beauties of Ronald Reagan was that he could communicate with people effectively in terms of patterns. It made him a good leader. He had a fairly clearly defined and short agenda, and his approach was a positive one: We can do things. He was a rather unusual combination—somebody who had some conservative ideas and yet was a government activist.

One of his favorite stories that I like was about the parents who had two sons, both of whom had extreme psychological problems. One was a pessimist who, no matter what happened or no matter how good the event was, would say, "Oh, that's terrible," and he'd be depressed and feel very bad about it. The other was an absolutely incurable optimist, so much so that no matter how adverse the situation was that he might be in, he always saw the optimistic side of it.

The parents consulted a psychologist who said, "We have the solution. For your pessimistic son, we'll put into a room everything he has always wanted—every toy, goody, and candy that he would want.

"For the optimist, who will see his brother open this door to this treasure trove for children, we will clean out one of the local stables and put in it straw and manure for him, so that when he opens the door he'll see nothing that is any good."

They tried the experiment, and the pessimistic son opened the door, saw all the toys, and said, "Well, there must be something wrong with this." Then when the optimist opened his door he said, "Gee, with all that straw and manure, there has got to be a pony in there."

Indeed, that was Ronald Reagan's approach to a lot of things, that there must be some good in it, and his lateral thinking proved to be of some historic significance. For example, one part of his view of the American dream is a great faith that Yankee ingenuity and technology can solve almost any problem. In thinking about arms control, he came up with the idea of a "Star Wars" defense, a technological umbrella that would protect the United States. All of his advisers assured him that it was absolutely impossible, and in my institutional role in the budget process, I assured him that we couldn't afford it. He responded, "It doesn't make any difference. Out of whole cloth we are creating an important bargaining chip to deal with the Soviet Union in negotiating arms control. They don't know whether we are going to have it or not; we don't know whether we are going to have it or not. But it is something to negotiate with that we don't have today, so I'm going to do it." He did it, and that made a difference.

The Reagan Agenda

Again, my initial impression of Ronald Reagan was that he had a fairly short, well-defined agenda and an approach that was optimistic, as well as a belief that government is manageable and that things could be done. First, there was Reaganomics, a different way of looking at things. Some people say it was all the same stuff in a slightly different package. However, he had goals, one of which was to do something about inflation, which was at 13 percent when he was inaugurated. The result of his policies was to bring inflation below 4 percent. Richard Nixon did something about inflation when it was raging at 4 percent: He put on wage and price controls, and they didn't work terribly well. Thirteen percent, however, is real inflation. Another accomplishment in the economic realm was President Reagan's bringing about the longest period of peacetime growth in the history of the country since World War II.

The second objective on that short agenda was to bring public opinion on the issue of national security back to the point where it was no longer an embarrassment to be in favor of national security and a strong defense. He came forward with the idea of a 600-ship navy. We don't have a 600-ship navy today, but it is still on the agenda.

He has changed the nation's agenda in that respect and in others. Ronald Reagan was in favor of deregulation. Is there less regulation today than before Ronald Reagan started? No, but it is not on the exponential growth curve that it was prior to his administration.

One of the things I became involved in was kind of a curiosity to me. I had heard a lot of politicians, including Ronald Reagan in his campaigns, talk about fraud, waste, and abuse in government. It is a great political issue, one that sounds good on the stump, but what do you do about it, really? You may catch the occasional wrongdoer, but does that make for government policy or does it achieve anything? Ronald Reagan brought this to the front burner as a constitutional issue. Congress had created inspectors general in a number of the domestic agencies. There were about 16 inspectors general appointed during the Carter administration. They were supposed to be nonpartisan, independent auditors. What exactly "independent" meant was one of the things that concerned the President. Thus he said to Ed Meese during the transition, "By executive order, on the first day of the new administration I am terminating all of the inspectors general, firing them all." This raised a fair-sized flap because many members of Congress felt that the President was dismantling a program they felt was very important in attacking the waste and abuse in government. Furthermore, it was the Congress's program, and it was the Congress's eyes and ears, its spies on the executive branch.

The President was not going to stand for that. He felt that the inspectors general were appointed by the President with the advice and consent of the Senate and therefore were part of the executive branch and not the spies of the Congress. This was the issue. He didn't ask my opinion. He did it and then said, "Here is your program, Ed. You're chairman of the President's Council on Integrity and Efficiency in Government." One of the originators of the program asked me why I wanted to do this. I said, "It wasn't my idea. I got here and they were fired, and we are now going to try to make the best of it." We did. We were able to hire 16 outstanding people, about eight of whom had been in the program before, appointed by President Carter.

That was not necessarily an easy thing to do because there were people around like Lyn Nofziger, whose job was to make sure that the party faithful, those who had participated in campaigns and who had done good things for Ronald Reagan and the Republican party, were appointed to those real plums in government. These 16 positions were pretty good jobs; they were fairly high-rated jobs that required confirmation. I had to take the qualifications of all 16 of them, one at a time, to Lyn (whom I consider to be a good man) and say, "This person is a good person even though he or she was appointed by President Carter, or has no political affiliation whatsoever—or might even be a Democrat. We've got to do it because it is the right thing to do. It is the thing that is going to make good on Ronald Reagan's promise to do something about fraud, waste, and abuse in government."

One of those people, for example, was June Gibbs Brown, whom President Carter had made inspector general in the Department of Interior. We fired June Brown. It was a traumatic experience for her. She told me about it; her husband told me about it. We then hired her to be inspector general at NASA. She did an outstanding job there, as she had done at Interior, and today she is the inspector general for the Defense Department and is doing a great job there.

Thus, we had some very good people, and the program went forward. That was a kind of crisis created by Ronald Reagan and handed to me, and I'm pleased to report that the point the President was trying to make from a constitutional perspective is now acknowledged: These people are part of the executive branch. The Cabinet secretary has recognized them as an important part of the management of the executive branch.

The Reagan White House/OMB/Cabinet

In the first few years of the Reagan administration, when I was there (1981-83), the administration operated differently from most other administrations. We were closer than ever before to the kind of Cabinet government that Woodrow Wilson and others have talked about. There was certainly no doubt that Ronald Reagan was the boss and the President. However, he liked to hear the positions discussed in his presence and to make a decision after having heard the various points of view. He encouraged the creation of Cabinet councils where the Cabinet members and senior White House staff could meet to discuss issues as subcommittees or with the whole Cabinet assembled. Some of the Cabinet councils worked very well; others didn't work. Overall, the Cabinet councils were one of the most important parts of the process for making policy in the early days of the Reagan administration.

Let me step back for a moment and talk about the life cycle of policy-making in a presidential administration and specifically what happened in the first year of the Reagan administration. I would suggest that there is an ebb and flow of creative policy-making in a presidency. The broad outlines of a president's program are defined during the campaign before he is ever elected. Clearly there are a lot of things that a candidate hopes will go away once he is elected president, but a lot of it remains and represents commitments that he has made to the electorate across the country—sometimes to the populace as a whole and other times to specific groups. They are all on his doorstep, even before inauguration day, saying, "Remember that speech you made in Keokuk where you promised X? We are ready to have that promise fulfilled now."

Accordingly, a lot of the first year of an administration is spent organizing the IOUs that the president has put out to an electorate and trying to implement what he said he was going to do. That takes 18 months or so, during which time you find out what can be accomplished, what can't, and you come upon the first interim congressional election. The Congress says, Mr. President, can you help me here and maybe twist things a little bit and not put so much pressure on terminating the Department of Education? (Ronald

Reagan didn't back off on that particular issue quite as far as some had hoped.)

Then, after that congressional election, most presidents—it must be human nature—begin to think about the next presidential election. There is then a new creative phase in policy-making that comes 18 to 24 months into a presidency. He begins to think, How is the electorate going to evaluate me as President at the end of four years in case I decide to run for reelection? Thus, he regroups to ask, "What are the things we are going to be able to fulfill that we promised last time? Which of those things are still relevant? What are the other things—the problems you've got to address today and the things that you can achieve by the end of that first term?" In that first year of the administration you are not creating a lot of new policy. You are instead going to the bank on things you've already created in terms of policy.

Another thing about that first year of the Reagan administration was that the President talked in crisis terms about the manageability of government, the manageability of the economy, and about what was happening with the federal budget. He created an environment in which the administration's theme was to hit the ground running, to move fast in the first six months to make the budget changes, and in fact to make the policy changes that were going to make a difference because lots of policies had to be changed to affect federal spending.

That's more or less where I came in. I had served some time in government but had not planned to go back. Marty Anderson, with whom I had worked in the Nixon administration, called and asked me if I'd come back and work for the President in the transition, and I said, "Well, if it is just for 90 days, because I've got a job and live in St. Louis and would like to go back to that." At the end of 90 days Ed Meese and Dave Stockman said, "Look, this is going to be a chance to make a difference. Here in the next six months is the time when this administration either is or is not going to be able to turn things around in terms of spending and in terms of a lot of these programs that really need an overhaul. We need an experienced team, people who know about the budget process and who know about the substantive policies, to work with us." I was pleased to have that opportunity to come for one year, which then was extended to three years.

When Marty left the White House in early 1982, the President asked me to come across the street to become assistant to the President for policy development. I was intrigued because that was the beginning of a cycle, building for the reelection, when we were beginning to set those policy decisions in place. It was a creative part of the cycle that I wanted to go back to.

In terms of the relationships with the Cabinet, we were not asking the Cabinet members to come in and start writing on a clean slate. The President had already determined what he was going to do about the Energy Department, for example. He had already determined what he wanted to do about the Education Department and a number of other areas. The Cabinet members were there to implement, not to create.

The new Cabinet officers arrived with suitcase in hand and lots of empty offices because not all appointees had gone through the clearance process. This process is becoming more and more difficult; its rigor was increased at the beginning of the Reagan administration with the new conflict of interest and disclosure laws that make it tremendously difficult to get people cleared.

On the other hand, at the Office of Management and Budget, we had our team in place on inauguration day, and the White House staff was in place. We knew what we wanted to do. Dave Stockman and I had spent a lot of time working on it during the transition. We knew what had to be done and were prepared to do it. The Congress was in an unusual position. There was a reconciliation bill, a legislative mechanism that really had never been used. Dave was very familiar with it and figured that under these crisis circumstances we could create a reconciliation bill that would involve hundreds if not thousands of changes in policy that would enable us to redirect the federal budget.

What that meant was that there was a huge locomotive going down the tracks and that the Cabinet secretaries would be lucky if they could jump on it as it went by. That, in fact, is what happened. Some of the Cabinet secretaries were not happy about it. Al Haig was never part of the team, as far as I could identify. He had his own program. He was a great individual but was not really a part of the team.

I remember well one meeting we had in the Roosevelt Room concerning policy and the Energy Department. Governor James Edwards, the secretary of energy, said, "Well, if the President understood his own energy policy he would change his mind and agree with me instead of you guys." We suggested that we thought the President probably did understand his energy policy and that we wanted to proceed with the program. Governor Edwards left not too long after that.

Sam Pierce, as you know, has only recently become controversial. In those days people would call me and say, "I'd really like to work in HUD. I've got a background in urban affairs. Would you recommend me?" I would say, "I'd be happy to do so, but let me tell you that Secretary Pierce has never accepted any recommendations from the White House on any personnel matter, so if you *don't* want to have the job, I'll recommend you. Otherwise I suggest you find somebody who doesn't have anything to do with the White House to recommend you." Pierce was otherwise reasonably easy to get along with, but on personnel matters he just would not give.

Some people got along very well with the White House. For example, Secretary of Commerce Mac Baldridge essentially saw my staff as his staff. A fellow named Dennis Kass was our associate director of the Domestic Policy Staff for Commerce and Trade, and I think Mac really did regard Dennis as a part of his staff. The only *contretemps* we had with Mac on rather unimportant issues was a big discussion over who leaked some of the budget information about the Commerce Department. He insisted that it was over in the White House complex or in the Office of Management and Budget, so we agreed to do an investigation. We satisfied ourselves that nobody at our end had leaked it. Then we said, "By the way, Mr. Secretary, do you realize that standard procedure in the Department of Commerce is that when a memo comes from the Office of Management and Budget to you as secretary of the Commerce Department, 24 photocopies are made the minute it comes into your office? Do you know where those 24 copies go?" He had no idea that 24 copies of every memo from the Office of Management and Budget were made the moment they came into his office. We suggested that he might have some reassessing to do about security over in the Commerce Department.

We had some controversies. In some ways, some of the fellows who were most prickly in public were relatively easy to get along with. The one that intrigued me was Jim Watt, who was always the picture of controversy and a fairly humorous guy. One time there was a big press conference in the Department of Interior. This happened to be about federal lands, oil royalties and what was happening to them, and several other political things about him personally. There were 500 reporters in the lobby of the Interior Building, and they were asking fairly hostile questions. At one point Watt said, "And I shall resign," and there was hushed silence. You could hear all the reporters writing this down and getting set to stampede to the telephones. Then somebody thought to ask, "Well, when?" Watt said, "Aha, that's the question, isn't it?" Watt and the President were on track in terms of what they wanted to do, which was curious to me.

There was a fellow named Don Crable in the Office of Management and Budget who was a long-term career appointee. Jim Watt came to me one day and said, "Would you mind if I offered Don Crable a job in the Interior Department?" I said, "Well, Jim, you are the most stalwart fellow in defending the conservative faith and only allowing those who have done important party deeds to get into these great presidential appointments." He said, "Yes, I know all that, but the fact of the matter is that Don Crable knows more than anybody else in the entire world about my programs, and I want him working for me and not you." Watt did have great respect for the people in the Office of Management and Budget.

There were some conflicts with the Cabinet, some things that worked well and some other things that didn't. One of the things that intrigued me was the relative political ability of some of our Cabinet members. At one point President Reagan had been saying, "No new taxes." He was certainly an unyielding, strong opponent of new taxes. When Secretary of Transportation Drew Lewis was coming up with the idea of a five-cent increase in the federal gas tax, I thought, this is going to be one of the more interesting conflicts that we are going to see. I knew at this particular Cabinet meeting that Drew was going to raise the issue, but what I didn't know was what Drew had done. The meeting started, and the President said, "Well, Drew, do you have something for us today?" Drew said, "Yes, Mr. President, what I have here is a proposal for a five-cent increase in the gas tax. I think we need this for highways, bridges, and so forth," and he finished his little speech. I was waiting for things to happen, and then the President turned to George Shultz and said, "George, what do you think about it?"

George said, "Drew has talked to me about this, and I think it is probably a pretty good idea." Drew had collared all the lead steers in the Cabinet ahead of time and sold them all. There was hardly a murmur of dissent, and this tax increase just shot right through. Drew had done a good job of preparing for the meeting.

The Future's View of Ronald Reagan

One of the most important things Ronald Reagan did was to erase an attitude of defeatism, not only about the manageability of government but also about the future of a planet. The Carter administration had bought the Club of Rome Report hook, line, and sinker. The Club of Rome made all kinds of dire predictions, saying that by the 1990s we would be turning out lights all over the world. We haven't yet, and maybe we are living on borrowed time, but we are still surviving. There was a defeatism in the last years of the Carter administration that we haven't seen since.

Ronald Reagan changed our attitudes about ourselves, our future, and our country. He believed that we do stand for some human values. There are social issues, and you can agree or disagree about his stand on any one or all of them if you want, but he at least brought the issue of values back on the table, and it wasn't just something that kooky right-wing people were talking about. Abortion is a complex issue. You can think of impassioned reasons to be for it and impassioned reasons to be against it, but it is something that we can talk about as a society and try to deal with openly.

A second important Reagan achievement is the economy. The economic changes Ronald Reagan brought about are important. He brought us back to an even keel. We did have a 13 percent rate of inflation at the beginning of the administration; we did have real questions about what direction the economy was going, perhaps toward a big crash. This was totally unchartered territory for the United States, and Ronald Reagan succeeded.

We have had a relatively controlled low level of inflation. We have had the longest peacetime era of economic growth, certainly since World War II. We have had deficits, but our deficits and debt as a percentage of GNP, when you compare them with the other Western industrialized nations, are about in line with where their deficits are.

A third accomplishment future historians might point to is that the President brought some discipline to federal spending. There are pluses and minuses. Defense spending as a percentage of GNP is about where it has been since World War II—some up and some down—but as percentage of GNP it is about where it always has been. It is business as usual despite the rhetoric about the 600-ship navy, "Star Wars," and so forth. Income tax revenue as a percentage of GNP is about where it has been in most years since World War II. Despite the big tax cut, it has returned to normal levels—again, business as usual. The big change is in spending for non-means-tested welfare programs: welfare for the middle class, social security, and other programs such as that. Those programs have not been curbed, and the aggregate amount of spending is rising. Federal governmental spending as a percentage of GNP is up about one point from where it was at the beginning of the Reagan administration, but Reagan's policies did put downward pressure on federal spending, and it would be a lot greater than it is now had he not done that. The deficit also leaves us with some discipline on spending; people think a lot more about introducing new programs now that we have pushed down spending, and the belief is pervasive that new taxes are something that we should avoid at almost all costs.

A fourth point, and one that we can assess only over the longer term, is Ronald Reagan's impact on the judiciary. It is too soon to assess the impact, but it may turn out to be very brief. There has been a tremendous number of changes in the federal judiciary around the country, not to mention the Supreme Court. The judicial activism that characterized the years prior to the Reagan administration was accelerating at a very rapid pace; it has since slowed down. How far it will slow down remains to be seen. The salaries of judges compared to their opportunities to make money in the private sector suggest to me that we are going to have a fairly high level of continuous turnover among our judges. Therefore, despite the large number of federal judges that Ronald Reagan appointed, a number of them are probably going to return to private practice in the years not far ahead.

I was pleased to have the opportunity to play a role in the Reagan administration. I've discussed some of the highlights and have maybe said some controversial things. I'd be pleased to discuss any topics that you find of interest.

NARRATOR: We've heard so much about David Stockman's role in the Reagan administration and about his evaluation of President Reagan and President Reagan's comprehension of the economic planning that went on. You must have been about as close to him as anybody could be. Could you comment on that?

MR. HARPER: I'd be happy to. A chief executive in any organization has people who are specialists working for him. They are in love with their specialty and think their specialty is the most important thing in the entire world. In the private sector, for example, you may have a guy in the transportation industry who is in charge of loading boxes on trucks, and he believes that he ought to report to the chief executive officer of the company. I say this to exaggerate the point that the broad outlines of the budget are fundamentally important to economic policy and to the direction of the administration. There are also nitty-gritty issues, which the director of the Office of Management and Budget can handle. When you've made all of these decisions, you are left with only hard decisions—hard decisions that either aren't very glamorous or are politically impossible. Thus, I can see why Dave would feel that the President didn't fully appreciate or fully understand what Dave was saying about every issue.

I have to admit that at times I was frustrated as well. I would say, "Mr. President, this deficit is going to add to the debt, and we are incurring fixed costs of an amount this nation has never faced before." I would suggest the analogy to the private sector that when you create those kinds of fixed costs you create the potential for disastrous economic downturns. He only said, "Well, my judgment is that the most important thing we can do is avoid a tax increase and avoid cuts in social security. We know where the people stand on that. We are not going to cut some of these other programs, so go back to the drawing boards and find something else." I think you can see why that would leave Dave and me with a high level of frustration, saying, "This man clearly doesn't understand the problem." Meanwhile, he had a different problem. As leader of the nation, he was responsible for bringing all of the pieces together. He came to a different conclusion, and so far it looks like it has done pretty well.

QUESTION: I was intrigued about how Stockman was caught by surprise by the Greider article, in which he spoke critically of the President in what he thought was an off-the-record interview. Was he less effective after that controversy?

MR. HARPER: It is easy for people to become blinded by the glow of publicity. Just as Richard Nixon wanted to make sure that history properly noted his contributions—and therefore he taped everything—I think Dave wanted his position in history to be properly acknowledged. He thought he had a deal with Greider such that the book wouldn't be written until the administration was over. Parts of that book were published shortly thereafter, and Dave's effectiveness was certainly reduced by that. The trust people may have placed in him diminished considerably. His reputation was tarnished on the Hill as well. He became known as somebody whom you could not entirely trust with secrets.

At the same time, the big deals that Dave could bag for the President in the budget process came in the first six to eight months of the administration with the Reconciliation Act of 1981 and the tax cut of that year. After that there was a lot of hard slogging. We had done the things that could be done quickly in an era of crisis; after that point, when the Cabinet secretaries were fully staffed, the competition was much more formidable.

Thus, there was a mixture of several things. Dave went from hitting home runs every time he was at the plate in the first few months of the administration, to hitting singles as time went on. He was still a very important player, and I wouldn't want to diminish his contribution at all. However, I think his effectiveness was diminished, and the environment in which he was working was much more difficult for him after that first eight months and after the Greider article.

QUESTION: Could you elaborate more on some of Mr. Reagan's personal strengths and weaknesses?

MR. HARPER: Ronald Reagan had a pride in his intellectual background. This was a little perverse in that he was both proud of having majored in economics at Eureka College and yet often told the story about how one of his professors came in one day, threw the textbook down, and said, "Look at what's happening around us.

This textbook doesn't have anything to do with what's happening in America today." President Reagan liked to say, "I have the training, but I have a great deal of skepticism about what economists have to say. They've been wrong before."

He did have a very good memory for numbers, but numbers can be fairly tricky and elusive. He remembered them well and took pride in that. Because of his confidence in his ability to communicate with people, he would sometimes wade into a lot deeper water than the staff wished. For example, in preparation for press conferences we would say, "Mr. President, we know that you are familiar with all these numbers about Social Security, but we would really urge a simple yes-or-no answer." One afternoon as we were briefing him for a press conference, he said, "Well, I know it is important for the people to understand some of the numbers behind the Social Security program." I said, "Mr. President, they won't understand it, and besides, it will only raise a lot of other more difficult questions if you answer that way." He said, "All right." That night at the press conference somebody asked a Social Security question, and the President said, "I've got to explain this to you." He threw out a pile of numbers. Of course there were half a dozen stories the next day about how he got the numbers wrong, and we spent the next week straightening that out.

He was tolerant, and that is good and bad. He was tolerant of some people who I don't think were very good and who didn't contribute much to the administration. He was tolerant of some backbiting and infighting that wasn't constructive.

Ronald Reagan was pretty good as a chief executive officer. You can say that he should have been involved in more detail, but Jimmy Carter was more involved in detail, yet he was not an effective CEO. One day during the Reagan years I sat next to Jim Schlesinger on the New York-Washington shuttle. Jim was secretary of energy in the Carter administration. Jim said, "I'll bet your President doesn't do what my President did." I asked, "What do you mean, Jim?" He said, "Can you believe that we used to sit in the Oval Office and argue about which deputy assistant secretaries had ridden first-class on the airlines?" Can you imagine the President of the United States doing this? Carter got into the details of cost cutting, but they meant nothing to the nation. Jim said, "I'm sure Ronald Reagan never bothered about that. He may be up in the clouds in terms of what the priorities are and have a few grand themes, but at least the rest of the organization knows what he wants them to do and what his priorities are."

By and large he was an easy guy to work for, certainly a lot easier to work for than Richard Nixon. Like Carter, Nixon liked to get into the details. One day I sent President Nixon a 140-page book with options on what he could do about policy on Indian reservations. He read the whole thing, cover to cover, page for page. You would never see Ronald Reagan do that. President Nixon also had a few focused priorities.

QUESTION: Were the adverse economic conditions of 1981 and 1982 completely necessary in order to get inflation down? This in turn makes one wonder about the relations between the President and Paul Volcker and other players in that arena.

MR. HARPER: The relations with Paul Volcker were good. Occasionally somebody would take a shot, but not very often. The President had the Economic Policy Cabinet Council, which was headed by Don Regan and for which Roger Porter of my staff was the chief support. That council met early and often and discussed every issue under the sun, and Don Regan enjoyed those sessions. You could learn a lot; they were great economic seminars.

The President also had something called PEPAB (the President's Economic Policy Advisory Board). George Shultz, Alan Greenspan, and many of the other people who had been the President's economic advisers during the campaign were on that board, and it continued through both terms of the Reagan administration. When Paul Volcker's term came up as chairman of the Federal Reserve, Ed Meese and the President asked me to survey the members of PEPAB to decide what we should do about Volcker's reappointment. The President gave me a short list of people he wanted surveyed, and all of the economic advisers to the President on the list said, "Reappoint Paul Volcker." Whether or not the survey was necessary, the result was certainly supported by the President and the economic advisers he trusted most.

Do I think that the adverse economic conditions were completely necessary? I would ask you the same question. I don't know. The net result has been that we have had a sustained period of growth with relatively low levels of inflation, at least compared to the late 1970s. We've had a fairly continuous rate of economic growth that appears likely to continue. By those standards, maybe it was necessary. I don't know. It would be tough to judge that. We tried to reverse the tides of resource allocation; maybe some of it was necessary.

A lot of good things happened; some of these things were funny. There was a Trade Adjustment Assistance Act that provided that if foreign competition adversely impacted any particular segment of the economy, we would make payments to the people and industries of that segment. Dave Stockman was set up on this one day by the "Today Show." The administration had been making these Trade Adjustment Assistance payments to steel workers, and we proposed that the program be cut back radically and then eliminated. Dave was on this show talking about how it should be cut back, and then the "Today" reporters cut away to a steel worker being asked, "What do you think about the Reagan administration cutting back on trade adjustment assistance?" He said, "I've been a steel worker for seven years, and for five years of those seven years I've been laid off. If it weren't for the Trade Adjustment Assistance Act, I wouldn't be able to be a steel worker today."

QUESTION: What concerns me is the debt that increased at such a terrific rate during the eight years of the Reagan administration, much of it because of defense spending. The conservative Reagan administration justified these large deficits by their percentage of gross national product. Isn't deficit spending something that liberals and not conservatives advocate? How can you justify these large deficits?

MR. HARPER: I would argue that the deficits didn't come out of defense spending. They came out of spending for all of the welfare programs for the middle class—that's where the deficits came from. They didn't come from defense spending.

COMMENT: Some of it must have come from defense spending.

MR. HARPER: Why is that?

COMMENT: It greatly increased.

MR. HARPER: Everything else greatly increased as well. Which is the first dollar? All of these dollars are fungible, so the matter of where the deficit comes from reflects your priorities. If you say there is no priority on defense, obviously it must be that all of the waste and the deficit came from defense. Or you could say it came evenly prorated across the board. The biggest increases came from areas other than defense, namely, Medicare and Medicaid, not from the defense area.

QUESTION: Coming back to my original question, why does the administration use the phrase, "in relationship to gross national product"? Isn't that simply window dressing?

MR. HARPER: I don't know if it is window dressing. When you look at the entire economy, how do you judge what is happening? When you look at the role of government in the economy, I believe that total government spending as a portion of GNP is a reasonable way to look at how the society meets its needs for roads, sewers, and health care. Security is a legitimate priority to have on that list as well. If the economy is growing, shouldn't spending for health care or the road systems be growing as well? In a business, we certainly analyze financial statements this way. When the business is growing, we would expect advertising expenses to grow, and unfortunately we would expect our overhead expenses for administration to grow because as a bigger company we need more people to process papers, send out bills, and collect money.

Therefore, the notion of looking at spending relative to the GNP—the size of the company, if you will—is a legitimate way to analyze expenditures. For example, if our company's R&D expenditures in an absolute sense are up $15 million, but as a percentage of our total sales are still less than 1 percent, is that the right dollar amount to put into R&D? We can build the R&D program up from the bottom and say that we need to have some research that deals with salt-free foods that still have the flavor impact of salt, or research on tomatoes that will maintain their texture and color for longer periods of time. Or we can build from the top down and say that everybody else is spending about 1 percent of sales on R&D, and we don't know which of these R&D programs are going to succeed and which are going to fail, so let's spend 1 percent on R&D. The dollar amount increases over time.

Likewise, as we are a bigger company, we have more customers, more bills to send out, and more money to collect. Thus, I don't think looking at expenditures as a percentage of GNP is an illegitimate way to analyze spending.

NARRATOR: Could you tell us a little about your relationship with Marty Anderson? Is his book about the Reagan administration and its philosophy, *Revolution*, one that squares with your account? Did you continue some of his major undertakings, or did you strike out in another direction at least in some areas?

MR. HARPER: First, although I have not talked to him in probably two years, I still regard him as a pretty good friend. He and I worked closely together in the Nixon years and in the Reagan administration. He was more than any other single individual the one who brought me into the transition and also recommended me as his successor.

With that preface, let me go back to the cycle of the creative development of policy in an administration. Marty was the architect of President Reagan's policy program during the campaign. He created it, developed it, and saw the first phase of its implementation during President Reagan's inaugural year. It is my impression that Marty is less interested in the bureaucratic infighting of implementing policy than he is in setting and creating policy. The things he was most interested in were done in the campaign and in the initial year of the administration. He then chose to go to the Hoover Institute.

I was intrigued about the possibility of coming over as his successor because I saw us moving into the next creative phase of policy. Marty and I are probably fairly consistent on most policy issues, and he wrote an excellent book on the administration.

QUESTION: Isn't gross national product a rather misleading figure? When you and I sit in our cars waiting for a traffic light to turn green and the motor is running, the gasoline we consume increases the gross national product. When Exxon spends nearly a billion dollars cleaning up its oil spill in Alaska, it increases the gross national product. Whether that is a true figure is a real question. When you look at this whole question of the tremendous increase in the deficit and an unbalanced budget, shouldn't you look at what is happening on the international side? We financed this long period of prosperity to a great extent by borrowing abroad. Eventually we will have to pay back what we borrowed either through inflation or through a reduction in our standard of living.

MR. HARPER: I don't profess to have the expertise to stand toe to toe with you in this argument. I have read some articles which say that it looks like we are borrowing abroad, but we really haven't borrowed abroad as much as some of the figures indicate. I can tell you from the Campbell Soup Company's point of view that we have found it cheaper to borrow all of our long-term debt abroad in the last four to five years. I'm not afraid of that. Our company is better off for it because we pay less for our capital when we borrow abroad. If we were going to borrow money today, however, it would be cheaper to do so in the United States than overseas.

Overall we have to look at a continually reestablished balance in the international economic system. I don't think we are ever going to be able to go back to—nor would we necessarily want to go back to—the situation in the early 1950s when 20 percent of the world's population had 50 percent of the world's gross domestic product. That is not a sustainable situation.

Will our standard of living go down relative to other people? Our per capita income is still in pretty good shape. In 1987, the U.S. per capita GNP, adjusted on a purchasing power parity basis, shows that the United States exceeded all major countries, including West Germany by 35 percent and Japan by 41 percent. Is that good or bad? I don't know. What it suggests, though, is that we are still in pretty good shape relative to the rest of the world.

QUESTION: Does it suggest that we are taxable?

MR. HARPER: Yes it does. I mentioned earlier that there was one thing I was concerned about that didn't get resolved during Reagan's tenure, and that is the issue of financing health care. This has come up in our own company a number of times. As some of you may be aware, the Financial Accounting Standards Board has proposed a new way to account for post-retiree medical benefit FASB 106. For many large companies, for example, if you are with the company for ten years and retire at any time after age 55, you are eligible to stay in the company's medical care program until death. The Financial Accounting Standards Board says that is a liability of the company, and since it is a liability it must be recognized on its books. Some U.S. companies estimate that they would have to establish a fund of $500 million to fund post-retiree medical benefits on the same basis we fund our pension plans. That's a lot of money. Many of my colleagues are now coming to me and saying, "If we are going to have to come up with an extra $500 million on the books, as opposed to a pay-as-you-go system, we are going to be at a competitive disadvantage with other countries. We are virtually the only major country in the world today that looks to the private sector to fund most of its health care. This has a profound effect on our costs, vis-à-vis the other countries, or companies in other countries, and we ought to take another look at it."

This issue is far from resolved, but it is an important one that didn't get resolved in the Reagan years and is one that is on our doorstep right now.

QUESTION: Herb Stein had an editorial in the *Wall Street Journal* a few days ago arguing that given the size of our gross national product, a $100 billion a year tax increase was so easily feasible that it was ridiculous not to do it. Did you read that?

MR. HARPER: No, I missed that, but I've heard Herb make that argument before. Not having to defend any administration program, I think that we are going to have to consider the possibility of taxing ourselves. The long-term debate is over what the most effective kind of tax is: one that raises revenues without distorting excessively the allocation of resources in the country. I have my personal preferences, but I don't know if that proves anything. A value-added tax or a sales tax or some sophisticated version of that may make some sense; a lot of other countries use it. I'm not particularly inspired by it, and I guess I'm satisfied for the moment to be in the foot-dragging crowd that is not in any hurry to raise taxes.

NARRATOR: You've mentioned several times that in comparison with Carter, Reagan did see the forest rather than the trees and dealt with basic issues. I suppose the question that has been asked of others who have come here is, Did that lead to the Iran-contra affair? Are there areas where you can't have a hands-off approach to crucial strategic issues and still expect to have a viable policy? Is that a fair criticism, or would you defend the hands-off approach even there?

MR. HARPER: There is a fundamental maxim of managing the White House that was ignored in this case. Twice it has created great embarrassments for presidents. That maxim is: Do not operate any programs out of the White House. That's what got Richard Nixon in a lot of trouble, and that's what created a great deal of grief for Ronald Reagan. Operatives don't belong there. The White House is for policy-making. It may be for monitoring and supervising, but no matter what it is, it is just not a place to run operations. If somebody had tried to run that operation out of the agencies created for operating in the international sphere, there would have been enough seasoned judgment applied to avoid some of those mistakes.

QUESTION: You stated that one of Reagan's objectives was to reduce fraud in government. Yet now we face two situations that may, before it is over, be the most costly examples of waste and fraud in the history of our country. One is HUD, and the other is the savings and loan industry.

You mentioned earlier that Pierce did not like to accept recommendations for personnel. Am I to assume that he was given almost a free hand to run his department without answering to anybody about the way he handled its funds?

MR. HARPER: It will be interesting to see if there are indictments out of the HUD discussions and what those indictments are. I look forward to seeing whether or not they involve Pierce.

This reminds me of a story. A friend of mine, not in the Reagan administration, was an intern with HUD in the city of Philadelphia. As an intern, my friend had to go to staff meetings. He went to a staff meeting one Monday morning, and the HUD regional administrator said, "I have several announcements this morning. The first is that the assistant regional administrator for administration"—who was at the table—"is hereby put on administrative leave and is not to take any further actions because of the back-dating of HUD applications for the city of Philadelphia.

The assistant regional administrator for this program is also relieved of all duties and placed on administrative leave." Those were two of the four people at the staff meeting. He then said, "I would also like to announce that I have been nominated to become regional administrator for the Environmental Protection Agency. Today is my last day, and I'm leaving to go to Washington immediately." Everybody got up from the table and left, and the only person left was my friend, Jack Berger, the intern.

There is always fraud, waste, and abuse, even in our company. We have 55,000 employees and an audit staff of 22 people, and there is probably not a month that goes by that we don't find somebody somewhere in the 50 countries in which we operate who is trying to steal money from us. It's a sad fact of life, but you've got to be alert to people doing wrong things.

There may be some wrongdoing in the HUD case. Maybe Sam Pierce was too hands-off and let bad things happen. It would surprise me if Sam Pierce were involved in any wrongdoing.

The savings and loan disaster is another matter. That's another problem of major proportions that Ronald Reagan didn't solve. Its roots go back to the 1930s, when we created a system of financial institutions that borrow short and lend long, and it just doesn't work. You must have government intervention to sustain it. It is a system that we let ride for many, many years, and the problem just got worse and worse. The Reagan administration did not deal with it. I was pleased that President Bush took the initiative early in his administration to try to bring it under control. It probably is going to be one of the most costly things that has ever happened. There is some fraud, waste, and abuse, but I think it is sporadic rather than systematic. Fundamentally, it is an economic problem; you are borrowing short and lending long.

COMMENT: It is great to blame the executive branch for the savings and loan fiasco, but we certainly have to put some blame on the Congress.

MR. HARPER: Yes, and in addition we created a nonmarket institution in the economy and then pretended that it was a market-driven institution. It just doesn't work over the long term, and we are having to pay the price for it right now in order to bail out the savings and loan associations and put them back on a sound economic footing. You recall that during the 1960s we had crunches on a periodic basis, when the short rates at which S&Ls borrowed went very high and the S&Ls were earning low returns on the long-term rates they had lent.

The Congress created legislatively an S&L system that was weak at its core because it was not based on market economics. Its survival required continuing intervention by the Congress and the executive branch. When you have a weak system, fraud is probably more likely to bring it down.

NARRATOR: Fritz Mosher has argued that the Office of Management and Budget has become politicized and that when the top 16 positions became political appointments, it was more difficult for the OMB to operate on the basis of the original nonpolitical standards that were established earlier.

MR. HARPER: If I had my choice I would like to see a reduction in the number of political appointees at OMB. Also, I believe that the director of the OMB and the deputy director should not be confirmed by the Senate.   The concept of the Office of Management and Budget as the president's professional staff is an excellent concept. The only problem is that I'm not sure how to unwind what we've got now.

NARRATOR: We all thank you for this informative discussion.

CHAPTER 8

THE REAGAN PRESIDENCY: CAMPAIGNING, MANAGING, AND GOVERNING

PETER D. HANNAFORD

NARRATOR: This morning we have the opportunity to speak with someone who knew President Reagan for many years in California and then continued, outside the White House, to be in touch with him in Washington. Peter D. Hannaford is chairman of the board of Hannaford Company, Inc., formerly Deaver and Hannaford, Inc.

After attending the University of California, he became an account executive for the Helen Kennedy advertising firm. He then served as either president or vice president of a series of leading advertising and public relations firms. He was assistant to the governor and director of public affairs in the California governor's office in 1974. He was vice chairman of the California Governor's Consumer Fraud Task Force. He was a Republican nominee for the U.S. Congress in 1972. Mr. Hannaford has also been a trustee of the White House Preservation Fund. He is a member of the Public Relations Advisory Committee of the United States Information Agency and the Advisory Committee for Mount Vernon. He is author of *The Reagans: A Political Portrait* and *Talking Back to the Media*. He served as first lieutenant in the Army Signal Corps. It is a privilege, Mr. Hannaford, to have you with us.

MR. HANNAFORD: Thank you, Mr. Thompson. Since the Miller Center's projects are historical and interpretive in nature, I thought I ought to start at the beginning and tell you how I became involved with Ronald Reagan in the hope that this will give you some insights into how his policy ideas developed and the way his thinking processes work.

I first met Ronald Reagan in 1965 at a Republican state convention. He had been persuaded by some friends of his—who ultimately became what was called his kitchen cabinet—to travel to party gatherings around the state and to meet people and get a feeling for whether or not he could be a serious candidate for the governorship in 1966. In early 1965 I was at our annual state convention in San Francisco with some friends doing volunteer work for our local state assemblymen. We were in the mezzanine of the hotel where it was being held, visiting some of the commercial booths and waiting for the sessions to begin when Ronald Reagan walked in, flanked by a couple of aides. He would stop and talk to delegates and others and visit. He was a very pleasant, amiable man who seemed accessible and approachable.

I had been an activist in the party for several years, and I thought to myself, "He seems like such a nice chap; it's too bad he couldn't possibly be elected governor." Like many of my friends, I believed in those days that in order to beat an experienced and popular Democratic governor such as Pat Brown in 1966, we had to have somebody with a lot of political experience. This kind of thinking pointed toward the mayor of San Francisco, George Christopher, who had been an effective and rather popular mayor, as well as a seasoned politician. As I said, it didn't occur to me that Reagan could possibly win.

About a year later, a group of which I was a member called the Republican Alliance invited Reagan to speak to it. This was a group of business people in the counties around San Francisco Bay whose purpose was to meet with Republican officeholders and would-be officeholders to size them up. The group didn't endorse candidates; it provided them with a forum. We invited both Mr. Christopher and Mr. Reagan, who were by then declared candidates for the nomination, to speak to us on different days.

When Reagan came, he used a very effective technique he had learned years before and which he used in all his later elections. He did not give a long speech or a formal address. He spoke for approximately three or four minutes, and then said, "Let's open it up to a dialogue; I'd like to know what is on your minds." The rest of his time, almost an hour, was simply a question-and-answer session in which people would ask him questions about the various issues, and he would answer them spontaneously. I was impressed not only by the breadth of his understanding of the issues, but also by what he had to say about them in terms of policy. I still voted for George Christopher—that was partly regional loyalty; however, I was impressed by Reagan.

When Reagan became the candidate, I was happy to support him, but I didn't go out and work on his campaign. That year I was working on or managing a number of local campaigns—for assemblymen, state senators, and so forth—and there simply wasn't time to go out and do volunteer work for the governorship.

Reagan won that election by about a million votes. Pat Brown underestimated Reagan. One day, Brown was caught by a television camera saying to a little girl, "Little girl, you know it was an actor who shot Lincoln!" Brown had, and still has, a good sense of humor. Actually, Brown and the Democrats had hoped that Reagan would be the nominee, because they thought he would be very easy to beat since he was, presumably, only an actor reading somebody's lines. What they hadn't counted on was that Reagan, using the very technique that I described to you in the early meeting with the Republican group, persuaded everybody he met that he knew what he was talking about. He was very sensitive to the idea that he was an actor saying lines, which was a major reason why he did not give a lot of big speeches. He gave short presentations to start an event, and then the rest was questions and answers. Obviously, you can't memorize answers if you don't know what the questions will be, so Reagan believed this would demonstrate to people that he understood what was going on.

Actually, that technique went back a lot further. In the early 1950s as his movie career was waning, he got a contract to be the host of the weekly television program "General Electric Theater." Part of his contract was to visit General Electric plants as a spokesman during the course of the year. Years later he told me that at the first plant he visited people coming off a shift had assembled in the cafeteria to meet him. Even though he was still quite a celebrity and people were anxious to meet him, during his speech he said people's eyes were wandering and their attention wasn't staying with him. Therefore, rather than talking to them, he decided he should find out what was on their minds, so that they could talk back and forth. He felt that if he was supposed to be the management's representative to the workers, he should be learning what they were thinking and what they cared about. That is when he really started the short introduction and then the Q-and-A session. I don't think that was the beginning of his political awakening, but it certainly had a lot to do with the crystallization of his interest in politics and policy.

Reagan won that election in 1966 by a landslide and brought a lot of new people in. Several I knew and respected went to work in his administration, and I thought that was a good sign. Later on my wife, Irene, was appointed to a consumer oversight board for home furnishings by Governor Reagan, and then about a year later in 1971, I was appointed by him to be on his Consumer Fraud Task Force. Here again, I was impressed by the way he was going about planning policy. He had set out at the beginning of his first term to have about seven or eight task forces on key issues. The first one was a precursor of the Grace Commission that he created during his presidency. This was a government efficiency task force, and he called on accounting firms and corporations to send some of their management and administrative experts in for 90 to 120 days, free to the state government, to do an audit of all the procedures of all the state government agencies. They came up with something like 1,600 recommendations for streamlining procedures and saving money—everything from a better way to handle food service in the state prison system to standardization of file folders between state agencies. Many of these were implemented.

A few years later, one of the task forces that had yet to be done was the Consumer Fraud Task Force. The idea was to identify areas of fraud or potential fraud on consumers and make recommendations for both executive and legislative action. This was entirely a creation of the governor's office, not a dual responsibility between the legislature and the governor. Yet this governor, who was considered to be fiercely conservative and right-wing by his opponents, appointed a task force composed of business people, an assistant attorney general, a municipal judge, a television consumer advocate, Hispanics, blacks, whites, and Asians; about half of the members were women. I don't know what their political orientation was because we never had a "nose count"; some of them were Democrats and some were Republican. It was a remarkably diverse group, and we worked together for 15 or 16 months, meeting about once a month and visiting various sites.

Reagan's only charge to the group was to identify areas of potential consumer fraud and to recommend corrective action. Beyond this, we did not have a particular agenda, nor was the one ex-officio member, the assistant attorney general, given any special agenda to lay on our group.

This diverse group with strong personalities and ideas came up with a single report; there was no minority report. Instead we hammered out one report, and a great many of the recommendations in it were taken up by Reagan and implemented by executive action. Those that couldn't be implemented were submitted to the legislature, which took some of them and passed them; some they didn't get around to.

We were pleased with the way it had turned out and the fact that we had the ability to range anywhere we wanted. For example, we spent an entire day in a small claims court in Los Angeles because we had learned that there was one judge who had a very creative approach to making small claims a more accessible procedure. We watched this judge in action and were very impressed by him. Much of what we learned was incorporated into our report, stating that what this judge did and advocated made good sense and could make the courts easier and more accessible for people. We also recommended that courses be taught in the public schools to young people to learn how to balance checkbooks and read contracts and things of that nature, so they would be better informed when they became adults.

After we submitted our report to Governor Reagan in his Cabinet room in Sacramento, I asked his appointments secretary what happened to appointees who had finished their assigned jobs. He said that if they were pleased with my performance, they would ask me to do something else, and I said I was interested. About three months later he called and asked me if I would like to be Ronald Reagan's appointee to the Tahoe Regional Planning Agency. This was a two-state agency (Nevada and California) that had been created by an act of Congress to oversee the development of the Lake Tahoe basin in the High Sierra. Reagan and his fellow governor, Paul Laxalt of Nevada, had pushed hard for the creation of this agency because the ecology of that basin is very fragile. The mountains there are rugged looking, but the ecological systems are delicate and will only sustain a certain amount of human development; however, the pressures on the basin for tourism and recreation are considerable.

When they asked me to do this, the agency had already been working for three years, but its chairman wanted to retire, since he had been in charge through the whole process of creating it. I asked Governor Reagan's appointments secretary why they wanted me to take this man's place and he said, "We are looking for a Reagan supporter who is also a member of the Sierra Club, and you seem to be the only one in California." I said, "Sure, I'll do it." I liked Lake Tahoe very much, and had been there many times over the years, although I didn't own any property there. Therefore, I had nothing to defend one way or the other, nor did I have any preconceptions. At no time did Ronald Reagan personally, or through any of his staff, ever tell me what to do. I was his personal representative on this board that met once or twice a month and voted on projects that many times had the effect of either permitting or not permitting the spending of many millions of dollars for development. I was never told how to vote on anything, nor was I given a particular agenda. I was impressed by that. If you are not told what to do, you will be much more conscientious in listening carefully to both sides of an issue before making a decision that will not bring discredit to the person who appointed you.

I found more and more that this was the way Reagan operated. His idea was to appoint people he felt were capable of doing the job in whatever field it happened to be, and then let them do the job. If they didn't do well, it was his responsibility to deal with the aftermath. That turned out to be one of his greatest strengths, and this was true all the way through his presidency. This approach, however, contains a weakness: Sometimes you pick the wrong people, and they bring discredit not only to themselves, but also to the person who picked them. This happened a few times during Reagan's presidency, though not as many as the press or his political opponents would like us to believe. Nevertheless, it did happen and sometimes with unhappy consequences.

I had been on the Tahoe board for close to a year when I got a call from Reagan's office one day asking if I would consider going to Sacramento to become his assistant and director of public affairs for his final year in office as governor. This came as a complete surprise to me. It meant I would not only have to drop out of the

Tahoe board—Reagan insisted that members of his staff could not also serve as appointees on board commissions—but more importantly, I would have to spend time away from my new business. I had just run for Congress and didn't quite make it, so I had to go back to work in order to earn a living. I had started a small company, and it was off to a very good start. Accepting this job would mean leaving my company at least for a year, but I thought about it and called back to say that I would do it. It was the most fortuitous decision I ever made, and it was a marvelous year.

Although I had met Reagan on many occasions, I had never worked with him closely on a day-to-day basis. Suddenly I had total access to him all the time. I traveled with him a great deal and spent time with him virtually every day, writing and drafting for him and handling a lot of assignments. Reagan's final year presented a great opportunity, one that hadn't happened for a long time in California. He had already announced long before that he thought two terms was enough and he wasn't going to run for a third. A sitting governor hadn't done that for a long time. This meant that we didn't have to go to the barricades to defend his record against the onslaught of a political opponent in that year, because somebody else was going to run for office. All we had to do, as Ed Meese, his chief of staff, told me, was "Finish strong"—in other words, do the very best we could to dot the *i*'s and cross the *t*'s.

When I asked one of Governor Reagan's senior assistants, the director of legislation, what kind of program I should put together for the governor that year, he recommended I ask the governor what he had always wanted to do but never had a chance to do in his first seven years. I met with Reagan and asked him that question. From the meeting emerged a long list of things—some quite lighthearted, some more serious than others.

For example, in his earlier years as governor, he had stopped the construction of a huge dam on two rivers in northern California which would have flooded an Indian reservation, including their burial grounds. This happened to be a federal water project, and the federal government could have built the dam without the governor's approval; there was nothing in the law that would prevent them from building the dam. The Bureau of Reclamation, however, as a matter of course and policy over the years, wouldn't build a federal dam in a state over the objection of the governor.

Reagan was visited by a delegation of Indians from the Round Valley reservation, and they persuaded him that to build the dam would displace all of the Indian ranchers and farmers in this valley, as well as flood the ancient burial grounds. Reagan was persuaded that the greater good was to oppose the dam, and he did. They were very grateful. One of the things he wanted to do in that final year was go to the valley. The people who lived there had been asking him for years to come and see their valley and ranches. He went and had a wonderful day. The governor's plane was the first and maybe the last jet ever to land in that valley. It was kind of a sentimental journey, but it was a great event for him. We had many other things like that trip during his final year.

There were policies that he wanted to pursue as well. One was a continuation of the welfare reforms he had started a few years before, reforms that would streamline the application and approval processes for people who needed welfare. The reforms closed many of the loopholes by tightening eligibility. They also reduced the increase in the rolls. Until the time of these reforms, the rolls were growing exponentially, and at that rate the state would have been bankrupt in another 10 or 15 years.

There was a trade-off involved. Reagan had a task force of professionals to create the reform package; however, by Reagan's last year the Democrats, who had never lost their majority in the lower house, had regained their majority in the Senate. He asked the legislature for an opportunity to address them to announce his reform package and was refused. As a partisan matter, the Democrats said, "No dice; you can't come and talk to us."

Reagan took the issue in hand and said it was rather like a book banned in Boston—everybody wanted to hear the speech that the legislature would not let him give. He went up and down the state to all the civic forums to give the speech, and he started building pressure. One of his favorite sayings was, "When you can't make them see the light, make them feel the heat!" That is what he did—he turned up the heat and built pressure on the Assembly. Finally, the late Bob Moretti, a good politician, skillful legislator, and then speaker of the Assembly, came into Reagan's office and said, "Stop those cards and letters; let's sit down and talk."

Reagan could put some of his reforms through by executive order, but the most important ones required legislative approval, which he couldn't get without the cooperation of the Assembly. On the other hand, they ran the danger that if they didn't do anything with the governor, he would set them up as an example of intransigence in the next election campaign. Each side had to give, so Reagan and Moretti sat down without any aides at all and hammered out the basic elements of a compromise. The Democrats agreed to tighten the requirements and close the loopholes in exchange for Reagan agreeing to increase the grants for the people left on the rolls.

I asked Reagan about his view of this kind of compromise, and he said, "Any time I can get 70 percent of what I am asking for out of a hostile legislative body, I'll take it. I figure that it will work well enough for me to go back later and get a little more of it here and a little more of it there." That was a guiding philosophy of his in dealing with the U.S. Congress as well. He said he didn't think it made any sense, as he put it, "to jump in a ditch over the issue because I'm not going to get 100 percent. You have to be realistic; you have to get what you can get, provided you get enough of it so that it isn't crippled, and so that you can make it work and show that it works. Then people begin to have confidence, and they let you come back to get some more."

In his final year, he came up with another task force report to further improve and streamline the welfare processes. That time the legislature wouldn't do anything about it. They definitely weren't going to give him something major that he wanted in his final year; he was a lame duck by then and everybody knew it. This report, however, became a blueprint for some of the reforms that he wanted to work on when he became president.

During that final year in Sacramento, one of the things that became my responsibility was to look at some of the offers coming his way—mostly media related—for him to consider after he left office. Most of these were blind alleys that didn't amount to anything. A few of them required investigation, however, and when I was on various gubernatorial trips up and down the state, I would look into them.

One of these offers was from a radio producer who believed there was a real market for a short, five-minute radio program of commentary from a conservative political perspective. Also, there were a couple of newspaper syndicates interested in a regular newspaper column by Reagan. I mentioned this one day to another of his senior aides, Mike Deaver, the director of administration.

Deaver said that the scheduling office was receiving a lot of requests from people who wanted Reagan to give speeches after he left office. We were sending back form letters, thanking and telling them that they would be receiving responses from Reagan's private office. He then said, "Of course, the joke is that there is no private office, and nobody has done anything about setting one up, and unless somebody does something, on January 5, 1975 we are going to have Ronald and Nancy Reagan sitting in their hilltop home with nobody but Ann, the housekeeper, to deal with the schedules."

With that, the idea of putting a program together with the Reagans dawned on us. I said I was going back to my own business, which was declining because—without the principal there—the clients weren't sticking around. I asked Deaver to join me, and we had many talks and decided to join forces in making a proposal to the Reagans. Somebody had to run their program. Meese, Deaver, Don Livingston (the legislative director), and I took turns attending the monthly kitchen cabinet meetings which were usually luncheons in Los Angeles. The "members" were all good friends of Reagan—social friends as well as strong supporters—and were all trying to find something for him to do when he left office; he had to earn an income. Each month we would go to these meetings, and they would say that they had talked to this or that board of directors on which they sat, and the response from the board would be, "Sorry, we're afraid he is going to run for president. We don't want some candidate on our board who is going to leave three months after he joins." Well, that's logical enough.

As late as the fall of 1974, the kitchen cabinet had not yet put together a plan. Deaver and I had talked to five or six of our colleagues with different roles in the governor's office about our plan to set up a company when we left and going to talk to the Reagans about it. Our colleagues all agreed to join us if we created such a company. We flew down one weekend to Los Angeles to call on the Reagans, and presented our plan: speaking engagements, radio programs, newspaper columns, occasional articles, and maybe even a book down the road. The Reagans liked it and told us to go ahead with it. To make a long story short, the day after his term ended in Sacramento, Deaver & Hannaford, Inc., opened for business in Los Angeles, about 15 minutes from the Reagans' home. Ronald Reagan's office was within our suite of offices, and Mrs. Reagan had it decorated to look much like his governor's office in

Sacramento. All the furniture in the new office had been in his office in the beautiful state capitol park in Sacramento. The only major difference was the view—we were on the eighth floor looking straight out to Catalina Island in the Pacific and at the airplanes landing at LAX (Los Angeles International Airport) to the south. One of his favorite mementos that had always been in his governor's office and which we put in his new office was a round wooden disk with a couple of old shoes embedded in plaster of paris. The press corps in Sacramento had given him this. When he was campaigning for office in 1966, he said, "I'm strongly opposed to any new taxes on the people." Within his first year he had to raise the state income tax rates because his predecessor had left the state—which like most states is required by its constitution to have a balanced budget every year—losing a million and a half dollars a day. Something had to be done; they were cutting, squeezing, and trimming—as Reagan used to call it—everywhere they could to save money, but they still had to raise taxes. Thus, Reagan had said at one of his weekly press conferences, "My feet are in concrete over this tax issue," but the day he announced the tax increase he said, "Well, the sound you hear is the concrete cracking around my feet." The press corps gave him this pair of old shoes in plaster of paris, and he always had that in his office. He did not, however, take it to the Oval Office.

Mr. Reagan kept regular office hours at his new office at Deaver & Hannaford. He had many leaders calling and visiting him from all parts of the world during those years.

Reagan was by no means certain in January 1975 that he would challenge President Ford for the presidency in 1976. As he left the governorship, we did not have a battle plan to do this, but we were all conscious that it might happen. We left all options open in case he did decide to do it. Thus, 1975 was a very busy year. Reagan was much in demand on the lecture circuit with business, civic, and party groups; thus, we did a lot of traveling. (That was the year I learned that Lincoln Day dinners are held from January to July!) Either Mike Deaver or myself would travel with him everywhere he went, allowing us to see a lot of the United States along the way.

Often we would fly into an airport in a small city, and there would be a volunteer driver who picked us up who would say, "Mr. Reagan, the time I decided I really wanted to help you was when you gave the speech for Goldwater in 1964." I didn't hear that speech at the time it was given, but I have long since heard of it and read it several times. He gave this televised speech to a live audience in late 1964 in which he appealed for political and financial support for Goldwater. It generated a tremendous flow of money into that campaign at the last minute, but it also began to attract a national constituency for Reagan. We certainly found it in 1975 as we traveled around. People everywhere were saying that to him.

We also found that the radio broadcasts that he was doing every day, which at their peak were on 350 stations, were being heard and paid close attention to by many people around the country. On those trips I've mentioned that people would approach Reagan and say, "I heard your broadcast today and it was wonderful!" These broadcasts were having a very strong effect. We never knew which broadcast was being played in which city because we recorded these three weeks at a crack, and they were sent out on discs of 15 at one time. It didn't matter; we just knew it was having a effect.

He did, of course, ultimately challenge Ford. He announced this decision in late 1975, and both Mike Deaver and I went into the campaign full time. Our company was small, and we had a vice president back home who could take care of our other clients so we could be gone for long periods of time. The effort fell short, but it was an interesting campaign in every respect. We had so much faith in this man's appeal to the public—in this case the Republican public—during the primary season that I think it never occurred to us that we wouldn't win. To us he was light years ahead of Ford as a decisionmaker, a philosopher, and a policy promoter, yet we didn't quite make it in New Hampshire.

In the New Hampshire primary, the press always decides the ground rules, and they change from one election year to another, and from party to party. You would think that if you came within a percentage of winning against an incumbent president you might be declared the winner. When Gene McCarthy challenged Lyndon Johnson in 1968, I believe that Johnson won the primary with about 65 percent of the vote, yet the press declared Gene McCarthy the winner. It didn't work with Reagan, however, because I think they had assumed that Reagan would win New Hampshire, and when he didn't, they said it was a terrible blow to him.

We really thought we would mop up the landscape in Florida, the next primary. Our early visits were very successful, so we were confident that we would win easily. However, Ford's campaign decided to bring Stu Spencer on board in Florida. Stu and his former partner had run both of Reagan's gubernatorial campaigns very successfully; he was a very smart political consultant, employing very effective campaign strategies. One of these that they used in Florida was the "imperial presidency." Ford was bestowing federal grants for highways or hospitals, and we would fly into an area that had just received one of these grants. That was making all the local Republican politicians line up behind the incumbent, which was hurting us at the grass-roots level. In addition, Ford would campaign in these areas in a big limousine that would be flown in several days ahead of time; we would see it on the tarmac being unloaded from the government plane in city after city. Here we were bouncing around in a little motorcade, and Ford had a limousine. We lost Florida by quite a lot, but it could have been much worse.

Just before our final visit to Florida, we were back home for a few days in California, and I received a call from John Sears, the campaign manager. He said, "When we fly into Orlando for the final weekend, we'll have a news conference as soon as we land. Take off the gloves on foreign policy!" Our pollster was finding that there was an increasing number of people who were afraid that the United States was falling behind the Soviets in our defensive capabilities. John was always worried that during the primaries Reagan might be perceived as being too hawkish, because our polls indicated that people already thought of Reagan as very strong on defense. For fear that Reagan would appear too strong, we had stayed away from discussing the issue during the campaign; however, John said that the polls were moving in that direction and we had better take advantage of them. John wanted Reagan to have a strong opening statement followed by his basic stump speech at every stop. He then wanted Reagan to insert facts, supporting data, and quotes from experts in his speeches. Reagan always wrote his own stump speeches, but Martin Anderson and I pulled the other material together.

We would also alert the press as to when Reagan was going to say particular things in a speech so that the cameras would pick that up. I remember one speech in particular that Reagan gave at

Winterpark, the spring training site of the Chicago White Sox. Reagan was standing around the pitcher's mound talking to a small group of people. The big insert in his speech was that if he became president, he would replace Henry Kissinger as secretary of state. This was, of course, intended to create distance between himself and Ford, and to insure the support of the conservatives in the party. On this day, as he usually did, he was reading his speech from his note cards (he used 4" x 6" cards, with his speech written in his own version of shorthand; by doing it that way he learned the material). He was coming to a dramatic part of this particular speech when a gust of wind blew the cards all over the ballpark. We were scampering around collecting the cards, and after we did Reagan had to start his speech all over. The speech played well to the press, but much of the drama was lost. We narrowed Ford's lead from about 24 percent to 17 percent, but it was still a convincing win for him.

North Carolina was the next primary. We had the strong support of Senator Jesse Helms and his whole organization, which was important. We had always felt that we would do well in North Carolina, but in the meantime, the news came out that we had lost in Illinois, which we had not expected to win. With three losses, it was looking pretty bad.

We were in Los Angeles getting ready to leave for our last trip to North Carolina. We had chartered a United Airlines plane, but were an hour late in taking off. I asked Deaver why we were so late, and he said, "I just got a call from Sears in Washington. They have to open all the mail to see if we have enough money to pay for the airplane!" It was getting that desperate. They called back and said they had barely enough money to do it, so we were able to take off.

We landed at High Point, North Carolina, where Governor Reagan was going to give a luncheon speech. As was usually the case when you land in a state, the local press were gathered behind a rope line at the edge of the tarmac, and the press secretary would take Reagan over for a little five-minute news conference. This particular one had an extra kicker. The local news people kept asking Reagan what he thought about the comments certain politicians had made to the effect that Reagan had made his point and now should withdraw from the race. I could see Reagan set his jaw, and when he sets his jaw, that means he's angry. He does not reach a boil very often.

He went on and gave his speech, but you could tell he was fighting mad. Deaver took me aside and said, "You know what we ought to do? After lunch, we are going to drive to shopping centers and things where he hops on the flatbed trucks, says a few words, and then has the Q&A session." He said, "We ought to tell him to put his cards in his pocket, and then we should put Paul Laxalt in the back of the car with him and have Laxalt tell him just to speak from his heart." Laxalt agreed to do it, and he got in the back of the car with Reagan and said, "Ron, don't take those cards out when you get on that platform. Just say what is on your mind."

In the meantime, an interesting thing had happened. The chairman of the Reagan committee in North Carolina learned that on the last weekend before the Florida primary, a local station in Miami had offered both Ford and Reagan a half hour of free television time to give a speech. Ford's people had turned it down, but we were going to take anything we could get. Reagan did it, and it was broadcast live. Eventually, the speech became known as the "talking head speech" because it was only Reagan sitting at a desk and talking at a camera. It was basically the same stump speech Reagan had been giving throughout the campaign, except that it was much longer because he had to fill half an hour. He acquitted himself very well, but there were no flourishes, fancy touches, or stage set; it was just him talking out at the screen.

Our North Carolina state campaign chairman had received permission from the television station to buy a tape of that speech. He ran it on every station in North Carolina. The air time wasn't very expensive, so he could run it many times. This was during the final week before the primary.

We then left North Carolina for Wisconsin, thinking that we had done all we could do. Sure enough, at the airport from which we were taking off was Ford's limousine, just to remind us how much leverage the President had. He was coming in for the weekend to do one of his grand tours.

We went up to La Crosse, Wisconsin, did a couple of things in the afternoon, and attended a Ducks Unlimited dinner that evening. I said to Reagan, "Do you want me to do anything special to your speech for this evening?" He said, "After a few thousand duck hunters have had some drinks, they are not going to want to hear a serious campaign speech. I'm just going to tell them a lot of stories." He was right; they were in no mood to listen to policy issues. Reagan knew his audiences very well, and he regaled them.

Later that evening the late Frank Reynolds, who was then anchor of the ABC evening news, came up to some of the staff members behind the podium and said, "I guess you guys know you're winning in North Carolina?" We said, "Come on Frank, don't pull our leg." He said, "No, I'm serious; we just got the first reports and you are ahead." We called our headquarters, and they said it was absolutely true. Mr. Reagan won the state convincingly, and there was quite a celebration on the plane that night back to California.

You know the rest. It seesawed back and forth between Ford and Reagan, and finally we got to the convention. Nobody knew who was going to win. Ultimately Ford did, and that whole saga was interesting.

Reagan went back to private life after that, thinking that his days of elective politics were over for good. I remember Deaver and I were sitting right behind the Reagans on the plane going back; Reagan was in good spirits, having had quite an emotional send-off by his supporters at the various hotels around Kansas City. He stood up after we were in the air, turned to us and said, "Well, fellows, I guess it's back to work, isn't it?" I said, "Well, I guess it is. Your first taping is in two weeks and your first newspaper column is in two and a half weeks." He said, "You mean you guys have been planning this all along?" I said, "Well, you have to plan for contingencies." He did go back to work. He went back on the road with speeches and television appearances, and did quite a bit for the Republican ticket.

Deaver went on all these trips that fall with Reagan, and in January he said to me, "You'd better take the next trip, because there is something very different going on out there. It isn't just the host groups that are crazy about him. The maids in the hotels all line up and want to shake his hand and get his autograph; taxi drivers are honking as we go by and saying, 'Give'em hell!' and things like that. There is a different mood out there." By then we were traveling on commercial planes, and as soon as we reached the lobby of the airport, people were coming from all over to shake his hand. Deaver was right; there was something going on out there.

Soon after that, in 1977, a group of his supporters created a political action committee called Citizens for the Republic. This was not a committee to support Reagan, but rather a committee which Reagan would chair and which would support like-minded candidates. It provided activity for a network of his close supporters around the country in the form of workshops and seminars he would speak to.

By late 1978, it was quite clear there would be a 1980 candidacy. Deaver and I had a number of conversations in which we tried to decide who would go into the campaign. By then our company was larger; we had an office in Washington with many more clients. We couldn't both work full time for the campaign, and eventually we decided that he would go in and I would stay out. Fate turned a trick on us, and just the opposite happened. For the first half of 1980, I ended up being in the campaign pretty much full time. I ran the research and writing operations for the Republican convention in 1980, and my swan song was helping Reagan with his acceptance speech. Then Deaver came back in, went full time into the campaign, and ultimately into the White House. I didn't go into the administration. I did some supportive things as a private citizen, such as the USIA Committee and the White House Preservation Fund. I was also asked to edit the report of a task force on privatization which the President established in 1986. Working between 1986 and 1988, this task force had come up with some excellent and interesting ideas; however, few of them were implemented because they required the cooperation of Congress, and by that time Congress was not in a cooperative mood.

Some of the things Reagan did in office could have been easily predicted if people had paid closer attention to what he had been saying. Reagan has never thought of himself as a professional politician. I guess you would have to say that somebody who has been governor of California twice and President of the United States twice is, indeed, a professional politician. Yet Reagan has always thought of himself as the citizen who, having made his mark in a career, devotes some time to public service in order to pursue those ideas and policies that he believes would be useful for the country. He was always quite serious about pursuing policy ideas that he believed made sense. Many politicians and others who were on the opposite side of issues from him made the mistake of believing that Reagan was like any other politician—that is to say, everything is always negotiable—but he wasn't. As I said, he readily understood the value of compromise. Reagan believed that when you are dealing with a powerful group, such as a legislature controlled by the other party that can deprive you of much of what you want, you have to compromise. That is simply being realistic.

Nevertheless, there were some things that he believed were not negotiable and that he had to pursue with great tenacity. For example, in 1981 the air controllers went out on strike. The president of their union—PATCO (Professional Air Traffic Controllers Organization)—was a strong-minded individual who seemed to be itching for a confrontation. President Reagan told them to be back at their jobs in 48 hours or they would be fired. They didn't go back to work, and they *were* fired. That was the end of that. He carried through on what he said he was going to do. Of course, we had to rebuild the air controller's system.

The man who ran the union didn't know what hit him; he didn't think Reagan would ever do that. In the past, however, Ronald Reagan had said time after time that most public employee strikes are illegal, and the reason they are is that public employees have certain benefits and securities—the civil service system and so forth—to protect them from the vagaries of changing politics. In exchange for these, and because they provide vital services, they don't strike. Reagan believed that if a particular employee strike was illegal, as president you had to enforce the law. Illegal strikes should not be tolerated; you couldn't just wink and turn your cheek and let them happen. He thought that if working conditions for a particular public employee group needed improvement, then some kind of binding arbitration process should be used; strikes, however, were out of the question.

Reagan used to say, "If I were in a situation where public employee strikes were illegal and a group went on strike, I would give them 48 hours to get back to work." He had been saying it for years, and it was on the public record many times. The man who was head of PATCO, whose name I can't remember, chose to ignore that, and as a result, Ronald Reagan goes into the history books as a two-time president. The air controller system has long since been back to normal, and I don't think we'll have that problem again.

Let me also trace another of his policy initiatives back to his pre-presidential days. (My friend and former colleague, Martin

Anderson, who was the senior domestic adviser for the first two years of the Reagan presidency, traced this very well in a book entitled *Revolution*.) In 1979 Reagan was urged by a friend of his who knew a number of the senior officers in the North American Air Defense Command to visit NORAD headquarters located deep in a mountainside near Colorado Springs. Reagan visited NORAD on his way back to California from a speaking trip in the East (Anderson was with him). He was very impressed by this sophisticated early warning system that would tell us if enemy missiles were inbound. He became troubled, however, when after asking a general at NORAD what we would do if our warning system indicated an incoming Soviet missile, the general replied, "There is only one thing we can do, and that is fire our own. Because of the ABM Treaty we don't have any way to defend ourselves; we can just knock the dickens out of them in retaliation." Reagan then wanted to know what our response would be if the Soviet launch was an accident. The general replied, "Our system doesn't tell us whether it's by accident or on purpose; they don't have labels."

That bothered Reagan a great deal, and he felt there ought to be some kind of defense against missiles. This ultimately found its way into his announcement in 1983 that we would pursue a strategic defense initiative (SDI). At the time, SDI generated a firestorm of criticism. It was criticized by those who were dedicated to the only type of arms control known at that point: mutually assured destruction (MAD). They believed that deterrence had prevented a missile war between the United States and the Soviet Union, and that Reagan's proposed SDI would undercut this. Then there were others who didn't ever really bother to understand Reagan or what made him tick; they assumed that he was simply trigger-happy. The press dubbed the SDI "Star Wars," in part because the press must simplify complicated things and because some wanted to trivialize the importance of what Reagan was talking about. Yet Reagan was quite serious about SDI.

Initially what Reagan had in mind was that at least one-third of a three-stage defense system against missiles could be put into place with existing hardware. That is the third stage where the incoming missile has reached the top of its trajectory and is coming down. He learned from the defense people that we had the technology to throw up a lot of small antimissile devices which would trigger an explosion of those missiles coming in. The more complicated laser technologies that would hit the missiles as they were going up and hit them at the top of their trajectory required a lot of research and development. We are still not, of course, completely there.

You know the rest of the story. He went ahead with it. It is difficult not to reach the conclusion today that this announcement, and the actions that he took to implement it, coupled with the deployment of the cruise missiles by the Germans that same year (in the face of an enormous propaganda campaign against Germany and the United States by the Soviet Union) were what ultimately led Gorbachev to conclude that the race was over and that the Soviets had lost. They were bankrupting their economy and could no longer catch up with us. The only thing we had been lacking up to that point was the political will to create a defense system they could not match. We had the technology, the money, and the industrial prowess. We lacked the political will, and Ronald Reagan supplied that. That alone is a great testimony to the value of his presidency, not to mention his tireless campaigning for the principles of democracy and democratic capitalism.

I know from the experience he had this last fall when he went to Germany, Poland, and the Soviet Union that he went as a hero and was received as a hero by the people, including the Soviet people. He is very much liked and admired in the Soviet Union by the so-called democrats and liberals. He's not liked much by those regressive folks who are trying to surround Gorbachev these days, but then no Americans are.*

QUESTION: Is it fair to say that although Reagan had an agenda of perhaps seven or eight important items, he concentrated on only two or three of these, and that problems developed because he almost ignored the others?

MR. HANNAFORD: I think it is to a degree. Early in his administration, all of the emphasis was on tax reform and economic changes; everything went into that in the early stages. Defense

---

This chapter is taken from a forum presented at the Miller Center on 8 March 1991.

came along afterwards and then general foreign policy. With the single-mindedness by which his administration was pursuing the key points on his agenda, there was always the danger that other things of importance would not get the attention they deserved from the President himself; however, you could argue that if he hadn't used such single-mindedness with the major things, they might never have been accomplished. There were both strengths and weaknesses in his approach.

QUESTION: Why was Reagan so convinced upon coming into office that we needed such a large military buildup?

MR. HANNAFORD: I think it goes back to his growing concern in the 1970s that detente was working differently for the Soviets than it was for us. For us, detente was a time to reduce tensions, improve arms control measures, and to build some mutual trust and confidence between our two nations. Ronald Reagan believed, however, that the Soviets saw detente as an opportunity for them to increase their armaments very significantly and if not get ahead of us, at least put us at a relative disadvantage to them.

His concerns and doubts about this continued to grow, and when the SALT II Treaty came up in Carter's term, the White House asked if he would take a briefing from them, and he said he would be happy to. In addition to the White House briefing, he talked to a number of independent experts and got many different opinions concerning the treaty. Finally Reagan made his decision to oppose the treaty, stating, "Whatever its merits, all this treaty does is try to limit the *growth* of arms. What we need are treaties that *reduce* arms; that's what we should be talking about."

By 1988, with the INF Treaty we concluded the first agreement ever to actually reduce nuclear weapons. Thus, even though one might not think of Ronald Reagan as a national figure all through the 1970s, it is fair to say that he was thinking about national defense during that time and speaking about it when he was on the road.

QUESTION: Why is it that a man with tremendous political ability, conviction, and the ability to communicate like Ronald Reagan was unable to translate these into congressional majorities?

MR. HANNAFORD: I can give you my theory on that. You've probably seen many of these polls that are taken in which people are asked what they think of Congress. In about the last 15 years or so, the public's opinion of Congress as a body has continued to decline, and today is at a very low point. If a poll is taken in a single congressional district, however, and the people are asked what kind of job they think their member of Congress is doing, most of them say "Pretty good," not only because he brings home the bacon to that district, but more importantly he or she does excellent constituent service. Members of Congress hire very good, competent staff, and these staffs take care of the individual needs of the constituents, like the social security check that didn't come in on time or whatever it happens to be. When the constituents call and want help, that office is Johnny-on-the-spot, ready to help. Most members have learned to do this, and if this is combined with some federal grants for their district from time to time, it becomes very difficult to dislodge incumbent members of Congress.

The one time that Reagan really had coattails was in the 1980 election for the Senate. There was a real change in the mood of the country at that time, and in its course it caught a great many liberal senators. Reagan was the engine of that. Also, Reagan's view of the world and of America's role in it, along with the policy issues that he thought should be pursued, happened to coincide exactly with the views of the public in November 1980. Once he was in office, however, the basic "rules" seemed to apply again to the individual members, with a few exceptions. Survival becomes dependent upon good constituent service and the occasional federal grant.

QUESTION: To follow up on that, could part of the reason have been the fact that the local and state Democratic party organizations were better than those of the Republicans?

MR. HANNAFORD: Yes, I'm sure that was often the case; however, neither of the parties are very strong as organizational entities anymore, and television has a lot to do with this. It is as much the connection between the individual members of Congress or a legislative body and his or her constituents. They have transcended the apparatus of the parties.

QUESTION: You spoke of Mr. Reagan's ability to compromise and work with an adversarial legislature. I was wondering what happened to the Grace Report, which never seemed to get anywhere.

MR. HANNAFORD: No, it didn't get anywhere, and it should have. That may have been a victim of what someone was asking about earlier—when you have your eye on one or two key objectives, there are some other ones that don't get the attention they deserve. That may have been the case. He spoke about it many times, but I don't think that there was enough emphasis placed upon it. It might also have been a question of spending scarce political capital with the Congress, considering that both tax reform and the defense budget were high administration priorities. You can only win a few battles, so choices have to be made. In addition, you had changing leadership in the staff as time went on, with James Baker and Donald Regan switching jobs. Iran-contra complicated matters, and then there were further changes when Howard Baker and, later, Kenneth Duberstein came in.

QUESTION: Can part of the reason for the Grace Commission Report's failure be that many of its recommendations, if implemented, would affect too many projects in too many districts?

MR. HANNAFORD: That is a possibility. Also, without having pushed the program too much, Reagan and his administration could then beat the congressional Democrats over the head over the latter's failure to adopt it. You can use it politically, I suppose.

It's not that Reagan didn't believe in the Grace Commission's report. After all, the Grace Commission was simply his initial gubernatorial efficiency task force on a national scale. However, in his efforts in California, Reagan implemented everything he could administratively by executive order, yet he was able to save only about $100 million a year. Although every dollar helps, that was out of a budget that in those days was about $15 billion, so even then it was a drop in the bucket. Perhaps he had this in mind when dealing with the Grace Commission. Although I've not spoken to him about this particular issue, he may have been thinking that given how relatively little money the Grace Commission's report would have saved, it wasn't worth expending limited political capital in the Congress.

QUESTION: It has often been said that Reagan had a very strong antinuclear bias, and this influenced his decision to pursue an arms reduction treaty with the Soviets. Do you think this point has validity?

MR. HANNAFORD: I don't think it was antinuclear as much as it was opposition to our policy of MAD. Reagan thought that this policy was crazy and that it would be much better to have a good defense system instead. At one point he even said publicly that once we built our SDI system we would give the technology to the Soviets so that they could build one as well. I don't think he was being facetious about this. He believed that if we both had such defense systems, the threat of nuclear war would be greatly reduced.

QUESTION: At the end of his presidency, Reagan said that he wished he could have done more to reduce the deficit. Do you think that he was really aware of the bill that he was running up for America while he was in office?

MR. HANNAFORD: As he points out, presidents can't spend a dime; only Congress can spend the money. His biggest regret is that he never balanced the budget. He would send budgets to the Hill that would work in that direction, and time after time the Congress would automatically proclaim his budgets "dead on arrival." Of course, they would add a lot of Christmas ornaments to it before they passed it.

What he argued for then and continues to argue for now—in fact, he makes this the centerpiece of all his speeches now when he is out on the road—is that the president ought to have a line-item veto and that we ought to have a balanced budget amendment. We need the discipline to do that, because he says Congress will never do it on its own. After all, those dollars translate into votes, and members of Congress are not going to give that up. They like their jobs. If they have a balanced budget amendment, then they are forced to make difficult choices. The president can help them if he has a line-item veto, which about 40 governors have. He had it in California and thought it was excellent, because you could take out things that were egregiously wasteful without cutting out entire programs, and thus save a lot of money. He never had a line-item veto overridden when he was governor of California.

QUESTION: You mentioned Governor Reagan's sympathetic attitude toward defending the environment when he was governor. Was there any serious conflict between President Reagan and his first secretary of the interior, James Watt? Watt's positions seemed to be quite at variance with the President's.

MR. HANNAFORD: I agree, but I don't think Reagan or his staff paid that much attention to natural resources policy in those years. They were fixed on tax policy and the defense buildup. Watt was allowed to go off on his own. Things settled down a lot after he was replaced with Donald Hodel, but I don't recall Reagan getting personally involved in any natural resources policies or issues in those early years.

NARRATOR: The last question that we ask each of our speakers is, how do you think history will judge Ronald Reagan?

MR. HANNAFORD: I think it will judge him pretty well, particularly in the foreign affairs arena. I think his role in the great changes that have overtaken Europe and the Soviet Union and our relationships with that part of the world will outlast the domestic issues.

NARRATOR: We were told we would get a very intimate picture of Ronald Reagan if we could get Mr. Hannaford to visit us, and that certainly was borne out in what we have heard today. He will be meeting with President Reagan soon. We know that it will be a warm reunion, and we hope that you may be able to help us persuade Mr. Reagan to visit us. Thank you very much.

IV

PERSPECTIVES
ON LEADERSHIP

CHAPTER 9

REAGAN AND DEFENSE

EDWARD N. WRIGHT

NARRATOR: Our speaker is professor Edward N. Wright, who is now a professor at the University of Southern Colorado and served as assistant to the attorney general for national security affairs.

MR. WRIGHT: I was at the Justice Department from August 1987 until September 1988. As somebody who teaches political science, I was fortunate to have the opportunity to go to Washington and see more closely the things one teaches about.

My impressions of Ronald Reagan were very different from what one reads in the press with respect to his decision-making style, his detachment from issues, and so forth. One example of this difference involved the decision to permit the British to sell a submarine that had some equipment the United States had licensed to the British but had forbidden them from exporting that technology to anyone else. The British wanted to sell this capability to the Canadians, but the Department of Defense, the Joint Chiefs of Staff (JCS), and the Energy Department all opposed the transfer.

At a NSC meeting in the Cabinet room, the various representatives of the departments were preparing the President for an upcoming summit with Prime Minister Brian Mulroney of Canada. The Department of Defense, the JCS and the Department of Energy were challenging the President to hold firm and not sell this technology. Also, the other departments had their own particular list of issues that they wanted the President to take to Prime Minister Mulroney.

This was the first meeting in which I saw the President. He listened to each person around the table and engaged everyone with eye contact, which he often did, and he asked questions.

The Environmental Protection Agency (EPA) was there. It was unusual for them to be at an NSC meeting, but they were there primarily because of the acid rain issue. Ronald Reagan challenged the representative from EPA on his research, his statistics, and environmental issues. Mr. Reagan didn't have any little three-by-five cards so often described by others. He had a file folder or notebook, and it was obvious that he had done his homework. He cited research studies and quizzed the person from EPA.

Then came the Defense Department's challenge. The President told Frank Carlucci that there would be another meeting on the technology transfer issue. The President had talked to Margaret Thatcher that morning. It seemed to the President that if we couldn't trust the Canadians, we couldn't trust anybody. But Mr. Reagan said he would take up that decision separately from the present session.

It went around the table, and he listened to everybody's particular interests and concerns. Finally, in his very easy style, he thanked those at the meeting for helping him prepare for the Mulroney summit. He told us that he understood each of the departmental and specific concerns in the range of issues that were brought to the table. He told us he understood why they were voiced as they were (from very narrow departmental perspectives), but that his job was larger than that. He then proceeded to lay out to his Cabinet (at least a third there were Cabinet members) that his job as President was to look to the broader, larger relationships between these two governments. He cited the cultural affinities, and he cited—probably far more accurately than would have been my guess—how many miles of border there were between the two countries. He talked about the need to maintain this mutual relationship in the North American hemisphere with the Canadians, that we are not just two countries and that there are so many commonalities. He actually lectured his Cabinet and chastised it nicely for not seeing the larger view. He turned to Admiral William Crowe, who was across the table, and Carlucci, who was directly on his left, and he made the comment that if you can't trust the Canadians, by God, who can you trust? As we left that meeting in the car, I said to the attorney general, "So much for the guy who supposedly sleeps through meetings."

Of course, Ronald Reagan brought a lot of that image on himself. For example, it was he who had said in a press conference that he was working hard, "burning the midday oil." He had that folksy way about him, and he evoked that image. There are those who are drawing comparisons between him and Eisenhower in regard to the public image versus the real involvement in issues. My conclusion from working with his staff—I only got to go to a few meetings at which he was present—was that on those issues in which Ronald Reagan was interested, he knew what he wanted. He knew where he wanted to go. He knew the intricacies of those policies, he knew the issues, and he didn't balk at making decisions. For those issues that he chose not to be involved in—and that's *his* call, in accordance with his "cognitive style," as Alexander George puts it—he relied on his people to do the right things, which perhaps made him vulnerable with respect to certain issues. But, I clearly saw a man who knew what he wanted to do.

The other meeting I think that was very instructive about his style dealt with Noriega. (These are the two most vivid meetings for me because he was heavily involved; these were important issues, and there were lessons to be drawn from them.) It had leaked out, with respect to Noriega, that we might negotiate the drug indictments to induce him to step down from power. There was great unhappiness in the law enforcement community and in the Justice Department. These people felt it was the wrong signal to send during the fight against drugs, especially during the President's campaign and Mrs. Reagan's "Just say no to drugs" campaign. Making a deal with a man under indictment for narcotics was the wrong message, according to this line of reasoning. Two U.S. attorneys in Florida—and U.S. attorneys are notoriously political—were getting all kinds of great media coverage by opposing that kind of decision and saying how wrong it was in the fight against drugs.

The attorney general had prevailed on the President to have another conversation on that issue. The issue hadn't really been decided, but this was clearly a strategically placed leak to keep something you want on the table, and that certainly occurred. The attorney general called the President that morning and said, "Mr. President, we've got to talk about this again. The law enforcement community believes this is just not a good decision." It seems to me it was a Friday, so the President held up his departure to Camp David to convene an NSPG (National Security Planning Group—a "principals only" NSC meeting) with the attorney general. I got a message through his secretary that the attorney general wanted to talk to me. Meese said, "I need to know what the rundown is on the statute of limitations for the indictments against Noriega; I need the notes from all the meetings on Noriega, and I'll meet you at the West Wing at 11 o'clock." It was then about 9 o'clock in the morning.

I scrambled to pull all this data together and had all kinds of other people jumping as well. Then I wrote the briefing book for him. We met at the West Wing, which we had done many times. I gave him a quick, 5-minute data dump about what was in the book, how it was organized, and where the things were that he wanted. Then on his way to this "principals only" meeting in the Oval Office, he told me to come along, which was typical of Ed Meese. I have a lot of admiration for him for things like this.

So off we went to the Oval Office. I wasn't cleared into the Oval Office, but he took me right in. We got into this "principals only" meeting, and we were getting a lot of skeptical looks directed at me. Who's this guy? they seemed to ask. No strap hangers are allowed, and for good reason.

The President turned to the attorney general and said, "Ed, this is your meeting." So Attorney General Meese began to lay out the concerns: the law enforcement community's reaction to the leaked story that we were going to negotiate the indictments with Noriega, what was going on with the U.S. attorneys, and a host of other things. The attorney general argued that these things should be considered in making the final decision.

Then they went around the room and various people spoke. Jim Baker at that point was preparing to go to take over the campaign for Bush, who was not in that meeting and in fact was seldom in meetings like that. Jim Baker proceeded to talk about George Bush's view. Baker was thinking in terms of the campaign and the job he was about to take on, reluctantly.

The President said he knew what "George" thought because he had talked to him that morning on this issue. In fact, that was the nature of their relationship. George Bush never juxtaposed himself between a Cabinet officer and the President. He wouldn't do that.

He held doggedly to that practice. His input to the President was always on the side and in private. The things he said during Iran-contra are true regarding his relationship to decisions.

NARRATOR: How do you think he became identified so strongly with the issue in the media?

MR. WRIGHT: Two things contributed to that. First, he had a role with the crisis management group. He was given that task. Second, the Vice President's Task Force on Terrorism involved a lot of the same players.

Ronald Reagan listened to all this discussion, turned to the attorney general, and said, "Ed, tell me this—will we ever get him in a U.S. court?" The attorney general said, no, the statute of limitations on some of the charges would expire soon. Meese said that there was no extradition treaty that would bring Noriega here, and as long as we had outstanding indictments, Meese was sure Noriega would not leave the country and place himself in some kind of international jurisdiction where the United States could exercise jurisdiction to arrest him.

The President then turned to Elliott Abrams (of whom I don't have a really favorable view in most things) who said that the sticking point in negotiations with Noriega was these indictments, which undermined our efforts every time we got close to something in trying to get him out of power.

The President then looked around the room, looked every person in the eye in this circle in the Oval Office, and said, "What would you have me do?" He repeated, "What would you have me do?" Reagan said that it seemed to him that he had three options. He could just throw up his hands in frustration and say there was nothing we could do, that we were frustrated by the inability to extradite him. We would have to admit failure, that we couldn't do anything about it. He shook his head and said, "You all know what Manuel Noriega is"—and this is an absolutely direct quote—"that son-of-a-bitch has got to go!"

As a second option, Reagan said that he could send in the military. The State Department had proposed lots of harebrained schemes to use the military to snatch Noriega and then set up a government in exile—some really bizarre stuff. Fortunately,

Carlucci, and before Carlucci, Weinberger, argued against those kinds of things.

NARRATOR: Did Shultz support them?

MR. WRIGHT: It is my understanding that he did. Such options couldn't be raised without the secretary's approval.

The President then paused, looked around the room, and said he would not order an invasion, that Manuel Noriega was not worth one young American boy's blood. Then he said that if indeed the indictments were the sticking point, and if indeed that meant negotiating and dropping the indictments in return for his stepping down from power, he would do that. He then said he would take the heat for doing so.

Again, I thought, "Where is the guy who supposedly sleeps through all of these meetings?" This is a different insight to Ronald Reagan, and I expect that lots of people would prefer to believe the "conventional wisdom," but I just didn't see it.

Someone you should talk to is an Air Force Lieutenant Colonel named Donald Baucom. He used to be in the Air Force Office of History, was the editor of *Air University Review*, and is now at SDIO, the Strategic Defense Initiative Organization. Abrahamson hired him to do a history of SDI. In researching the President's decision to pursue SDI, Baucom interviewed a number of people from Reagan's days as governor to try to trace the original idea of SDI.

One of the things people would have you believe is that SDI was foisted on Ronald Reagan by a narrow group of people, and that he became enamored with the idea and in a very simpleminded way began to talk about this impermeable shield. Well, that's just baloney. What Baucom found was that Ronald Reagan had been concerned for many years and had read a lot about nuclear issues. He had a deep concern about the nuclear dilemma of holding the populations hostage. He strongly believed that there had to be a better way to structure the nuclear competition than putting innocent populations at risk. In this context, the idea of using science to reverse what science had created made sense. Reagan felt that we created the weapons, so we should find a way to mute their destructive capability.

It started when he was governor. He would go for a long weekend to the Hoover Institute, where among others he met Edward Teller. He would send up a list of things about which he would like to get experts together, and they would have a long weekend of argument and discussion, and he would listen.

One of the issues that was on that list frequently was nuclear weapons and policy. He had thought about this a long time, and in his conversation he asked, "Wouldn't it be possible . . .?" Of course, there were those who agreed with him, such as Teller.

It ultimately resulted in the addition of the idea at the tail end of a speech about defense priorities. He made his decision with the advice of some of the people close to him, but not many. It was his initiative to say that he was going to use the power of his office to try to move the scientific community down that road. Isn't it possible? And if it isn't possible, we are going to find out. He felt then that he could make it happen. This is an enormous insight into Ronald Reagan that is not popularly held.

Clearly my insights on things like that were very issue-specific and very narrow in terms of targets of opportunity. But I conclude something very different about his approach to decisions.

NARRATOR: Did Meese talk to you much about such things?

MR. WRIGHT: We talked a lot. In fact, Meese was a good teacher, and we spent a lot of time together. We traveled a lot. We were out of the country about a week each month, and foreign affairs generally fell in my area of staff responsibilities.

NARRATOR: We've heard two or three things about Meese so far in our other oral histories. First, because there was a political connection all along, Meese was closer than anybody else to the President for that reason. Second, Meese was the rapporteur at many of the sessions and he therefore had control of the agenda to the extent that no one else had.

MR. WRIGHT: I think that is true. In fact, he has the exceptional ability to synthesize, and he takes the best set of notes of anybody that I have ever seen in a meeting.

NARRATOR: Was it in shorthand?

MR. WRIGHT: No, it was longhand, but he would synthesize it down to be three or four specific phrases that captured the issue and the views of participants in the meeting. It was almost like an engineer's work. Actually it was more like a lawyer's brief. It was precise.

In fact, his notes were always far better than mine. After a meeting, he would give me his notes and I maintained the necessary files so that when there was another meeting, I had whatever he had. I would pull everything together and draw from it, and then give it to him in his briefing book and try to encapsulate all the things that had gone on, give a chronology, and those kinds of things. I used his notes a lot for such things.

People who go back through the presidential papers will see that he did have that ability, and he played that role. He also played that role with respect to access to the President. He told me several times that he saw one of his roles as trying to see that the President received a variety of views on an issue. Granted, the majority of people who had access to the President were on the conservative side. Other than Meese, few would go to the President and say that he was going to make a bad decision and needed to have some additional information or perspective.

A classic example of that happening was the issue of the Krasnoyarsk radar. Ed Rowney at the Department of State was very much on the outside, because the State Department and George Shultz wanted this arms control agreement to go forward. Every month in the first six months of the last year or so, Shultz had a new timetable to get an arms control agreement. This was to be the crowning achievement.

Ronald Reagan was saying that he would not de-couple SDI and that he would not leverage SDI to get an agreement. Shultz argued to do that and to moderate the U.S. position on SDI; so did the JCS.

In a morning national security briefing, Ed Rowney heard that it was going to be recommended to the President that he not declare the Krasnoyarsk radar a material breach of the ABM Treaty, but merely to raise it as an issue of concern. Rowney, of course, wanted to declare the radar to be a clear and material breach on the front page of the *New York Times*. He wanted to call it what it was—a manifestation of the Soviets' own strategic defense capability and the pursuit of that technology in violation of the

ABM Treaty. Rowney's staff called me and said, "Ed has to talk to the attorney general, and the subject is what is going to happen in tomorrow morning's national security briefing." I said OK.

I briefed the attorney general every morning at 8:30 or 9:00, after his staff meeting with all the assistant attorneys general. After my national security brief we would discuss what was going to happen that day. I told him what people in the department were participating in national security interagency groups at the second level down, what the issues were, and who our person was. He wanted to know, because he wanted to know what the Justice Department position was with respect to the issue, and who the person was out there representing him. I also gave him feedback the next day on what the outcome of the meeting had been. He wanted to know those things.

The call from Rowney's man had occurred after my meeting with the attorney general, so I went in between people on his schedule. I went to his office and said, "Ambassador Rowney has got to talk to you. There are serious concerns about a presidential decision on the Krasnoyarsk radar. It appears somebody thinks it's going to happen tomorrow morning. I've talked to some other folks at Defense and State, and it appears that what Rowney understood was probably going to happen." He said that we had not had a meeting on that. There had been some informal discussions, but a wider discussion was needed on that issue.

I set up a time for him to talk on the secure phone to Ed Rowney, who registered his concerns. The attorney general said to me, "I'll call the President in the morning before his national security briefing." He called the President the next morning. I wasn't there when the conversation occurred, but the result was that he told the President that he thought there probably needed to be a wider discussion before a decision was taken. That afternoon came the agenda for a national security planning group meeting and an NSC meeting the next day on that issue.

Meese saw his relationship and loyalty to Ronald Reagan as absolutely political; it wasn't social. They weren't in the same social circles, and didn't socialize except when it was the required kind of thing. There was a very high regard by each for the other. Edwin Meese was motivated by only one political ambition, and that was to serve the President. He subordinated two-thirds of the affairs of his life, which got him in great trouble. That is part and parcel of all his legal problems—his inattention to his own personal affairs in service to the President.

When the independent counsel sent over the discovery order, they found letters in Meese's desk from Bob Wallach that had never been opened. Edwin Meese was so consumed with serving the President and being the attorney general that he left his own personal affairs in great disarray, which is too bad because he was a good attorney general, in the law enforcement community particularly. There won't be another one like him.

Until Ed Meese, I think attorneys general have typically been the lawyer's lawyer: William French Smith, an elegant man; Griffin Bell, a scholarly man. Meese turned out to be a far better scholar than I thought when I first met him, but Meese was a law enforcement guy; he had been a prosecutor, which is also Thornburgh's background. I would venture to say that this is the kind of attorney general we will see for a long time—a criminal justice type as opposed to a corporate law type.

NARRATOR: Because of the nature of the problems?

MR. WRIGHT: That's right, and I think the role has been redefined by Meese in large measure.

NARRATOR: Given Meese's close connection and Weinberger's intimate association, why do you think Shultz won out and they lost on INF and on negotiations in general? Or did they?

MR. WRIGHT: I think Weinberger didn't. I think Meese initially opposed INF, but certainly by the time the two-track decision was taken, Ed Meese became a strong supporter and believed this was a major achievement, which I think it was. Meese would make the argument now that in fact that adherence and firmness is what brought about much of what's at work in Europe. It involved the Soviet Union trying to respond and being unable economically to do so. That, plus resolve in the West, resulted in the INF Treaty. Meese would make that argument.

Edwin Meese is a far more pragmatic man than most people think. Some people around him, however, were highly impractical or dogmatic as opposed to pragmatic. For instance, Brad Reynolds is a very bright man, and a very hardworking, committed person, but

I think he gave the attorney general bad advice at times. That advice tended to be, "Well, screw the Congress!" You can't be a Cabinet officer and take that attitude in your dealings with the Congress, because you have to work with them. You've got to push, prod, and compromise. Reynolds would rather put the stick in somebody's eye.

Meese certainly had a set of principles that were very well-founded conservative ideas, but they were absolutely attuned to Ronald Reagan. As the change occurred in Ronald Reagan with respect to the gut-level, personal decision concerning Gorbachev—much like the change Margaret Thatcher made in deciding that Gorbachev was a man she could deal with—this was filtered into Edwin Meese's view. He would still urge caution; he would try to ensure that it wouldn't go too far and that it was still underpinned by firmness and the conservative ideas about strength and the competition with the Soviets.

His duty was not to change Ronald Reagan's mind—Ronald Reagan was the President, after all—but to make sure that the President operated on the basis of a full understanding. We talked many times about this. Meese would say that his job was not to tell the President what he had to do. His job was to let the President be the President and to make that decision easy for him. He said it was the President's decision, not his. That's the role he played on the NSC, too. Meese wasn't a statutory member; he was a member because Ronald Reagan wanted him there, and he had been his counselor.

NARRATOR: Was he rapporteur for them too?

MR. WRIGHT: No. The NSC staff did all of that. Meese did, however, pay close attention that papers generated from the NSC staff and records of meetings were accurate.

NARRATOR: You used a phrase that explained a lot, but I don't remember Ronald Reagan ever using it in his public statements. The phrase you used was, "The Soviet Union is changing and is going to change, and we can shape it."

Whenever the President answered reporters on this question, he always explained it by saying of Gorbachev—"He's different." I have sometimes wondered whether any of you who were in the picture said to him, "Well, why don't you use phrases like . . ."

MR. WRIGHT: I think there would have been a great reluctance to say that publicly for fear of what that would do with respect to Gorbachev's own standing back home; I think he was always viewed as being on very tentative ground. I think there was a real desire not to make that worse for fear of what a successor would be like. And what I described is my analysis of the moderation of President Reagan's views of the Soviets—and Gorbachev.

NARRATOR: Did Meese ever talk at all about the conflict between Weinberger and Shultz?

MR. WRIGHT: It's true that Weinberger and Shultz wouldn't speak to each other oftentimes. But Meese would never talk about it, nor would those who worked for Meese. During Iran-contra, with respect to Don Regan and all those things, Meese *never* criticized anybody in the administration in the presence of anybody else. He wouldn't do it, and he wouldn't let you do it. That was a rule.

He is a very different person from the person painted in the media; he really is. I heard him curse twice in a year. He met once a week in a prayer group in his dining room before work. It shows, I think, how important it is that the appearance is just as important as the substance with public perception, and Meese didn't spend the time to shape his own personal public image. He made the decision to avoid doing so long before he ever became attorney general, when he was still at the White House.

NARRATOR: Didn't he have any public relations or public affairs officer working with him?

MR. WRIGHT: Their job was to write speeches and to answer questions about the Justice Department. Pat Korten, in fact, became his public affairs guy, and Pat would say, "You've got to do this; you've got to do that!" But Meese was not particularly interested in his personal public image. He was much more concerned with serving the President.

We went on a 13-day swing through all the drug capitals of South America. It was a marvelous trip in which the attorney general tried to persuade and strengthen the resolve of the leaders to hold firm against narco-terrorism and against the cartel and to enforce the rule of law. He told them we would do everything we could to help them, and that we could give them expertise, for example, in special courtroom security. (Of course, there had been and still are killings and kidnappings of judges in Colombia.) Pat Korten asked the attorney general why we didn't take a press group with us. Korten thought we should.

Meese finally consented. We had a pool of about six people—one from *Newsweek*, a reporter from the *New York Times*, and others, including a CNN camera crew. They spent 13 days with us. It was a great thing to have done, because before that if you had asked any of them if they wanted their picture taken with the attorney general, their answer would have been, "Not me! Somebody might see it!" But in the end, they couldn't wait to have their pictures taken with the attorney general. They said things like, "This isn't the same guy, is it?" But it was him. They saw him every day for 13 days, and that was the real Ed Meese. They came out with a far different view, after having seen him interact and have serious discussions, always on the record, with people like President Barco of Colombia.

Another rule Ed Meese had was that he would never give background interviews—nothing on background. He refused to leak and was absolutely adamant about such things as leaks. We weren't on his staff to give background interviews either. That was a rule. The attorney general said that if the press wanted to talk to with us, we should tell them to talk to our public affairs office, unless there was some specific thing we needed to do; if so, we were to coordinate with public affairs so there wouldn't be any misunderstandings or crossed signals. Of course, the media didn't like that. If they can't talk to you on background, they can't talk about the kinds of things they want to talk about.

NARRATOR: Did Meese feel the President defended him in every way he could? Do you want to say a word about the President's loyalty to subordinates in general and how that affected his ability, not in Meese's case, but in general, to hire and fire people?

MR. WRIGHT: I have great admiration for the attorney general, and I consider him a real friend. I see him when I'm in

Washington. I have come to know his family. I would say to him what I'm going to say here.

There was probably a time when I think Mr. Meese might have served Ronald Reagan better by stepping down earlier, saying, "I don't want to detract from the important work of this administration. I don't want to be an issue; I don't want to be a thorn in your side."

I don't know that he ever had that kind of conversation with the President. I wouldn't be surprised if he had, and if he did, the President would have said, "No, I don't want you to do it." But I don't know that.

However, it is important that there was a point in time after which he had to stay, because if he had left, he would have done equal damage to the President. There was a point in time in which the decision had to be, "I will stay." In his own mind he knew he would be vindicated by the independent counsel's report. Also, he had to do it to recover his legal fees. There is a practical side to that too.

I know that he had a meeting with the vice president when it was about time to begin working on his presidential campaign. I'm convinced—but Meese never said this to me—that he said to the vice president that he would not be an issue in his campaign. The attorney general was very concerned about the timing of the independent counsel's report, and as soon as it was out, there was an announcement that Meese would be leaving the administration. I think that was a clear commitment to George Bush so as not to be an issue in his campaign, and I believe there was a commitment back from George Bush not to make statements about the attorney general and whether or not he should step down.

I don't know that the President was steadfastly loyal to people other than those who were at the highest levels, but his sense of loyalty to high officials was seen as rewarding their loyalty to him.

Concerning the degree to which this commitment to loyalty clouded his decision making, I think it probably did. Again, there was a time when he might have been better served in asking Meese if it would not be better for him to resign. But the independent counsel's report validated the President's continued support—though it came at some cost in moving forward. I believe the principle is important and in the end Meese and the President were right.

As soon as Meese resigned, one of the first things that happened was that presidential personnel called and said that the President wanted to know what kinds of things Ed wanted to do—what kinds of advisory committees, councils, presidential appointments, etc. Meese was then appointed to the West Point Board of Visitors, and he had a couple of other interests. In fact, he said to me, "The President wanted to know what I wanted to do."

It was awfully difficult for him to say no, and Meese had that same problem with Bob Wallach. As people described him to me, Bob Wallach was an entrepreneur who would use anybody's name. I only saw him once. It was Bob Wallach who wrote a letter saying, "I've got this friend at the White House, and I've got access." And he did. The relationship went back many years to law-school days.

Edwin Meese would not say no to anybody. He would always make time to hear somebody. The people who came to talk to him represented the conservative constituency, but he believed that government needed to be open. He was one of the few Cabinet officers to make a point of being available to academics. That was not the case in other departments like Treasury. When Baker became secretary of state, the answer to academics was likely to be maybe in the third or fourth year—or even second term. Meese was committed to being open to the academic community. He believed public officials had to be open to academic research and those who study government.

NARRATOR: Was he open to people of all points of view—all academics?

MR. WRIGHT: Anybody that would ask—I promise you. I never saw him say no to anybody who was doing research—graduate students or anybody. A lieutenant colonel from SDIO wanted to come and try to track down and verify some of the meetings that occurred in the President's days as governor of California. Meese gave him two hours the first day and three hours the second day. He was open to that, and he thought that was a commitment people in public service had to make.

NARRATOR: Meese never talked about getting jobs for people who had done things for him, as far as you know?

MR. WRIGHT: No, but he was always interested in the same kind of things that all people are—trying to put good people in good positions, spread throughout the political network. As counsellor, he saw that role from the political aspect much more strongly than as attorney general. As counsellor, that probably is part of his job, but not as attorney general.

There were some people who worked on the campaign and also worked for him in Justice, like Ken Cribb, so he lobbied to get Ken Cribb a job at the White House. In terms of favors for people outside, I didn't see any of that. However, I would not necessarily have had the chance.

I had an interesting relationship with him. When I went there, there was a lot of concern on the political side that they wanted a political appointee, someone whose loyalties were unquestioned. In my resume, I had worked with Les Gelb at the Carnegie Endowment for International Peace. Les Gelb had been assistant secretary of state for politico-military affairs in the Carter administration. He was a reporter, and people on the attorney general's staff considered him a notorious leaker when he was at the State Department. Les is now back at the *New York Times* and is a great guy. That was another assignment, a job—as this was.

I'm told that my previous work with Les Gelb was questioned in light of the need for a proper "political fit." Meese said to his staff, "Hold on a minute!" He said he wanted two things in his special assistant for national security affairs. He wanted a serving military officer who knew the Pentagon, who knew defense, and who could get around town and tell him what other people were thinking on these issues. Second, he wanted someone who was not a lawyer. "There are plenty of lawyers in this building," he said.

I went to great lengths not to be involved in political discussions, because I saw that as subverting my own ability to be objective with respect to what I told the attorney general. I have a very strong view about Oliver North and what you do as a subordinate to a principal figure. My job wasn't to tell him what he ought to do. When Meese described to me his previous job as counsellor, he said his job was to give the President the widest range of information that he could and to tell him what the temperature of the water was and how different people felt about the issue; what the positions were; who was opposed; who was for; what the consequences were; and then allow him to make his decision.

I also found that approach useful. Thus, I wouldn't participate in the political discussions of who you could or couldn't trust in representing the department at a meeting. That occurred a few times, and typically, Brad Reynolds would say that politically he didn't think someone was the right guy. My answer was, that wasn't my decision. Based on his position at Justice he was the person to go to the meeting. If the attorney general wanted somebody else to represent the department, he would say so. Seldom would the attorney general do that. I should add that such political advice from attorney general's counsel was probably appropriate. But it wasn't my place to do so. Impressively, Meese kept his finger on everything; he knew exactly what was happening in the Justice Department every day.

He was very different from Thornburgh. Meese met with all assistant attorneys general who were in town at 8:30 every morning in his conference room. He would have a few words to say about what the issues were that day or whatever was going on. He would go around the table for questions—anybody got a problem? If they needed guidance, they got guidance. If they had an issue, they could bring it to that table. That is the way every day started when he was in Washington.

Thornburgh had a very different style—he operated like a governor. He had a little group of three people who were the watchdogs of the office. If an assistant attorney general wanted to talk to Thornburgh, he would talk to them, and then they would bring him the issues. Were there staff meetings every morning? No way! That was gone after Meese.

Meese was involved in the day-to-day operations and he believed in that style. It's a little bit like the White House style: the 7:30 breakfast with all the elephants (Darman, Sununu, and back in those days, Baker, Meese, Deaver, and Clark) getting in a room together and thrashing out the day. It was a different style.

With respect to national security things, he wanted to know what the agenda was for every meeting that involved an assistant attorney general. He wanted to know what issues were raised in national security meetings concerning the Office of Legal Counsel, interdepartmental programs, covert action, and should the Office of the Legal Counsel have to make a judgment, he wanted to know what the issues were and what the results were.

The first item on my brief every morning was the National Security Principal Group (NSPG) and sub-Cabinet level meetings for that day. Then he would pick up the phone and say, "Let's talk before you go." He and I and the third person would get together, because he would want to know what the issues were. Everybody knew that if there was an issue, they could raise it with the attorney general and would receive his guidance and backing as the Justice representative.

I would go to meetings called by the NSC staff as the Justice representative. I remember once we were talking about the immigration quotas and refugee status for Armenians trying to get out of the Soviet Union. We had representatives of the Immigration and Nationalization Service (INS) as well as the assistant attorney general for that area. We all met, and the attorney general decided what the department's position was based on the input from the assistant attorney general and INS. Allen Nelson wasn't particularly enamored with Meese's position, and attempted to get it changed three or four times. Meese made his decision, and I went to the meeting and sat down at the table with Ty Cobb of the NSC staff, a very competent guy and a Soviet-East European specialist who was a deputy assistant to the president and a senior director on the NSC staff. We had three functional areas from the NSC staff sitting around the table and three different representatives from the State Department sitting there, and I said, "I can't talk to you guys! I'm here to represent the Justice Department position. When the NSC gets a position and when the State Department gets a position, then we can talk. But I can't handle trying to make the decision for what the State Department position ought to be. So you have got to come to the table with just one position." Well, that was bizarre. They just don't do those kinds of things, but you did those kinds of things at Ed Meese's Justice Department.

NARRATOR: How did Meese find you?

MR. WRIGHT: When I did my dissertation research, he was counsellor, and I interviewed him them. I was a Ph.D. student at Georgetown, writing about defense mobilization concerns and presidential superintendence of a lethargic policy area. That is what the dissertation was about—how Ronald Reagan structured the mechanism to try to invigorate or reinvigorate a very lethargic policy area.

I had tried to get on Meese's calendar several times while I was attached to the NSC. (I did a project for them as my quid pro quo to get access for the interviews.) I was attached to the NSC for about nine months, and Bill Clark was the national security adviser at all meetings of this group. Every time I got on Meese's calendar, I was bumped off. It was then time for me to leave town to get back to the Air Force Academy where I was on the faculty. I still hadn't had two interviews that I wanted. Meese was one of them. He was coming to Denver to make a speech, and I got a call which asked if I wanted to have breakfast with him, and I went and spent the morning with Meese. It was terrific. The day of our meeting was three days after Grenada, and it was a marvelous morning.

I later saw him, because he was very active in the Center for the Study of the Presidency. I would see Meese, and he always remembered me. It was amazing. We would talk about trying to keep the research current and how things were going. He later visited the Air Force Academy in October of 1986 for two days and spoke at a seminar at the law department and to political science students. I was his escort because our department ran the distinguished speakers program, and I knew him. At the end of the second day, he said that he had a special assistant for national security affairs who was a military officer and who would have to be moving on soon because the Navy kept saying that they had to get this person into a command. Meese asked me, "If that person leaves, would you be interested in the job?" I said yes, and he said, "Well, I think the chemistry is good and it would work." About February or March, I received a phone call from my predecessor who said that he was leaving and asked if I would come, and I said no. That didn't sit very well! I said, "I realize that a lowly lieutenant colonel in the Air Force does not push around a Cabinet officer, so by saying this to you, I realize that I'm off any list." I was very flattered to be asked, but I didn't want to leave my family in Colorado. Because we had kids in high school, we didn't want to move the family.

A couple of months went by and I figured it was over. Then he called and said, "The Navy has agreed to give me six more months if you will split the difference." My answer was, "Yes."

NARRATOR: The one thing that you touched on a couple of times was the relationship between President Reagan and Vice President Bush. What do you think Ronald Reagan really thought about George Bush?

MR. WRIGHT: I have often wondered. I really have, because Bush was not a big player in outward appearances. Dan Quayle is far more outwardly involved in policy than George Bush was as vice president. He wouldn't be if George Bush didn't want him to be: You do what your President wants you to do. I think that was defined early on, and Meese probably helped to define what that relationship ought to be in the early formative years. In the end, though, I haven't a clue of what Reagan thought of Bush. I do know that Bush made his input, but always in private, as a counselor, and typically not in meetings with the Cabinet as we already discussed.

NARRATOR: You said Meese never talked about it.

MR. WRIGHT: No, we never talked about personalities. We did talk about Bush near the end when we were talking about the campaign. Meese would never say that George Bush would be a good president. He would say Bush was a great candidate, and that he certainly was one of the most qualified there had ever been. In fact, at Meese's going-away party at the White House, Bush and Meese were very friendly and chummy, but seldom would Meese say anything about Bush. I think he just considered Bush to be the vice president and not particularly involved in most issues. Meese had a significant portfolio with respect to terrorism, and the vice president chaired the vice president's task force on terrorism, but I don't think he saw him as a big player.

Meese certainly respected Bush. The relationship Bush had with the President was that Bush would make his own views known to the President. I don't think Edwin Meese would ever have considered George Bush's views as being more important than anybody else's, and that wouldn't be the case with respect to all people.

As you look at Quayle's staff compared to Bush's staff, Quayle's staff is much more competent and more involved in the interagency process, particularly the national security matters.

Most, if not all, have Ph.Ds, and they are all very conservative—right out of the book.

I think the jury is still out, although a lot of people give the National Space Council credit for doing a lot of good work. It has, but I think it has more growing to do in terms of making things happen.

NARRATOR: Meese never expressed an opinion, did he, on the selection of Quayle, or on other personalities?

MR. WRIGHT: No.

NARRATOR: Do you think he was surprised?

MR. WRIGHT: I would venture to say that he probably was surprised. Meese never said anything that would cause you to think he had anything other than the highest regard for Jim Baker. On any given day, I probably spent more time with Edwin Meese than any other special assistant other than his counsellor, his chief of staff, and one other special assistant. By that I'm merely trying to say that I was around him a lot. We had a friendly relationship; he was very much like an academic mentor and really saw me differently in that regard. We would talk about academic kinds of things—about process and structural kinds of issues. In fact, on our way to the principals-only meeting in the Oval Office, while in the car I said to him, "I know that was a high-risk decision" (to take me to a "principals-only" meeting). His only comment was, "I thought you needed to see it." Well, that says a lot.

NARRATOR: Why don't you like Elliott Abrams?

MR. WRIGHT: I feel about Elliott Abrams the same way I feel about Oliver North. I think it's very dangerous to have zealots in policy positions where the cause becomes more important than the constitutional oath one takes. I think it comes down to that. I think people like Elliott Abrams are dangerous because I think that the cause can get in the way of what's right.

NARRATOR: You have said a number of things that put Meese and the President in a different light than the way that perhaps 95 percent of the public saw them during that time.

MR. WRIGHT: I realize that many of my observations run counter to much of the conventional wisdom that grows out of over-simplification, superficial media coverage, and a caricature of Reagan and Meese, which is a caricature. What I've described are my personal observations and conclusions. I hope to expand my limited snapshots in the Reagan presidency as archival materials become available to better analyze and define the Reagan presidency, which I was privileged to serve in a very insignificant way—an opportunity for which I continue to be gratified as a teacher and as an American.

CHAPTER 10

THE PRESIDENT'S HEALTH

T. BURTON SMITH, M.D.

NARRATOR: We are very pleased to have Dr. T. Burton Smith with us today. The Commission interviewed many of the presidential physicians in the postwar period, but you were rather busy at the time, so we weren't able to meet with you. We are benefitting from the fact that you came east at this time.

Dr. Smith was born in Hermosa Beach, California. He served as presidential physician in the second term of the Reagan presidency. He is a graduate of UCLA, holds a medical degree from the University of Southern California Medical School, and served as an intern in Los Angeles County General Hospital. He did a postgraduate residency at the Jefferson Medical College Hospital in Philadelphia. As a medical officer of the U.S. Coast Guard in World War II, Dr. Smith had combat service as beach party medical officer in five amphibious landings in the South Pacific. He has taught at various places, including the United States Veterans Hospital in West Los Angeles, the UCLA Medical School, and Santa Monica Hospital. He was chief of the Department of Urology at St. John's Hospital in Santa Monica as well as chief of staff. He is a member of a number of professional medical associations, and for those of you with extra medical interests, it is interesting to note that he was a member of the Citizens Advisory Committee of the United States Olympic Committee in the medical area. Dr. Smith was team physician of the Peoples-to-Peoples Tennis Team, which visited—as far as I can tell—almost every country on the globe. So he has had a wide international as well as national experience.

He is going to talk for a bit, and then I am sure he will be happy to answer your questions about the Reagan administration and share his impressions and experiences.

DR. SMITH: I certainly do wish to thank you for the opportunity to be here and share some time. I hope it is meaningful. It is a pleasure for me to share the experiences that I think are quite unique. Virginia, I think, is the place to do it because this, after all, is the cradle of our nation.

I think your foresight in setting up such a center and commission is commendable. You are probably unique in that regard. I certainly think the arrival of Burton Lee, the new doctor for the Bush administration, has caused some confusion for the White House since we both have the name Burton. In any event I did have a chance to meet him, and we had a chance to share some experiences. I gave him fatherly advice, but whether he accepted it or not, I don't know; we will see. I know that Dr. Lee has been in contact with you. I know you helped him a great deal, and I also know that because of your committee, President Bush, Vice President Quayle, Mrs. Quayle, and the attorney for the President have all met and reached an accord over a protocol on how to invoke the Twenty-fifth Amendment. There was no such understanding when I arrived, so you have done a service already.

As far as I am concerned, I feel that I was very privileged to have had this unique experience. Not many doctors get to have a White House experience. I served only a short period of time—two years—and was called home because of family matters. Nevertheless, those two years were quite eventful. We had numerous political experiences; we had a lot of personal experiences with the President; we had many medical experiences; so we did have a lot going on during that period of time.

Through it all it was my observation that President Reagan remained—at least in my eyes—calm and assured. Perhaps it is the actor in him—I'm not sure—but I really think it is the person. So as of this moment I still think he is a wonderful person, and I'm glad to have had that opportunity.

I suppose the first thing you want to know is: How was I ever invited to go to the White House? I was a Californian in the field of urology in 1966 when Ronald Reagan was on a campaign tour to depose "Father" Pat Brown as governor of California. You know

from television that campaigning is a very arduous affair, physically
and mentally. During that period of time Ronald Reagan–the
person Ronald Reagan–got into some medical problems related, I
think, a lot to fatigue. In other words, he was tired and his
resistance went down. He would get urinary tract infections and
needed a urologist. I was called in to see him. His family used my
hospital; I happened to work in a certain hospital, and that was the
connection. Otherwise, there is no connection. It was a medical
coincidence.

I said to him, "Look, you are established, you are an actor, and
you have a family. I don't know about your wealth, but in any event
maybe you don't need to become governor. It seems to me the task
of becoming governor might get you into medical problems." I
realize looking at it now that if he had obeyed my advice at that
time he never would have been the governor or president, but he
overruled my suggestion and became governor. He continued to
have problems after his governorship and we then elected to
undergo a surgical procedure to try to stop these problems. It was
successful.

I often looked at him in awe thinking that if I had not called
the right shot and if my operation had not been successful, he
probably wouldn't have become president, in which case I wouldn't
be sitting here with you today. As it turned out the operation was
successful, and it did make a difference; he was no longer impaired.
It allowed him to be governor for eight years, and after a brief
interim period, serve eight years as the President of the United
States.

My first trip to Washington was in 1981, when he invited me
to come for the inauguration with my family, which I did. It was
interesting to see him at a parade and at a distance, like at a gala
with dancing and so forth, without being able to go up to him and
say hi. I felt it. I thought possibly that I'd never see him again; I
would certainly never be on a one-to-one basis with him. As a
consequence, I felt he was on a different cloud than I was. Little
did I know, of course, that I would be seeing him again in an
intimate relationship. So it was an interesting speculation at that
time.

In 1982 he began to have another set of urological problems,
and he called and wanted to know if I would come back in
consultation, which I did. So that led to my being there and

meeting Dr. Daniel Ruge. I think Daniel Ruge liked his work for four years but did not want to go on for eight. I think he saw me as an opportunity or a ticket out. I believe he groomed me to consider coming back to Washington to replace him. Otherwise the question was, Who would replace Dr. Ruge?

I began my tour of duty after Ronald Reagan was elected for a second term, which began in January 1985. I had anticipated staying there four years, but my younger brother, who was a surgeon, was dying of cancer, and my mother was dying as well. My brother had been taking care of my mother, but after he was no longer able to care of her, I had to go home. I think it's proper that I did. When I talked to the President about it, he said, "You have to do what you have to do," and so I went home, leaving him under the care of an army colonel, Dr. John Hutton, who was my assistant while I was there.

How did I look at this position, being a civilian and never having taken care of a VVIP? I shouldn't say that; I had cared for quite a few movie actors and celebrity types in southern California, but never with this awesome feeling that the world would know about it if I didn't do the right thing. I looked at my new position and tried to analyze where I could get into trouble. In other words, you look at the scene and ask where you are likely to get into trouble. It seemed to me that a sudden heart attack would be the one emergency that anybody would want to be prepared for. Often we were one-on-one; that is to say, at Camp David I was the only doctor, or at the ranch in Santa Barbara I would be the only doctor there for a month at a time. If something happened during the night or day, you are a long distance from help, so I tried to prepare myself as well as I could for that situation.

During my medical career I had a lot of trauma experience in the emergency room; I am a surgeon. All of you must want to know the criteria for a good White House doctor. I personally think he should be surgically oriented. I felt comfortable being a surgeon; I felt capable of handling accidents, including gunshot wounds, explosions, bombings, auto crashes, helicopter crashes, or anything traumatic. I wasn't as comfortable with heart attacks, but I thought I could handle that. I spent my last month in California preparing myself. I stayed in the hospital for a month, working strictly on heart problems, to prepare myself night or day for a one-on-one encounter with the President in the event he had a heart attack. A stroke is another thing, but I don't think a stroke requires the degree of emergency care that an acute heart attack does. Injuries, I thought I could handle. As a consequence, I spent the last month, while my wife was packing and closing the house, trying to prepare myself for an eventuality that never occurred.

When I arrived at the White House, I continued to have these drills, drilling myself and my unit to try to be prepared for any eventuality that occurred. So what did I find when I arrived and opened the door? There was a military White House medical unit in place. This had been set up previously, but after the shooting in March 1981 it was doubled in size to afford more coverage. Also, the vice president was never covered with the doctor. After President Reagan was shot, he said that he did not want Vice President Bush having second-class medicine; therefore, he wanted him also to have a doctor assigned anywhere he went. That was not true prior to 1981. So we doubled and quadrupled our doctors; we had three when I arrived, four when I left. We had six nurses and a total staff of 14. I was the only civilian.

When I arrived I found that there was no continuing medical education among the staff. They simply were assigned and sat there. They were OK. They were alert and well trained. I went through the whole list of people to see if they were qualified or certified for ATLS (acute trauma life-support) and ACLS (acute cardiac life-support). A few of them were certified, but for the most part they were not certified. I therefore insisted that everybody on my staff be well versed in all these. They had to be recertified every year. That was something that caused great turmoil because half of these people could not qualify.

I did set up the criterion that any new person coming aboard had to be certified before even opening the White House door. That caused a lot of heat, but it still applies today. I think it was a good move. Also I found that a lot of people had been there five, seven, ten years. They had not contributed very much; they were there, but they were certainly not very keen. So we set the criterion that nobody would be there longer than two years.

What does this do? These are by and large younger people; they owe a lot to the military. It's wrong if they sit in the White House and not contribute. I also think if you sit that long, you are not keeping up with new medical techniques. I reduced the maximum period of duty to two years so that there wouldn't be any setting up shop and staying indefinitely. I also felt that they ought to contribute back to the service. Many of these people were sitting there, and their talents were not being used. They were people who were not growing in medicine. To grow in medicine you have to do things; you don't just sit. So I insisted that each one go back to their particular unit: the Navy personnel would go back to Bethesda Hospital, the Army people back to Walter Reed, and the Air Force people back to Medcom Grow. Even the doctors would have to go back and run clinics and then could come back and contribute something to us. I was the only one that didn't return to a unit. I was a civilian medical executive and kept up my skills by attending courses.

We began continuing medical education sessions in the White House, with drills of one kind or another every week. When I arrived, the Secret Service and the medical unit didn't communicate, despite working hand in hand. I found out that they had never drilled together. There had never been a medical drill on Air Force One, at Camp David, at the President's ranch, in the White House, in the motorcade, or in the limousine; there had never been an actual drill for communications, protection or medical procedures. For example, when the President was horseback riding at the ranch, the nurse and the doctor rode together, not on a horse but in a jeep, so that in the event the horses would bolt, we wouldn't get carried away from the scene. But when we did drill, we found out that if you are "taken out," as they say in the Secret Service language, you lose both the nurse and the doctor. So we separated them. In the motorcade now you will always see us way down at the end, because otherwise you can take out the ambulance and all the help and everything together. You have to separate all this, and we found out all these things during realistic drills and critiques.

During the winter, we would drive by motorcade from the White House to Camp David, which is about a two-hour run in the snow. There was never an ambulance with us in case somebody tried to ram the motorcade or there was a bombing or something like that. There was really no medical help other than myself. So we changed that and added an ambulance. We made many changes to improve our effectiveness.

Curiously enough, if you want to change anything in the White House—I don't know about other departments, but I'm sure it is the same—you run across a lot of resistance. The mentality is, it was not done before, so why should we change? Coming in as a new person a I found certain amount of resistance to change. I'm sure that's true at the University of Virginia as well.

Anyway, I stuck by my guns. I tried to show people how it would help. In the long run, the Secret Service and the medical units were much closer together. After all, while they were protecting us, we were helping them in the event of a problem.

Why are we so worried about problems? In 1985 the threat level was quite real and growing rapidly. The threat level was determined by how many crank phone calls and crank letters you received per day. What does the FBI tell you is happening? Are there people coming across the border to get you? This is the age of terrorism. We became, I suppose, overly sensitive, but that was our role, and we were there for that purpose. As a consequence we may have "overkilled." We didn't use these drills to a great extent, but we conducted them in the event we needed them. This is called "contingency planning," and I think it is worthwhile.

I didn't have any power as to where the President traveled when I first arrived there, but I certainly became aware of the need for a doctor or medical input on the President's traveling. The first experience was with the island of Grenada. The President went down there on the day of independence for Grenada, which was one of his pet interests at that time. We went there beforehand to see what medical assets were on the island. The hospital and the prison are one and the same, so you can imagine. Can you take the President of the United States into a hospital in Grenada? No, you can't. What were we to do? We said, "You can't go to Grenada." He said, "But I want to go to Grenada." It was up to us, then, to set up something without bothering him. What did we do? We "commandeered" an aircraft carrier to serve as a hospital and floated it six miles off the island of Grenada within easy helicopter distance. Emergency care would be provided for the President, and/or me or whoever is in the party of approximately four hundred people. That would be provided there right on the spot. Then you have to have some place to go to for definitive care. From the island of Grenada, the nearest place is Miami Beach, which is about a four-hour flight, so the intermediate care provisions were indeed necessary.

Worse than that was the trip to Bali in Indonesia. When they set that up, the President was to go to Bali and then to Tokyo for the Tokyo Summit. We surveyed the medical assets of Bali and the Indonesian group, and they were woefully lacking. What do you do with our group of 600 that went on that trip? I was responsible for 600 people's care. So here again we thought about an aircraft carrier. Manila at that time was more or less under siege and was six hours away, which was too far for an effective medical evacuation. Tokyo is nine hours away; the island of Guam, which is a U. S. possession, is eight hours away, but they only had minimal facilities. Singapore, which is six hours away by air, had good facilities.

What do you do? We again made our own hospital by using an aircraft carrier with our medical team aboard. The military likes to do this because, after all, it serves as a drill. We have the assets anyway. You might as well use them in that regard so that it is not burdening the taxpayer with additional costs. It is simply using what assets you have. They are there but not being utilized that way. The President is commander-in-chief, after all; he, and therefore I, can command such actions.

This is where I think a doctor should have been involved in policy-making. I have an idea that Dr. Lee, the new White House physician, may enter into this after the discussion we had. But recently they have been traveling to Hungary, Poland, and Paris. I don't know how he handles medical problems there. I'm glad I'm out of it. I don't think the average person considers those things, but I'll tell you, as the White House physician I used to wake up at night in a cold sweat wondering what we would do if anything happened.

My first experience with that was flying across to Bonn for the Bonn Summit. I was in a small airplane, Air Force One, and was the only doctor for about 50 people. What do you do if there is a problem aboard over the middle of the Atlantic? You are four hours from Europe and four hours from home, and it's pretty lonesome to be the only medical person there. With the new 747, there will be another medical person. A medical emergency team is a team; it's not just one person. You have to have help. You need about six hands all at once, and I only have two. I used to worry about that. If something happened and I hadn't done the proper or right thing, would I have been under criticism? I'm sure I would. Would my medical colleagues come to my defense in case of a trial? No. Considering class-action suits against the physician for the President, yes, that would have happened because as you know he was terribly popular. If I had allowed anything to happen to this wonderful idol, the world would have come down upon me, and I worried very heavily about that and how I was going to bail out of these things. Fortunately, everything went along all right. We had problems, but not anything massive, so we did get through with that, and I was pleased to get out of that clean.

NARRATOR: Dr. Ruge mentioned regarding this travel business that from 60 years on it is forbidden—according to medical practice—to cross more than three times zones without stopping.

DR. SMITH: Jet lag?

NARRATOR: Yes. He said he raised that issue every time the President was to go more than three time zones, and every time the political people overruled him.

DR. SMITH: That's right. The President once said after we came back from Tokyo, which is a nine-hour time change, "From now on we will never travel east to west. We'll only travel north to south." I was going to abide by that suggestion of the President, but it didn't work out.

The other thing that bothered me about airports was that everybody wants to get on and ride with the President. I'm talking about senators and other political figures. Some of these people are pretty tottery and wheeze along as they come up the gangway. I'm responsible for their care while they're on the plane. What do you do? You can't say, "Get off." I've worked with the head physician of the Congress, Admiral Narva, and said, "If I'm going to take care of these senators or congressmen or political types aboard Air Force One or a helicopter, I've got to know something about them. Are they diabetics? Are they epileptics? How do I prepare?" I'm just one little guy, so I really wanted a medical dossier on everybody, but that never came to pass. Whether it will come to pass with this present administration, I don't know, but I couldn't get it.

Also, Air Force One takes a certain number of various types of people, and there is no room for another medical seat. In other words, you only have 50 seats. The Secret Service has to go; the press has to go; the hairdresser has to go. There is no room for another medical person. As I say, fortunately nothing did happen. Maybe I was overanxious, but I really think I had a case.

QUESTION: President Reagan only went to Bethesda when he needed inpatient care. Just out of curiosity, when the President goes into a hospital like that, where do your responsibilities end, if at all, and the medical staff at the hospital become counsel?

DR. SMITH: I think Dr. Ruge's adage was that "I'm his doctor until he enters the door, and then he's your patient, and then in so many days he is mine again." I tried to keep overall command. After all, he wanted me as his physician and by golly I was going to be his physician. Before, during, and after the operations I was there in the recovery room from the time the surgery was over until he was alert.

QUESTION: You didn't have any trouble with the hospital staff doctors?

DR. SMITH: No. The reason I didn't have trouble with the staff is because I said, "Well, next time I won't come here." One of the nicest things about these hospitals is that they are all vying to get the President. Walter Reed wants to have the President; they have a suite there for him. Bethesda has a very nice suite with a Cabinet room twice this size sitting there all the time with the telephone wires all in; the communication center is there at all times. Walter Reed is the same way. As a consequence, they are all trying to get you to bring the President there.

President Reagan was an army reservist, yet I realized that I wanted to take him to Bethesda because I feel more comfortable there (I'm a Navy type). Dr. Ruge was also Navy; Nixon and Ford were Navy. FDR went to both hospitals but he was Navy, and Kennedy and Johnson were Navy. Most of the Presidents at least since FDR have been Navy, so going to Bethesda was normal.

QUESTION: Why don't you go to a civilian hospital? When the President was shot, he was taken to George Washington University Hospital (near the White House) because it was only three minutes away.

DR. SMITH: George Washington Hospital has three wings; one five-story wing was assigned to the President. It was completely sealed off from the rest of the hospital and had its own elevator, Secret Service, dog sniffing, and its own telephone wires running up and down the hall. That destroys a private hospital, I think. The private hospital loves it because it is great publicity, i.e., "The President came here; therefore, we must be good." But it is no place to put a president because it destroys the hospital as far as the working of the hospital. I don't know about reimbursement from the fiscal point of view, but I would doubt they'd ever recoup the loss. As I said, they all like the publicity; it is very positive. On the other hand, it is very destructive for the hospital and very hard for the Secret Service and ourselves to organize. Where do you put his secretary? Where do you put the head of the Secret Service? Where do you put communication and all the telephones? He's got to have a secure phone if he wants to talk to Mikhail Gorbachev or someone like that, and you've got to install all those things and also protect him while he's there. It is very difficult.

You can do this at Bethesda. Since Bethesda is a military establishment, the average hospital worker doesn't talk too much. You know there aren't rumors. The press is always paying people to find out little things, so we felt it would be better in a military setup. That's why we use them. I think my advice would be to continue to use that facility.

For President Reagan's prostate operation, which was early in 1987, we did bring in a Mayo Clinic team. People asked me, "Why didn't *you* operate on him?" I had not operated on a prostate for three years, so it wouldn't have been right for me to operate on the President. It is just like saying, "Well, play the violin at the symphony." If you haven't practiced for three years, you are not going to do a very good job, and that was the position I was in. I could have done it, I'm sure, but I didn't think it was proper that I do so.

We looked at the facilities the Navy and the Army had for that particular operation. It was very difficult. There must be a hundred urologists in the United States who could have done a superb job, including some at the University of Virginia, but somebody wanted us back at the Mayo Clinic, so we imported a team from Mayo, using Bethesda's facilities. You can do that with no problem, and everyone is happy.

While the Navy chief of surgery set the team up when we did his colon surgery, we also imported civilian teams because I wanted to mix the civilian and military. I think everybody was very happy and comfortable with that.

QUESTION: Security is much easier to maintain in a military hospital, isn't it?

DR. SMITH: Yes it is, because you can give orders and they are usually followed. A lot of people run around and wait for souvenirs of this and that; it is a problem. As I say, the press pays people to dig up information, to watch and give bleeps, and so forth. It's also a problem, but he is very comfortable about it. The military hospitals are also close to Washington and close to the White House. It is an extension of the White House; it's only about ten minutes away.

QUESTION: I was wondering if in addition to your very lucid discussion of acute problems, you would talk a little bit about the sort of thing that you would be concerned about with regular examinations or evaluations. I was thinking particularly with respect to neurological status. Also, the country at large has been made aware of the use of memory aids and the avoidance of unstructured question periods and that sort of thing. I wondered to what extent you would, in the course of evaluations, evaluate the President's recent memory and see to what extent that was holding up.

DR. SMITH: I feel, although I'm a surgeon, I am somewhat of a professional observer. I've been observing people, both in good health and bad for many, many years. I felt reasonably comfortable. I realize I am a friend of his and that makes me somewhat biased. But I would see him every morning at nine o'clock because he came down the elevator from the family quarters and went over to the Oval Office. I would be standing there, not to say, "Hey, how are you doing? Take your blood pressure, take your pulse," but simply to watch him and say, "Good morning." For the two years I was there, every morning at nine o'clock he was absolutely alert, pleasant, well groomed, well dressed; then maybe we'd make small talk at that point. At five or five-thirty or six in the afternoon, he would come back from the Oval Office to go back upstairs; he would say, "Remember what we were talking about this morning? I just thought about the answer to that," or something like that. Here is a man who had seen maybe a hundred different people all day long who were involved in discussions and so forth. I felt that was a little way I had of discerning. I think on a day-to-day basis I thought I could tell. We didn't run any memory tests per se. These are personal observations.

QUESTION: How frequent and how extensive were your regular examinations?

DR. SMITH: As extensive as we wanted. We would do a general examination. The first time I was in charge, I found that a stress test had never been performed on him, a stress test to evaluate his cardiac status. It is not 100 percent accurate, but at least it is helpful. I was preparing myself to handle things. If you know a person is a diabetic then you can focus on diabetes; if they are an epileptic you can focus on that. But I knew nothing about his cardiac status, nor did he know anything about mine, for example, so I had a stress test to be sure I was OK. He doesn't want an impaired doctor, right? Anyway, we did perform the first stress test. I was criticized rather strongly for this because they said, "Well, now what if we find something? How are we going to handle it?" I said, "Well, we'll handle it if we find it." We didn't find anything, but it made me more comfortable on transpacific flights of eight hours between Guam and Hawaii that probably nothing would happen to him from a cardiac point of view if you believe in the stress test. We don't have many tests to prove this. You know the old story about the fellow who left the stress test, went outside and fell over dead. Well, this can happen, but I think by and large the test is helpful.

We ran through all the systems; we had an ophthalmologist check his eyes; we had a hearing doctor check his hearing because his own hearing doctors were on the West Coast. We'd go out there for Christmas and New Year's, and the doctor would run another hearing test out there. It was quite complete.

There is much discussion concerning the annual physical examinations. I think the public must know. I think I must know, so maybe we overdid it. We were landing once at Bethesda, and he said, "How many times have I landed in this hospital?" I said, "I think it's 28 to be exact." To move him for a physical exam was a big undertaking. You don't do it lightly. We couldn't carry out all these things in the White House because we really don't have an X-ray machine. We could do an EKG and certain other things, but we couldn't do them all. I tried to stick to the annual physical so it would be done and in place, and it does establish a baseline for the future.

NARRATOR: How often do you do colonoscopies?

DR. SMITH: After his original operation it was done every six months for a year and a half, and then once a year. The 13th of July will be his third-year anniversary for this particular operation. He will have one this year, and it will probably be annual from now on. It has been four years now, but there has been no evidence of recurrence to date.

QUESTION: Do you think there should be a second opinion? I've read or heard somewhere that a second opinion is necessary for determining when the President is able to resume his duties, say after a heart attack, accident, or operation.

DR. SMITH: Oh, yes. I think everything like that is done by committee. We never did anything unless the four White House doctors got together and made a decision. Our White House doctors considered me as a surgeon. Dr. Hutton was a surgeon, Dr. Lee was a cardiologist, and Dr. Gasser was an internist.

QUESTION: Was there just one decision?

DR. SMITH: No. This is done by committee within the White House. We discussed it, added our input, and then made the decision. We'd go out to Bethesda with him and work together in concert. So there is not one head, never has been, and I'm sure never will be.

QUESTION: We are becoming more cholesterol- and diet-conscious all the time, and I was wondering whether you recall what the President's cholesterol level was, whether the Mayo Clinic took care of this particular thing, and whether he was on a special diet.

He seems to maintain his weight very well. Would you care to comment on that?

DR. SMITH: I remember his cholesterol extremely well because the first time they came out with the cholesterol test was in March 1985, which was my first annual physical with him. Somehow the numbers came out entirely wrong; they would have classified a patient in the dying stage. They were as low as 90 or 60, something completely wrong. It should have been 160 instead of 60, and I got calls from all over the United States asking why the levels were so low. Anyway, his cholesterol is fine, and his blood pressure was always good. I'm not medically involved with him anymore, although I see him in a personal relationship.

As far as nutrition, he is very moderate in everything. He used to smoke a pipe, but his older brother Neil developed cancer of the larynx. He got rid of the pipe, and that was the end of that. He does not smoke. He drinks only for toasts, that is, he sips some wine for toasts and things like that. He doesn't really drink. He exercises daily in the morning and the afternoon. Later, he takes a shower and puts on his pajamas and bathrobe, and they read and watch television. He does a lot of reading. He leads a very moderate life; he sleeps very well. I never saw him asleep in the Cabinet meeting like some people reported. When I was at the ranch with him he rode every morning, and we worked very hard every afternoon chopping wood and clearing brush, so I know he didn't sleep in the afternoon.

QUESTION: He got calls from all over the country about his cholesterol. How did everyone find out what his cholesterol was?

DR. SMITH: Unfortunately, it came out in the paper.

QUESTION: How did the paper find out?

DR. SMITH: When I first arrived, nobody told me how to handle the press with medical issues. There was no book written for me. Dr. Ruge was OK, but he said, "Call me if you have any problems. I won't call you," and that was that. Larry Speakes was the White House press secretary at that time. After the physical he sent down his deputy who said, "OK, give me everything." I said, "Yes, sir."

Well, I didn't know. I thought they would take what they wanted out of this and put in the media what they thought was proper. They put it all in. The first lady didn't think that was quite proper. Anyway, I learned my lesson. I became very ambiguous after that, and they had a hard time getting anything out of me because I thought I had been taken. The cholesterol level, however, did come out in that one.

The way we did it was in generalities: "All his tests were normal, and no further examination is required." That way, we didn't put all the numbers down, because if you put a number down and it varies from the earlier one, everybody is going to get upset.

QUESTION: Having been a president's physician, how much privacy do you think the president should have? I think the country and the government go way too far in exposing everything about him. The president's intestinal story is one example.

DR. SMITH: That's the media. They want to know everything, and they put it in.

QUESTION: Why not contest the policy?

DR. SMITH: I think you have to have a certain amount of privacy and a certain amount of dignity. I don't think all these little details are important in the functioning of the presidency and setting policy. A certain amount is: What's the future look like, how is he today, and so forth.

I was sitting with the President, and I said, "You know, all this teaching the masses about all these things, that is, how the cystoscope works, how the colonoscopy works with the red light flashing on the end of it, all the graphics that came out on TV, does this bother you?" He said, "Well, if you think it is helping anybody and it does any good, then it is not bothering me."

To follow up on that, colonoscopies have gone up 300 percent from the mid part of 1985 until the present time; hearing aids have gone up 75 percent; sigmoidoscopies have doubled in number in the United States. Many, many doctors have called or written to thank me because now when a patient comes in they say, "You need to have this done." The patient says, "Oh, like the President?" The doctor says, "Yes, the same thing." I had people calling me from

Peru, Egypt, all kinds of places about how things went and what could I suggest to them. Publicity is fantastic.

When you see that the use of colonoscopies has tripled since 1985, that has to be good. We are saving some lives because of this. So I think the President should be pleased. There is more to being a president than the political aspects. I think as a model for medicine, he has been absolutely superb.

Take into consideration colonoscopies, cystoscopies, prostate operations, skin surgery, and Mrs. Reagan's mammograms for diagnosis of cancer of the breast—all of them have been laid out, discussed, and pontificated upon. There is really very little left to discuss, so the public has truly been educated, not only locally but internationally. I think it is a very positive thing. I can't imagine any better medical education in the world that's occurred since 1985, not of my doing, but because of his problems. It was not only well publicized, but he bounced out of all these things beautifully, both medically and physically, and I think gave a good example of what can happen. It has been very positive for a lot of people.

NARRATOR: Could you give us any reaction to this spat between Donald Regan and the first lady? It had to do with how soon he should go on the road, as I understand it, after the cancer surgery. Were you drawn into that?

DR. SMITH: Oh, yes. I have certain rules that I developed during my practice and I think they are valid today. Don Regan wants to portray the President as a viable, decision-making personality for the media, either by traveling, by TV, or by giving talks on the radio. So that is his mission. My mission was to keep that down, and the first lady's mission was to keep that down. That's why after a prostate operation my rule in private practice was no activities, including golf and so forth, for three weeks, and that's exactly what they did. The only thing he did at the end of the third week was to give the State of the Union message, which I mildly opposed, but statutorily speaking, that's when the State of the Union address must be given. It turned out to be the 21st day after his prostate operation, by coincidence.

He wanted desperately to go to the ranch to recover from his colon surgery, which is an abdominal operation. He wanted to ride a horse; I wouldn't let him ride a horse because if you do something wrong, your incision may be weakened and then you have problems the rest of your life. It is not worth it for a week.

But the politician wants him to look viable, ready, eager, saddled up, and ready to go so that the doctor has to hold him back. The first lady, in deference to her, did hold him down because they would run with him. The demands on him are terrible, and somebody has got to say, "Hey, stop." I think that was her job and my job. I think we had a nice balance.

QUESTION: Did you establish or initiate any special or routine preventive medical measures?

DR. SMITH: No, other than common sense things you probably practice yourself, such as a reasonable amount of sleep.

QUESTION: So there was nothing special?

DR. SMITH: No. He didn't do anything that was extraordinary. He didn't eat twenty pounds of peanuts a day or anything like that. He is a very conservative person. They both are, and I think they led a normal, easy lifestyle.

QUESTION: Did you take care of the President's wife?

DR. SMITH: Yes. The President, Vice President Bush, Mrs. Reagan, and Mrs. Bush were my four sole responsibilities. As I say, Vice President Bush was never given a doctor until after the March 1981 shooting. Because of the rise in the terrorist threats, they wanted to have good security and coverage, so we upped our staff to give them both coverage. We ran their physical examinations, and they could come to us with any complaints. I didn't, for example, perform gynecological checkups and such; we brought in a gynecologist for that. Eye exams were conducted by an ophthalmologist; skin problems were handled by a dermatologist, and so on. I was responsible for administrating them, organizing them, timing them, and performing other similar services.

Anybody else in the White House who wanted to stop by and discuss something, such as visitors who poured through there during the day, were also my responsibilities. These people would come from all over the country; they'd fly in without eating breakfast or sleeping. They'd come in and collapse. Others would collapse while meeting the President. It is awesome to meet the President. Big, strong people would meet the President and get clammy and would wilt and get pale. It is a problem, including doctors. I met two doctors who came in and said, "What do I do when I meet the President?" I said, "Don't do anything. The President is very disarming. Just stand there, smile, and he will take the conversation." And he did; he made you feel at home instantly. But afterwards they said, "You know, just meeting this man, I feel weak." People do things emotionally. Although he's not a king, just to be in the Oval Office and meeting the President of the United States is an awesome thing for a lot of people.

The White House medical unit is responsible for the military personnel stationed there. The military are entitled to medical care, and there are a lot of military in the White House. We are responsible for all the honor guard, all communications, and security who are not military. We are responsible for about 2,000 people.

We also try to do what is called "first aid in the working place" to keep people on the job. To leave the White House, go out and park your car, see an outside doctor, and come back consumes approximately half of a day. So to keep the White House working efficiently, we tried to do what we could. For example, we give allergy shots to people on their doctor's prescription, mainly to keep them on the job. We did all that; we did any courtesy requested to try to make people happy. We gave advice and suggested referrals.

QUESTION: On the long plane trips, did you make sure he exercised?

DR. SMITH: He did that a lot. He didn't sleep well on airplanes, although he and the first lady had the only bunks on the plane. He did roam around and read a lot. They had many meetings: speech-writing meetings, decision-making meetings on policy, and so on. Air Force One was simply an extension of the White House, as were his ranch and Camp David. Anywhere he goes the White House goes with him.

I think one of his best statements was: "The job never changes, only the scenery." In other words, the harassment never stops. He was always in communication. They were always handing him papers and people were always running in telling him things.

It really never changes, night or day, the whole time. He never can escape the responsibility of the office.

QUESTION: How about visiting heads of state? Did they have their own doctors or were you responsible? How did you handle that?

DR. SMITH: They bring their own doctors, by and large. It depends.

QUESTION: Take Mrs. Thatcher for example.

DR. SMITH: Mrs. Thatcher? No. But Princess Diana and Prince Charles brought their own; other principals brought their own doctors. Interestingly enough, being a doctor on these tours, you are kind of left out in the cold. They all go in a meeting room, and you sit out in the hall because you are not a politician and you don't belong in there in a state meeting. You have nothing to offer, and so you belong outside. Dr. Ruge didn't like that, but I didn't mind it. I think he prepared me for it. As a consequence, I accepted that, and I thought my role was to be a doctor and not to be a politician. They never asked me for any input, and I never gave any input. That's the way it worked.

I did find lonesome doctors on these other state visits. So I set up a deal with the State Department and said, "Now, when this group comes, if there is a doctor call me, and if he comes to the White House for a lunch or a state party that night, be sure and contact me, and I will put him under my wing. I'll take him to lunch." Because, you see, doctors are unique. I can meet a doctor from Afghanistan, and while we do not we talk the same language, Latin is a common language, and we have medical things in common. We can look at instruments, we can look at techniques, we can look at how you do things and get along OK.

I invited these people in and took care of them, and before the two years were out I had met 30 doctors who came through. In fact, I was going to start a VVIP Medical Association because every time I went to the summit I'd see the same five or seven doctors: Mitterrand's doctor, Kohl's doctor, etc.

COMMENT: Then you get a free lunch anywhere in the world.

DR. SMITH: That's right. These doctors have unique problems, VVIP problems, because they are dealing with heads of state. Wouldn't it be interesting to form such an association? So I started to set it up for the Tokyo Summit where we would all be together, but everybody was running around so fast. President Reagan was meeting with President Mitterrand, Mitterrand is meeting with Thatcher, and they are all running around to these one-on-ones, so you could never get the doctors together, and my association kind of fell through. But I still think VVIP care is a very interesting facet in the medical world.

QUESTION: Does the President as a rule require of his personal physician advice on national medical matters, say Medicare?

DR. SMITH: Yes he does, particularly people who write him, friends of his who have, say, cancer of the prostate or something similar. He would come to me and say, "Read this letter and tell me tonight what you think about it."

Medical legislation is handled by a policy-making committee; these are medical doctors on that policy-making committee, such as Otis Bowen, the secretary of health and human services. They handle the policy. I think the President approves or disapproves it, but by and large on a day-to-day basis I don't think he is too aware of it.

QUESTION: Does the surgeon general handle that?

DR. SMITH: Surgeon General Koop?

COMMENT: Yes. I mean the political end of it.

DR. SMITH: No, not policy-making. That's handled by Health and Human Services and Medicare, for example. It has nothing to do with Surgeon General Koop, although he could have some influence. The President does get medical briefings; that is, the White House invites experts from all fields to meet for luncheon sessions with the President and brief him, and I was asked to sit in on those. In other words, there is a surgeon, an immunologist, and a pediatrician all giving a little information so the President will know what is going on. This is done for all facets of any particular field to try to keep the President up to date because it is very difficult for him. So a great effort is made to keep him, not entertained, but keep him informed as to what is going on. Most of the decisions are made, and then he approves or disapproves, I think, is the way it works.

COMMENT: You've made it clear that in your view President Reagan was in excellent mental health.

DR. SMITH: Yes, sir.

QUESTION: What kind of preparation did you have or what kind of plan did you have in case there should be a depression or a panic state or perhaps substance abuse, something of that kind? How would you have dealt with that?

DR. SMITH: Well, I don't know where he'd get his substance, because I wouldn't give it to him, and he didn't drink.

QUESTION: I understand, but you are a representative of a line of doctors for the President. There is no guarantee that any given president is not going to become depressed or have an anxiety attack. What kind of policy did you have?

DR. SMITH: I would just have to have addressed that as it arrived, to be honest with you. I can't imagine him coming down in the morning smashed or seeing him drunk at a party. I've never seen it, and I've known him for 22 years.

QUESTION: So you really individualize that. You were thinking of President Reagan and not thinking in terms of others?

DR. SMITH: In the old days I think Dwight Eisenhower and his doctor used to have scotch together before bed, and I never did that. It wouldn't be appropriate, and I don't think he'd want it. But I think FDR and his doctor used to sit around and drink together, and I'm sure Churchill and his doctor sat around and drank brandy together and smoked cigars.

I think I'd just have to handle that as it came up. I don't know where he'd get a chemical substance anyway; I guess it could be brought in to him. He never took a sleeping pill in my tenure and never requested medicine. He ran his own show. I'm not sure I answered your question.

QUESTION: Well, I was just wondering what would be the appropriate role of the President's physician in the event of that problem?

DR. SMITH: You are thinking of temporary disability?

QUESTION: You don't always know whether it's temporary or not. Suppose that Secretary of Defense Forrestal had been president and trouble had occurred?

DR. SMITH: But he had a track record of depression, you know, long before he dove off the Bethesda Naval Medical Center. I didn't believe, however, that the President had any track record that should have worried me. I suppose he could have. During the Iran-contra affair I doubled my surveillance because I thought it was a time he might become depressed. I couldn't detect any such signs.

COMMENT: They say that there are three chances in four that the suicide attempter has seen his physician within a week before it happens, so possibly there are some indications.

DR. SMITH: I think you have some indications, but I never saw any. I personally feel I was keen to that. If he had been disabled, I would have invoked the Twenty-fifth Amendment. I would have had no hesitancy. I prepared myself for that, and I would have—unlike FDR's doctor, unlike Wilson's doctor, unlike Grover Cleveland's doctor—because I had the Twenty-fifth Amendment with me all the time. I could practically recite it, and I think I would have used it if necessary, because I had the country's interests at heart.

NARRATOR: Maybe we should let you in on a dirty little secret. The man who has just been questioning you was head of psychiatry at the University of Chicago.

DR. SMITH: Maybe he can tell me something, I don't know. I think during the two years I was there I made it through.

QUESTION: If a president becomes comatose, how does the transfer of power begin?

DR. SMITH: That's in the Twenty-fifth Amendment; it's automatic. The vice president and the Cabinet transmit a letter to Congress, and that's it.

QUESTION: Even if the president is still breathing it, it takes effect?

DR. SMITH: Oh, yes. If he can't sign his name, you can impose the Twenty-fifth Amendment. As I say, I got into trouble during my two years during the four-hour colon operation when he didn't invoke it. Everybody says, "Well, where were you when the decision was made?" I was at his bedside.

We didn't expect to have to have this operation. On Friday afternoon we took a look, and at three o'clock there it was, a tumor. So I was busy preparing to get ready for surgery the next day—Saturday noon. Honestly, I didn't think about the Twenty-fifth Amendment. I left it up to the chief of staff, Don Regan, because I was busy laying out our plans. During that evening we ran special tests to be sure it hadn't spread. It gave no time to think about the Twenty-fifth Amendment. According to your governmental affairs group here it should have been handled by this protocol that was set up by the Twenty-fifth Amendment. But in that instance it wasn't, but I think from now on it will be.

QUESTION: What do you do in a dental extraction where a local anesthetic is used? Do you invoke it then?

DR. SMITH: No. They asked me. Nor do you do it, for example, on a colonoscopy where he is given sedation but not a general anesthetic. They asked me, "What's it like?" I said to Don Regan, Larry Speakes, and the President's counsel, Fred Fielding—and I've been taken to task in Larry Speakes' book because I was looking for an example that a layman would understand—"It's like having a martini." Well, they said, "It depends on how many martinis." I said, "That's true." One person said, "Well, if I had three I could still sign my name." I said, "I couldn't." So it is an individual problem, but I was trying to give a layman's idea of what sedation is like. It affects people in different ways.

Should you invoke the Twenty-fifth Amendment in such a case? I would say no, because I think he is still arousable like somebody who has had two martinis and dozes off. Now whether they could make a correct decision is an individual problem.

This came up, as I say, in the books that have been written by Don Regan and Larry Speakes. They think I was ambiguous and flippant about this, but it was about the test; it was not about the general anesthetic. They got their wording wrong in their books.

NARRATOR: Does this sedation issue make it even more important that the physician know the President?

DR. SMITH: I think so, his capabilities. Would you agree? Some people can handle things differently than others.

NARRATOR: They told me the other day I was going to go to sleep after the sedation; instead of that I talked more than I've talked in a long time.

DR. SMITH: Could you have made a rational decision on whether to retaliate for an atomic bomb? No, this is the problem. This is what you are thinking about. That's what I was thinking about.

I don't think historically there were many cases that happened within a period of only three minutes. Three minutes, three weeks, three months, three years—in the old days it didn't matter. Now, three minutes is vital, and it's a different ball game. But it is fortunate nothing has happened in so short a period of time that you couldn't get over sedation, like two or three hours. Some people do get hyper, as you say. They could make a bad judgment there as well.

NARRATOR: We are very grateful to you for spending this time with us.

CHAPTER 11

THE REAGAN PRESIDENCY

EDWIN MEESE

NARRATOR: It is a great pleasure to have former Attorney General Edwin Meese with us. He will make a few opening statements and then will respond to questions.

MR. MEESE: I am particularly appreciative of the oral history program at the Miller Center. As a former professor, I share your interest in history. I believe the question-and-answer format of this and other oral history programs makes an important contribution to the historical record.

Much can be learned about contemporary policy from each presidency. For example, with the Iraq and Persian Gulf problems, there is a great deal that can be learned from the policies of the Reagan administration. President Bush would not have been able to perform the rapid military mobilization and deployment in the Persian Gulf ten years ago. The planning, policies, and decisions that were made during the last decade have contemporary as well as historical value.

NARRATOR: Many in the Reagan administration have talked about your role as rapporteur within Reagan's federal and state administrations. Did you share that function with anybody else? And what relevance does it have for other administrations?

MR. MEESE: All presidents, like all governors, have their own style, and their staffs develop in response to that style. In the case of the president's staff, the president must feel comfortable with

223

each staff member chosen. In the gubernatorial days, from 1967 through 1974, there were really two of us who acted as rapporteurs.

The first person who had this role was Bill Clark, who later served as the secretary of the interior and before that as the assistant for national security affairs. He was Governor Reagan's chief of staff in California in 1967 and 1968. I took over that role in 1969 through 1974.

One of the things we both found as the respective heads of the governor's staff was that Mr. Reagan liked to have many people in on decision making. He developed his Cabinet concept in California with about half a dozen people who comprised the Cabinet. Together, these six people had all of the agencies and departments of state government under their management supervision. The President liked to call this his board of directors. They met with him regularly to provide their input on policy decisions. The role of the chief of staff, which developed during the six years that I was there, was to summarize the views at the end of the discussion and to identify the Governor's options so that he could decide which of the alternatives he preferred. When Ronald Reagan became President, he liked this system, and we adapted it to his federal administration. This was where the idea of Cabinet councils developed on a federal level.

In state government, there is much more interdepartmental activity which more or less encompasses everyone in the Cabinet. In the federal government, it would be a waste of time to have all the members of the Cabinet in on every major decision. For example, the secretary of education is not usually interested in setting foreign policy or defense policy, and conversely, the secretary of state is not interested in what is happening in Health and Human Services. Thus, the President developed the idea of Cabinet councils, which was a group of the Cabinet less than the whole that advised him on those areas of which that council had knowledge. Therefore, my role in the first term, which carried over from the California days, was to summarize at the end of the discussion what had been said and to lay out the options for the President and let him make a decision. While I was in the White House as counselor to the President (from Inaugural Day in January 1981 through the time that I left to become attorney general in February 1985), I carried out this role.

After I left and took on a Cabinet position, it was less appropriate for me to be a broad summarizer since I was, in a sense, an advocate for a particular part of the government. Don Regan, as the new chief of staff, performed my old role. With Regan, however, the role was different, largely because of the many years of experience I had with the President prior to his taking office.

QUESTION: You knew the President personally and officially for a longer period of time than almost anyone who has the capability of judging his career. Do you think the picture of President Reagan presented by the media was truly representative of the man as you knew him?

MR. MEESE: The media accurately presented his ability as a communicator. He was called the "great communicator" as far back as the beginning of the 1980 campaign. It was an accurate perception by the press of one of the President's greatest strengths. He had the ability to directly communicate with people during the entire time that I knew him. He could be talking to an audience of a few people or 3,000 people, and most people would get the impression that he was talking directly to them. He communicated directly to all kinds of groups.

Probably the most glaring inaccuracy of the press was the deliberate attempt to project him as being laid-back. The public was led to believe that somehow he was only playing at the role of President rather than being deeply involved. This portrayal came from the fact, I think, that he recognized that the federal government is such a large enterprise, that if he wasted his time on the minutiae, he would not be able to concentrate on the big decisions. Contrary to the press's perception, he made every major policy decision in the government. These decisions, of course, were not made in the presence of the press. The Cabinet process that I mentioned was not open to the press.

President Reagan did not try to grandstand. As a result of this, many people in the government, particularly some on the White House staff, tried to magnify their own positions and importance with the press, which I guess is a natural human trait. However, the important policy decisions were made by the President, primarily through the Cabinet-council process.

Because he was different from some prior presidents who had not used the Cabinet as much and who made most of their decisions through their contact with one or two members of the White House staff, Ronald Reagan was perceived by the press as being an inactive president. Ronald Reagan was active, but he had an ability to delegate the implementation of decisions, because he felt this was something that other people could do.

The President was a very good conceptual thinker and had his eye on the big picture. He felt he should give a vision of where the country ought to be going, what the government ought to be doing, and what the broad policy guidelines should be. Then he expected others to carry this out, sometimes to his detriment when people didn't do what they should have.

In Don Regan's book, for example, Don says that he felt he didn't get adequate direction from the President during the time he was secretary of the treasury. However, all the things he did as secretary of the treasury were the things that Ronald Reagan wanted done. The economic policies were policies that were outlined in the election campaign of 1980. So whether Don realized it or not, he had policy guidance. Part of this guidance was derived from Ronald Reagan's speeches to the public, part was derived from the Cabinet meetings, and most was derived from smaller group meetings in which the secretary of the treasury and others participated. I think this was true of the other Cabinet members as well. The longer each Cabinet member worked with Ronald Reagan, the more they appreciated his style.

The idea that he wasn't a direct participant in decision making was not accurate. At times, he could get very deeply involved. One of the best examples of this was in the first year of his presidency. We had naval exercises at sea at a time in which Gadhafi had said he was extending the territorial limits of Libya into the Mediterranean Sea beyond the normal 12-mile limit. He was going out 200 miles or so and, in effect, he was saying that part of the international waters belonged to Libya. He warned that if our planes or ships traversed that area, he was going to shoot them down. We felt, after conferring with our allies, that we could not allow any country to claim for its own what had clearly been international waters in which every country had the right of navigation.

During this time, because it was such a key issue, the issue of the rules of engagement was brought to the President in a National Security Council meeting. I remember that meeting very well. The admiral asked the President, "Suppose the Libyan planes shoot at our planes and then flee back into Libyan territory. Do you authorize us to follow them?" President Reagan said, very clearly, "You can follow them into their own damn hangers if you have to!"

It was more than just a flip remark. He was making it clear to the Navy that they would have full backing. If they were attacked, they could take full, complete action to defend themselves, which meant they could fire upon Libyan planes. Therefore, when a commander and his wingman were fired upon by the Libyans, they didn't have any questions in the back of their minds as to whether they would be fully backed by the commander-in-chief. This was how the President operated. He made it clear what his position was.

That's kind of a long answer to your question, but I think the press didn't get it right as to the degree of his involvement in the presidency. It was much greater than the general conventional wisdom among the news media.

QUESTION: If ever a man was qualified to be an associate justice, it was Robert Bork. What went wrong when Robert Bork's confirmation was denied?

MR. MEESE: There were several things. I agree with you. In the history of this country, it would be hard to find anyone who by intellect, background, and experience was better qualified. Several things came together at one time which kept Judge Bork from being confirmed. The ultraliberal left wing, who have an interest in the Supreme Court decisions, had been spoiling for a victory since they were defeated previously when Scalia was confirmed and Rehnquist was made chief justice. They had suffered defeats on several legislative issues. They also tried to keep me from becoming attorney general. So, they were spoiling for an opportunity to defeat the President and score a political victory.

A second factor was that the Senate had changed shortly before Bork's appointment from control by the Republican party to control by the Democrats. Bork's was the first major confirmation hearing and the most important appointment that had come before the Senate Judiciary Committee after that change. So there was an eager group of Democratic senators, led by Senator Joseph Biden (Del.) and Senator Edward Kennedy (Mass.), who were anxious to challenge the appointment.

A third aspect was the political action group called the People for the American Way, which had a tremendous amount of money. What had been historically a dignified confirmation process was turned into a political contest with TV ads in the home states of the senators on the committee and grass-roots mobilization of people like there would be in a presidential campaign.

Finally, Judge Bork was a person who had been unusually candid in his writings as a law professor, because he was not grooming himself for a position in the Supreme Court. As law professors do, Judge Bork wrote law review articles, magazine articles, and other commentaries in which he set forth his views in great detail. These ultraliberal groups did not agree with his views, so they opposed him. The combination of the political nature of the confirmation process, the extreme lengths to which the opposition groups went, and Bork's own candid nature led to the denial of his confirmation. Even with all of these negative factors, the vote on his confirmation was 58 to 42, so he came close.

COMMENT: There was quite a critical comment that President Reagan failed to take a stand on Bork.

MR. MEESE: I saw that comment. Most of it was after the fact. My own view is that this was not true. I think it came from the perception that the White House had gotten into the fray too late. In retrospect, I think that was an accurate perception. However, this was not due to any lack of support by the President. I was in meetings with Bob Bork, his wife, his family, and the President during that whole period. There was never any doubt as to the President's total support and willingness to go to any length that he could legitimately go on Bork's behalf. The President thought that this was going to be a hard-fought confirmation battle. No one realized, however, at the start, that the process would turn into a political contest involving TV ads and all that. I think if there had been a perception that the nature of the contest had changed, then the White House would have done more for Judge Bork at the beginning. Instead, work was done to prepare Bob Bork in what they call "murder board" sessions, practice sessions for the tough questioning expected in the confirmation hearings. It wasn't until Congress came back from the recess, just prior to the start of the hearings, that the political campaign against Bork began. Even if the President and the White House staff had been prepared for the negative campaigning, as governmental institutions they would not have had the money or the resources to match the People for the American Way, who had virtually unlimited funds. Millions of dollars were put into defeating the confirmation, so it would have been difficult to get Judge Bork confirmed even if the opposition had been anticipated. However, there was no lack of presidential support. It was just a matter of the other side going to unprecedented lengths to put public pressure on the senators to reject him. Not only has this not been done in the past, but I think it is an improper use of the confirmation process. The senators are supposed to look at the qualifications of the individual. A confirmation hearing is not supposed to be a political contest.

QUESTION: Mr. Reagan was perceived by many as avoiding ad-lib comments on issues and as being considerably reliant on his cue cards. In your view, is this perception correct? If so, did this have to do with lack of preparation or with problems involving short-term memory?

MR. MEESE: Again, this is an exaggeration by the press. I think it came from some mistakes that were made by the people in the White House staff who had the responsibility for handling the media and who scheduled too few press conferences.

When we were in California, then Governor Reagan held a press conference every week virtually without fail unless he was out of the country or out of the state. As a result, his relationship with the press was ongoing. He took whatever questions might come up each week, and in addition, he had a press conference with editors of high school newspapers or leaders of high school groups every other week. As a result, he remained current on every issue of state government. I used to schedule a luncheon every Monday with all the Cabinet members and top members of his staff at which we would kick around what was going on in the state government and issues that might come up at news conferences.

There was no systematic preparation for press conferences in the White House to the same extent where he could assimilate this information. Instead, the press conferences were very rare. As you saw, they were held in prime time with him coming down the red carpet. Because of their infrequency, they became almost gladiatorial contests between the President and the news media. As a result, instead of trying to elicit information, the press tried to ask him questions that he couldn't answer. It became more of a contest than it did an informative conference. Also for him, the preparation sessions lasted only two or three hours for the two days preceding the conference. You cannot cram everything that is going on in government into two hours. It would have been much better if they had kept the pattern that we had used in California. Actually, the idea that he was dependent on cue cards is not accurate. There is no way that he could have gone into that one-on-one negotiation session with Gorbachev, for example, when they first met in Geneva and on other occasions if he was dependent on cue cards. They were all-day sessions and there was nobody there to coach him. He was fully prepared. Time after time in meetings with foreign leaders or others, he would display his tremendously retentive memory. As a matter of fact, one of the things I felt as a staff member was that I had better be sure the information I gave him was correct, because he would remember it virtually word for word and would use it that way.

QUESTION: When President Reagan took office in 1981, the savings and loan industry was in dire straits because of the high interest rates experienced during the Carter years. Your administration made several attempts to try to alleviate that situation. Can you give us some reflections on efforts you made at that time to try to correct the problem and your perspective now on the situation?

MR. MEESE: The savings and loan industry's problems when we first came in were different from the problems experienced since 1986. In 1981, we were concerned with coping with the high interest rates. The savings and loans were funding home loans that had been granted during the 1970s when interest rates were low. They were getting small returns of 5 and 6 percent or less on their loans and were having to pay—because of the sky-high interest rates during the Carter administration—as high as 17 or 18 percent to get their money and as high as 9 or 10 percent to attract savers. So, they had a problem.

A couple of things happened. In 1980, still during the Carter administration, the limitation on deposit insurance was raised from $40,000 per account to $100,000 per account. Then, in order to cope with the high interest rates, the Garn–St. Germain Depository Institutions Act of 1982 allowed savings and loans companies to go beyond housing loans into other, more speculative forms of investment.

After these changes, several things happened. In some cases, you just had errors of judgment. Savings and loan officers and directors with no experience in these other investment areas frankly made investment mistakes in granting loans. Secondly, new people who were attracted by the new freedom in investing came into the savings and loan industry without experience in that industry. These people were speculative in their nature. In many cases, they not only made bad decisions, but they also gave loans to people who were not worthy of those loans. Finally, quite frankly, you had some people who were not as honest and ethical as they should have been. They found ways to skim a lot of the profits off the top rather than plow these profits back into the business as had been the traditional practice in the industry.

There was one mistake, I think, that the administration made. There was a general feeling that we should deregulate business to the greatest extent possible, that regulatory reform meant that there should be less governmental regulation, only what was necessary for the public health and safety, because overregulation throughout the government had crept up over the years. The difference in regulation of the savings and loan field—and it would be true of the banking field as well—is that the federal government has a different relationship to those industries. The administration should have regulated, not as a government for whom a minimum level of regulation was necessary to protect the public, but as an insurance company or a guarantor of any sort would have regulated the industry or the firms that they were guaranteeing. This would have meant a much higher level of audit and examination.

To say the savings and loan crisis is the fault of one administration or one party, whether it be Democrats or Republicans, is inaccurate. Unfortunately, there is enough blame to go around. The crisis happened not through any desire of the federal government to have it happen, but because many problems were not seen in time. Hindsight is always perfect. If some problems had been foreseen in 1982 and 1983 as they later became visible in 1989 and 1990, then we would have had a far different result.

Personalities sometimes play a big part in how policy develops. In the Reagan administration, there were some basic disagreements occurring between Ed Gray, the chairman of the Federal Home Loan Bank Board, which had the responsibility for savings and loan associations, and some of the people in the White House. I think this friction added to the unwillingness in the Office of Management and Budget to grant more bank examiners. However, it is interesting that when the FBI in 1986 and 1987 requested more FBI agents to work on these cases as they started to unfold, which OMB supported, the Congress turned down those requests for additional investigators.

QUESTION: Could you comment on the relationship between George Bush and Ronald Reagan?

MR. MEESE: The relationship between George Bush and Ronald Reagan was probably unique between a president and a vice president. As a result of this relationship, I think that George Bush was the most qualified person in history to become president. I say this because for eight years he had the actual experience of seeing everything that went on in the presidency.

Even in his California days, then-Governor Reagan felt that he and the lieutenant governor ought to actively work together. He felt that there should be no information kept from the lieutenant governor, because he might have to take over some day. Ronald Reagan does not have an ego problem; therefore, he does not have to exclude other people in order to play up himself. He was very comfortable with working closely with his lieutenant governor.

When George Bush became vice president, President Reagan literally brought him into every meeting. The first thing each morning, the President met with Jim Baker, Mike Deaver, and me, and he had the vice president sit in at those meetings so he would hear even the small details of the President's office or the White House. Then at 9:30 a.m. when the President had his national security briefing, Vice President Bush was always a participant, and so on throughout the day. He was included at every major meeting. In addition, the President and Vice President had a private lunch every Thursday during which they talked over their views.

The press had the impression that Vice President Bush was not very active. However, the reason for this was that George Bush did not want to step on President Reagan's lines, as it were. He did not seek any of the limelight for himself, so his advice to the President was given in private. He did not give speeches saying what the President ought to do. He felt his role was to provide advice privately and, whether his advice was followed or not, to understand that the President makes the final decisions. I was present on many occasions, particularly as the 1988 elections approached, when the vice president told the President what he thought the right thing to do would be. In one case, he was giving advice on a few appointments which could hurt him politically because it would alienate some people who might have been counted on to support him when he ran for President. Vice President Bush felt compelled, for the President's and the country's interest, to give the President his best advice even though it was counterproductive personally. As a result, I think their relationship was excellent, and it was tremendous preparation for now President Bush to have had eight years of seeing exactly how the presidency operated, and I think that preparation is why he was so sure-footed in taking on the presidency and has done so well.

QUESTION: Would you comment on the role of the special counsel and its activities?

MR. MEESE: The special counsel, or the independent counsel as it is now known (it was originally called the special prosecutor) was part of the post-Watergate syndrome. It was mandated by the Ethics in Government Act of 1978 and was used only on one or two occasions during the Carter administration involving very few people. It was not until the Reagan administration that the institution was used to a great extent. The purpose behind it was good—the idea of having someone totally independent so that there could be no feeling on the part of the public or even political opponents that an administration was whitewashing its own people in cases of alleged wrongdoing. What the creators of the special counsel failed to incorporate was the principle that the Founding Fathers had in mind in 1787, which was that for every agency there has to be some counterforce, that there has to be a system of checks and balances. What we have now is an independent counsel that has no checks or balances. Therefore, they literally run wild, conducting at great length investigations that any competent prosecutor could conduct in 30 to 90 days at most, but which the special counsel goes into for a year or even two. Special counsel investigations have become like IRS audits of each person investigated and everything that he or she has ever done. I think it has gone far afield from what it should have been, and I think there have to be arrangements to curb it or abolish it entirely. It certainly has gotten out of hand.

There have been times, for example, when people have had to go to court to keep the independent counsel from going beyond the bounds of the investigation. In one case, Ted Olson was accused of a minor violation, and it took nearly two years before he was finally cleared. During that time, the amount of money spent by both sides was horrendous. Hundreds of thousands of dollars are spent during these cases, and during that whole period the press plays the cases up as major news. One of the unfortunate aspects of the investigation process is that the counsel is supposed to work in complete secrecy until it is time to render an indictment or to give a report. However, there are so many leaks that there is almost a leak of the week as far as the press is concerned, all of which are disadvantageous to the individual under inquiry because that person cannot say anything publicly. The accused are precluded from saying anything both for practical and ethical reasons, yet leaks by others are reported in the press, many of which are completely inaccurate. So, I think it is a process which has gone badly wrong. Also, it plays into the hands of those in the Congress who try to use it for political reasons, by demanding the appointment of an independent counsel or special prosecutor to investigate cases. They use this as political leverage and try to make, as in the Iran-contra case, political differences into criminal violations. I think that it really needs changing.

QUESTION: Is it possible that we would not have had the special counsel if Archibald Cox and Elliot Richardson had not virtually been forced to resign?

MR. MEESE: It is possible. We say that "hard cases make bad law," and it is entirely possible that if there had not been the so-called Saturday night massacre when Archibald Cox was fired, but only after Attorney General Elliot Richardson had resigned rather than fire him, the independent counsel might not exist. I think we have seen that the counsel was not necessary. There was a special prosecutor appointed, namely Archibald Cox, and when Cox was fired, the next special prosecutor, Leon Jaworski, appointed by the acting attorney general, Robert Bork, did the things that Cox was supposed to have done. The idea of having this special prosecutor subordinate to the attorney general for procedural, administrative, and budgetary purposes maintains the separation of powers and the authority of the president who can then be held responsible for the results. Presently, if the independent counsel does something wrong, the President cannot be held responsible for it because he has no authority over them. I agree with you that this was part of the almost hysterical reaction to Watergate.

QUESTION: You mentioned the Olson case. Would you analyze that for us?

MR. MEESE: Justice Scalia had by far the better argument in that case. I have a feeling, and this is just a personal view, that there are times when the majority of the Court is unwilling to take on what they perceive to be public opinion, even though there may be constitutional issues at stake. In the first Reagan administration, for example, there was a case on whether the IRS, without any statutory authorization, could take away a tax exemption from a private school that was alleged to have unfairly discriminated in their policies. The position of the Reagan administration was that no one should have a tax exemption if they unfairly discriminate, but that such authority needed to be expressly given by Congress to bureaucrats. Bureaucrats should not be able to take away an exemption without statutory authority. When the case got to the Supreme Court, the Supreme Court backed away from it. I think they felt they could not take what might be an unpopular view on as tough an issue as racial discrimination.

The same thing was true of the *Morrison v. Olson* case. The Court was not ready to take on such responsibility. Justice Scalia thought it was silly to call the independent counsel an inferior officer, and therefore able to be appointed by someone other than the president. If anyone had even more authority than Cabinet members, it was the independent counsel. I think Justice Scalia was absolutely right, and that is the way the decision should have gone. But the Court was not willing to take on what they thought was public opinion, so they looked for a way out with this contrived notion that the independent counsel was an inferior officer and therefore subject to Article II, Section 2 of the Constitution. Their interpretation is questionable, but at least they found some basis in the Constitution.

NARRATOR: Would you comment on the so-called troika and why it worked?

MR. MEESE: The troika was the name given to Jim Baker, Mike Deaver, and me because we were all given positions of relative equality in the White House in the first term.

I think it worked well for several reasons. First, there is plenty of work in the White House to go around. I think it is surprising that there have not been more problems when there was less than a troika in the White House handling the workload. Procedurally, there were some reasons the troika worked well. Each of us had access to the President. His personality was such that he did not like internal strife, and therefore I think all of us went out of our way to cooperate, even though we had different views on particular issues.

I must say that our differences generally were not philosophical or policy-related. They were really differences on procedural issues on what specifically ought to be done. Ours were more tactical differences, rather than the basic, deep-down philosophical differences of the conservative versus liberal type that the press liked to report we had, which was a gross oversimplification. There was no real difference on ultimate goals and objectives among any of us. The only differences were on the best ways to achieve those objectives. Still, I think we tried to sublimate those as much as possible and reach a consensus, because that was what the President wanted.

Another reason why the troika worked was that there was a delineation of who was responsible for what. As the counselor to the President, I was the White House member of the Cabinet. I was responsible for policy, for the administration of the Cabinet, and for strategic planning. Jim Baker, as chief of staff, had the responsibility for the internal administration of the White House and dealing with the press and the Congress. Mike Deaver was responsible for those things directly affecting the President as an individual—security, scheduling, travel, and the White House residence. There was a good understanding of who did what.

So, I think for these reasons we were able to function relatively effectively, at least in the minds of those who observed us, even though the troika did violate the principle of unity of command. When there were differences, obviously the President had to and did make the ultimate decisions. However, we tried to present the different options, even where we disagreed, in a civil manner without having ongoing antagonisms between us, and then the President ultimately made the decisions.

QUESTION: How did Don Regan manage to replace the three of you?

MR. MEESE: Don felt that one person could do the job, and I think the reason he had a difficult time was that he could not (and no one can) replace three people. I think he needed two or three others, even if they were called his deputies, so it was clear that they were subordinate to him, but who nevertheless had regular access to the President. When we were there, there were four people in the White House staff who had unquestioned immediate access to the President any time they felt like walking through his office door. They were myself, Jim Baker, Mike Deaver, and the assistant for national security affairs, who at that time was Bill Clark, and later was Bud McFarlane. During Don Regan's tenure, everyone had to get clearance through him before they went in to see the President, and that was simply too big a job for one person. Whatever the relative equality of the people, there has to be more than one person who can not only see the President, but also take on major responsibilities and get them done.

Don was an able guy and an excellent manager, but I think there is a big difference between what happens in the White House and what happens in even the largest companies in business. In business, while there are many challenges every day, at least those challenges are limited by the nature of your business. At least most of the situations that occur are going to be fairly similar to what happened the year before and the year before that. In the White House, conditions and challenges change all the time and you have to be responsive to many different occurrences. Problems occur in the running of the government. Other problems occur with congressional policy. Still other purely political problems occur. All of these problems happen in a fishbowl-type atmosphere with the press reporting on everything. Even the best corporate executive would have a hard time working under those conditions. This was one of the problems during the second term. When Howard Baker became chief of staff, he found he needed more people, and he brought in Ken Duberstein and Tom Griscom who both enjoyed the same access we did.

QUESTION: Did Jim Baker want to be secretary of the treasury so badly that he talked Regan into making the switch?

MR. MEESE: I don't think he talked him into it. I think Don Regan was ready to make a switch. He had been secretary of the treasury for four years. He thought he could perform well in the White House after having seen what went on there. Jim Baker was certainly ready for a change. I think all of us in the White House were ready for a change. I know I was, as was Mike Deaver, so I think change was inevitable. Don Regan indicated an interest in serving in the White House. Jim always had an interest in heading a department, and I think that their two minds had interests which happened to coincide at that time. They talked about it over the course of a couple of months, then they went to the President and he was agreeable to it.

QUESTION: Would you comment on the number of negative books which have come out of this administration?

MR. MEESE: In one sense, it is an indication that Ronald Reagan is perhaps too nice a guy. In most cases, people felt they could write these very self-serving books with impunity and the President would not get back at them because he was not that kind of person.

In other cases, people were naive and did not realize what they were getting into. Once one person had written that kind of book, it became easier for others to do it.

The first one was David Stockman's book, and quite frankly, I believe Dave Stockman should have been fired the first year after he made those untrue but certainly revealing statements to a reporter who then published them. Then, he wrote his book, which was filled with untruths and misinterpretations. Stockman made it easier for Larry Speakes and Mike Deaver. In many cases, people were lured by the money of publishers who were willing to pay big bucks in order to get something that was negative about the administration. I personally am very chagrined that those books were written.

Martin Anderson wrote a different type of book, *Revolution*, which is probably the most accurate account of the Reagan administration that anyone has written. Martin's book is now coming out in paperback, and in that edition he added a chapter dealing with these other books. His opinion of them is more or less the same as mine, but in much greater detail.

QUESTION: When you look back on your tenure both on the staff and as attorney general, what do you consider to be the highlights and the disappointments of your service?

MR. MEESE: The highlights of my White House service were the accomplishments in the first year of many of the major objectives that President Reagan had talked about during the campaign, namely revitalizing the economy and rebuilding our national defenses. We were able to achieve those two things and develop a single-minded agenda. I helped develop this agenda during the campaign and helped implement it afterwards. I think those were really the greatest achievements of that first term.

I think the greatest disappointment I had was that we were not able to do more to curb the growth of federal spending. We slowed it from what the rate had been, but certainly not nearly as much as it needed to be slowed. This was largely because of the inability to get Congress to go along with cuts. One of the items that should have been cut, for example, was the Department of Education. We saw no reason to have a full department, with all their regulations and red tape, hamstringing our schools, when all that was needed was a disbursing agent for whatever funds were going to be devoted to the schools. That could have been done by a small office in the Treasury Department where they could disburse money and have auditors who make sure it is being spent properly. Instead, there was this whole bureaucracy. We couldn't even get the senators who had voted against establishing the Department of Education in 1978 to vote to abolish it in 1981 or 1982 because of the pork-barrel syndrome that goes on within the Congress. Therefore, being unable to stem the growth of federal spending was the greatest disappointment.

As attorney general, I think the greatest achievement (there were two really) was the contribution of information to the President on the appointment of judges. I was very pleased with the quality of the judges that we were able to assist in having the President appoint.

Another achievement was the progress we made on the drug issue. During the time that I was attorney general, drug abuse in the United States declined by a little over a third. I think that was a tremendous achievement, not due solely to our work, but we did provide the leadership for a nationwide effort for the prevention of and education on the dangers of drugs. This started in 1982, but the coordination of the federal agencies was tremendously enhanced from 1985 on.

Finally, I was particularly satisfied that we put down the largest threat to public safety that has ever been encountered by the federal government without anybody being killed and with over a hundred hostages being returned. Most people probably cannot remember what I am referring to, and the reason they cannot remember is because we were successful. If we had not been successful, everybody would remember it to this day. What I am referring to are the two prison riots that went on simultaneously at the Oakley Correctional Center in Louisiana and at the Atlanta penitentiary. There were, I think, 120 or so hostages taken. We had to employ the hostage rescue team of the FBI and the Delta Force, a specially trained unit of the Department of Defense, but we were able to put down both of these incidents without any of the hostages or any of the people participating (law enforcement people and prison guards) being killed. I think that achievement was definitely a high point.

I cannot identify a particular disappointment during my tenure as attorney general. I guess one of the disappointing things was the lack of communication between the Justice Department and the Congress. We had several congressional people whom we took great pains to brief on different issues relating to the drug field. The next day we would see those same people on television saying the opposite of what they had heard the day before. I think the inability to have a better rapport with Congress, which was not entirely the fault of the Justice Department, was one of my greatest disappointments. What I found, unfortunately, was how little respect some congressmen have for either the truth or for some kind of balanced approach to issues. Our work was constantly impeded by partisanship and incivility.

QUESTION: You referred to several situations with the Congress where, if it were in effect, the line-item veto might have been used by the President. What is your opinion of the line-item veto and do you think it will ever be put into effect on the federal level?

MR. MEESE: I think the line-item veto would be one of the most constructive constitutional changes that could be made in order to balance the control of the budget between the Congress and the presidency. Currently, no one has control of the budget. There is no control within the Congress, because the budget is subject to three different sets of committees: the appropriations committees, the authorization committees, and the budget committee itself. The President has no control because, without the line-item veto, he receives an ultimatum from Congress saying, "Either you sign this bill with these appropriations in it, or the government comes to a halt."

I think the line-item veto would be tremendously valuable as it has been for the 43 governors out of 50 who have it in their own states. Ronald Reagan, who had the line-item veto ability in California, was never overridden on a line-item veto in eight years as governor. This is interesting, because in California it takes two-thirds of the legislature to put an appropriation into the budget, and it only takes two-thirds to override a veto. Therefore, even though the state legislators had a two-thirds vote to put something into the budget, when Governor Reagan vetoed it and brought that item to public attention, there was never a two-thirds vote to override him when it came back to the legislature. So, I think it would be extremely valuable in cutting out unnecessary expenditures.

I do not know if it will ever be put into effect at the federal level. There has been talk that Congress would finally give up and legislatively give the President a veto, leaving him with the responsibility of cutting the budget. I think this is a possibility, but there are tremendous pressures against it within the Congress. Allowing the line-item veto means that some pork-barrel items that they all like would be eliminated by a presidential veto, and then they probably wouldn't be able to restore those by overriding his veto in the spotlight of public opinion.

I think, and the polls show, that the public feels that a line-item veto would be a good thing. It is possible that if the line-item veto is not approved in the next two or three years to curb federal spending, we will see various state legislatures call for a constitutional convention to provide for a balanced budget amendment with the line-item veto. If they do that, the Congress may well be so scared of a constitutional convention, which we have never had even though it is provided for in Article V of the Constitution, that they might pass such an amendment and let it go to the states for the three-quarters ratification rather than risk having a constitutional convention. I think this is the only way that it will ever be attained.

QUESTION: Would you comment on the role of Mrs. Reagan during your years at the White House?

MR. MEESE: It is difficult for me to comment because you've seen the different stories from different people. She did not, as some first ladies have, attend Cabinet meetings and she did not have any official, quasi-official, or formal role. The real role she provided was what any wife would provide to her husband, and that is as a good sounding board for the President when he was at home thinking and talking about things.

There are stories that she tried to influence different members of the administration. I don't know whether these stories are accurate or not. I know she never did with me the entire time, either in the White House or in the Justice Department. As a matter of fact, going back to the Sacramento days, she and I had an understanding that I was working for her husband and had no desire to be thought of as a family retainer. I held a position in the government working for her husband, and if she felt that I was doing something wrong she could talk it over with the President and let him tell me. Indeed, that was our relationship, which I think was the correct one. If she did have direct communication with some people, it was because they made the mistake of forgetting for whom they were working.

QUESTION: In view of the difficulties you pointed out about getting a real budget through Congress the way it now functions, do you think President Bush will be able to do it?

MR. MEESE: I don't know whether he will or not. Certainly there is no sign so far that any real progress has been made despite the days and now weeks of meetings that they have had. I think it would be very advantageous for President Bush to do two things particularly. One is to refuse to raise taxes. As long as he is willing to raise taxes, there will not be a satisfactory budget agreement. There has never been a time in history when raising taxes has helped the deficit. It has only increased the deficit ultimately, because the new monies created by the increase are spent by Congress on programs that start small because funds are available, and then gradually grow and demand much more money later on. Therefore, I think he should take the tax issue off the table and simply say that the Congress must limit the growth of spending.

At the Heritage Foundation, where I am working now, we have what we call the 4 percent solution. The solution allows 4 percent growth in the budget every year, which is quite a bit when you have a trillion dollar budget. This could be done because tax revenues grow that much each year.

The Congress has all kinds of gimmicks to increase spending. For example, you hear talk that if we don't raise taxes, the budget will have to be balanced by spending cuts. The press makes this sound like there will be less money for a particular function, but that is not true at all. When Congress develops a budget they take the last year's budget, add an inflation or expansion figure to it, and then it is from that higher number that they propose cuts. Therefore, even though they are "cutting" from the increase of the budget, they are not cutting below last year's budget. Thus, an actual increase is portrayed by the press as a cut in the budget. That is why, I think, the only way one can control the budget is to limit it by decreeing a 4 percent maximum overall increase.

The other thing that the President should do, and the Persian Gulf situation illustrates this, is refuse to hastily cut the defense budget to the point where the United States is no longer able to defend its national interest and its citizens. There is something to be learned from the Persian Gulf situation, because if the cuts in the defense budget that are being suggested by the Congress this year had been made two years ago, our ability to deploy troops rapidly to the Persian Gulf would have been seriously affected.

QUESTION: Would you agree that by accepting such a large fee to speak in Japan Mr. Reagan adversely affected his popularity?

MR. MEESE: Yes, I agree with you. I think the trip was not handled well at all. However, much of the $2 million he was paid was used for many purposes other than his remuneration. I know part of it was given to the Reagan library, for example. I think it should have been explained to the American people that the Japanese often pay that kind of fee for speakers. It was not something that President Reagan sought. In other words, he did not propose that his fee for going to Japan be $2 million. This was something that was offered by them, and I think the American public should have been told about the many other things that the funds were going for. I don't think it was handled well at all, and I think that is why it made him look to some people like he was available to the highest bidder. He let the Japanese determine what they thought his speaking program over there was worth. They heard the same speaking program that other audiences around the world have heard for much less, but they felt it was so important to have him there that they offered that amount. It was not something he sought; it was something they offered. If the American public had known this, they would have reacted differently.

QUESTION: Would you care to comment on the failure of supply-side economics?

MR. MEESE: Supply-side economics didn't fail. I think it was oversimplified by many people, including the press. Actually, it was a very sophisticated theory put forth by Milton Friedman and many other economists, including Art Laffer. Essentially it did work. Basically, it proposed that if you cut the tax rates, you will ultimately get more revenue. This is in fact what happened. Every year from the time these policies went into effect in 1983, which was the year the past phase took effect, the federal revenues increased.

Supply-side programs were not the reason we had to borrow. Nor was our defense budget why we have had to borrow. We borrowed because the domestic spending enacted by Congress increased much faster than the revenues. Tax revenues have increased. In addition, the top taxpayers, as a group, are paying a much higher percentage of the total tax revenues than they were before. The reason for this is that the loopholes that were used–tax shelters and that sort of thing–are no longer available. People are making more money by not using tax shelters, because they are making better investments with the lower interest rates. As a result, the total intake for individuals is greater, but so is their tax revenue. So, supply-side economics really has worked.

NARRATOR: We are very grateful for the opportunity to have you with us today. Thank you so much.